MW01051099

FATAL ABSTRACTION

FATAL ABSTRACTION

WHY THE MANAGERIAL CLASS LOSES CONTROL OF SOFTWARE

Darryl Campbell

W. W. NORTON & COMPANY
Independent Publishers Since 1923

Copyright © 2025 by Darryl Campbell

All rights reserved
Printed in the United States of America
First Edition

For information about permission to reproduce selections from this book, write to Permissions, W. W. Norton & Company, Inc., 500 Fifth Avenue, New York, NY 10110

For information about special discounts for bulk purchases, please contact W. W. Norton Special Sales at specialsales@wwnorton.com or 800-233-4830

Manufacturing by Lake Book Manufacturing
Book design by Daniel Lagin
Production manager: Lauren Abbate

ISBN: 978-1-324-07895-1

W. W. Norton & Company, Inc.
500 Fifth Avenue, New York, NY 10110
www.wwnorton.com

W. W. Norton & Company Ltd.
15 Carlisle Street, London W1D 3BS

1 2 3 4 5 6 7 8 9 0

To Mom, Dad, Amanda, and all the professional flyers in the family.

"History is a constant race between invention and catastrophe."

—FRANK HERBERT, *GOD EMPEROR OF DUNE*

CONTENTS

FATAL ABSTRACTION

INTRODUCTION

The Wrong Kind of Logic

I joined the tech industry in the summer of 2010, before it entered its Messianic phase. My first job was downright predatory. I worked for a company that promised to open up the world of ecommerce to small businesses around the country—and then sold them barely viable, prefabricated websites for $100 each. For every new order, I'd fire up our site builder program, slap the buyer's name and logo across the top of the page, and underneath I'd write paragraph after paragraph of text that was meant less for human readership and more for Google's search algorithm ("Bob's Dealership Sells New Toyotas and Used Toyotas").

In the white space between sections of this uncanny-valley copy, I'd place obnoxiously animated CONTACT US buttons, which would allow visitors to call directly from their computers—if the client paid us a small monthly fee, of course. If they didn't pay, I would still add the CONTACT US buttons to their website; they just wouldn't do anything when clicked. Invariably, about half of our clients would enable the buttons, while the other half would tire of having a useless element on their website after a few weeks, and buy the click-to-call functionality anyway. It was, by any standard, a kind of mild extortion.

Then again, so was our entire business. There was no proof that the websites did a whole lot for our customers. The vast majority only got a few dozen hits per month. Still, the price was low enough—and the click-to-call technology flashy enough by the standards of Web 2.0—that no one really complained. Our clients evidently thought it was better to get in on the next technological revolution, even at the bargain-basement level, than to have it pass them by entirely. And I enabled their behavior.

My job was deeply unsexy. I earned $10 an hour, with no benefits. After six months, I was eligible to convert to full time, which meant a $2-an-hour pay bump and the most basic health insurance permissible under Washington State law. I knew of only one person—our supervisor—who had lasted long enough to become a permanent hire.

Still, I had no intention of staying at the company for very long, so the arrangement suited me just fine. I had left graduate school that spring after three years of futility. I studied history because I thought it mattered somehow; but the academic job market, and the bored reaction of the undergrads I was teaching, indicated otherwise. So I moved back to my hometown of Seattle into an illegal sublet in the sketchiest part of the Capitol Hill neighborhood to look for real work. I had no clear prospects and no specific plans for where my career reset might take me. I answered a job posting for the website company because the bar for entry was low and I needed the money, not because I felt a special calling to work in tech. The company seemed just as ambivalent about expending effort to vet me or my skills. After a brief test to ensure that I could write HTML and construct a grammatical sentence, I was in.

Like many tech workers in the pre-social media era, especially in Seattle, my coworkers and I did not fit the modern Silicon Valley stereotype. We weren't die-hard evangelists for every new gadget, we didn't run in the same circles as venture capitalists, and we tried as best we could not to identify with our employers. I sat in one of the company's many copywriting "pods," and about the only thing that I had in common with my fellow pod dwellers was the expectation that this was only a temporary landing spot on the way to something better. One of my fellow contractors was a self-described serial entrepreneur who boasted openly about his failures, as if by doing so he would turn them into a mark of persistence rather than of bad luck or incompetence. He was only slumming it alongside us, he claimed, until his next investment came through. Next to him sat a middle school teacher who had finally reached her limit of teen rage-angst the year before. Overall, she said, the pay was about the same but the hours were better, given that she didn't have to take her work home with her every night. Our boss sat next to the only doorway to our work room, and scowled every time we ducked out for a bathroom break or a snack. He spoke to us rarely, and only to give us a correction or a reprimand: *add more keywords*, he'd grunt, or *you're behind pace*. When he was in an especially bad mood he'd threaten to not renew our contracts, which expired at the end of every month. But he never followed through; there was too much work to do, and apparently too few people willing to do it for the money we were getting paid.

Very quickly, we learned that the company was designed to exploit the gap between those with technical skills—that was us—and those without. Each of the pod dwellers had a quota of six complete websites per hour of work. And there were nearly a hundred of us in the bullpen on the sixth floor of our high-rise on Pike Street, all making websites for eight hours a day, five days a week. At that level of productivity, we'd produce $21 million a year in annual revenue from website sales, plus just as much for click-to-call subscriptions. For every dollar in revenue we generated, we only cost the company seven cents. We enabled the fat operating margins that most companies can only dream of. It didn't occur to me until much later, but the way we exploited clients, and the way our company exploited us in turn, unlocked the true moneymaking potential of the digital age.

Where all that profit went, we had no idea. I never once saw our CEO, and we certainly weren't reinvesting in the product or the workspace. Our websites never got a facelift, and our site builder never got easier to use, even as the rest of the internet was rapidly modernizing around us. Entire sections of the floor remained unlit and unpopulated for cost-saving reasons. Once we asked for a raise to $12 an hour, to help offset Seattle's ever-increasing cost of living. Our boss, who had once been a contractor like us, dismissed our request with a wave of his hand. *No chance.*

So we carried on, making our websites that didn't work for buyers who couldn't afford anything better, until one by one we, the workers, hit our limits. Some people lasted only two months. Others nearly a year. When someone left, we did not mourn their departure but celebrated their escape from the drudgery.

It's been fifteen years since I moved on from that job, yet in many ways I have never quite put it behind me. I've since worked at brand-name companies such as Amazon, Expedia, Tinder, and Uber, as well as others that you've probably never heard of. I have participated directly in the launch of a half-dozen apps, two physical devices, more feature releases than I can possibly remember, and yes, even a cryptocurrency. I've picked up more computer languages than human languages in my lifetime, from teaching myself BASIC when I was eight years old so I could tinker with my favorite text-based *Star Trek* adventure game to slogging my way through Swift twenty years later in order to stay relevant in the age of apps. I even learned a new one, Ada, while researching this book. I have spent time at almost every level in the org chart, from a very junior analyst in a thousand-person division to a C-suite role at a tiny startup. I have even met a handful of tech billionaires in my time, one of whom yelled at me, personally.

Despite the variety of roles, levels, and types of businesses where I've worked, the tension that I felt in my first job has been a constant. On the one hand, the tech industry has always urged me to think of all its products not as mere tools, there to boost our efficiency and expand our abilities, but as something more—a path to liberation from all the hardships inherent to the human condition. On the other, I have also seen firsthand that rhetoric of salvation lead not only to petty disappointments but also to society-breaking catastrophes. Most critiques of Silicon Valley, no matter how many damning details they get right, ascribe its fundamental sickness to greed or incompetence or, simply, "capitalism." They miss the reality that Big Tech's defining product—software—has opened up an entirely new category of risk. The speed with which software can be created and disseminated around the world seems to open up opportunities to create prosperity and efficiency on a global scale. Yet in our haste to innovate our way out of every problem through software, we have inadvertently created new and terrifying problems. The promise of the digital age has turned to ash in front of our eyes. What do we keep getting wrong?

⁝⁝⁝⁝⁝⁝⁝

THE ISSUE IS NOT SOFTWARE PER SE, BUT THE COLLISION BETWEEN SOFTWARE and the prevailing theory of how companies should be, must be, run: "managerialism." This is the notion that every part of a business can be abstracted into its financial components, and therefore optimized according to scientific principles. The uniform flattening allows professional "managers"—who lack special expertise in what an individual business actually does, but who have significant expertise in the operation of businesses in general—to parachute into any operation and quickly understand how to balance the competing demands of customers, suppliers, employees, and investors. Managerialism distills the vast responsibility of running a business and all of its products down to the straightforward management of cash flows, key performance indicators, and second-order financial metrics such as the price of a company's stock, or its return on invested capital. It is corporate strategy, organizational design, and a philosophy of leadership, all rolled into a single unifying theory of business.

The American sociologist James Burnham coined the term in a personal letter he wrote in 1940, and expanded this offhand remark into his landmark sociological study, *The Managerial Revolution*, in 1941. In the book, he argued that new inventions alone could not bring about great economic progress; rather, people needed to change the way they ran their businesses before they could truly harness the power of technology. Modern society began only when professional managers learned how to organize human capital on a large scale, to accurately measure the performance of their business, and to build their corporate strategy using financial analysis rather than gut instinct. He called this philosophy "managerialism."

Managerialism, he argued, had many benefits. It gave people the intellectual toolkit to run the kind of global, nongovernmental, profitable businesses of the sort that did not exist until the mid-nineteenth century. This toolkit was easy enough for a new department head to learn, yet flexible enough to allow that same person to eventually run the entire business without learning anything substantially new. Its tactics were equally suited to companies both large and small across every sector of the economy. Most of all, it created a replicable method for producing sustainable growth in a world of fallible humans, complex markets, and unpredictable disruptions.

Burnham's book was retrospective. The managerial revolution he described had been underway for almost a century by the time he wrote it. By that point, it had already transformed the business world in three important ways. First, it centralized power within a new command-and-control layer at the very top of the company, the executive C-suite, which was populated entirely by members of the new managerial class. Over time, the C-suite model was replicated further down a company's organizational chart, in the form of middle management. As these managers took over, they imposed the second major change in business: the rise of financialization. To do their job properly, managers needed a consistent and universal framework for making strategic decisions, even as their businesses got bigger and more diverse. Finance quickly became a kind of lingua franca of the corporate world, as it allowed managers to summarize everything into a neat quantity, and then compare those quantities across lines of business and levels of command. Everyone from the CEO to the most junior manager could understand their relationship to a company's bottom line. Strategy now became entirely synonymous with finance, and vice versa.

This led to the last key change: the intellectual homogenization of the managerial class. These business leaders learned to think broadly and quickly, but not necessarily deeply. Their main task was to understand the priorities of the business as a whole, and leave the details to their underlings. It became impractical—irrational, even—for a general manager to develop domain expertise when they would only ever operate at the abstract layer of finance. Ignorance was not just bliss. It was good business.

The triumph of managerial economies over centrally planned ones, first in World War II and later in the Cold War, cemented this corporate philosophy as the only acceptable one for the developed world. Immediately after World War II, the total after-tax profit for all American companies was the equivalent of $316 billion in today's money. By 2000, annual corporate profits had increased more than tenfold to $3.5 trillion. Over the same time period, the Dow Jones Industrial Average grew six times in value, the total market capitalization of all American public companies grew nearly twenty times, and the American gross domestic product per capita grew nearly thirty times. Some of this was due to technological innovation, economic development, and regulatory changes. But decades of research on tens of thousands of firms shows a strong positive relationship between the adoption of managerial practices and the success of a business. Across all industries, companies can reliably increase their productivity, profitability, and shareholder returns—in some cases doubling them or more—through "good management" alone.

What's good for the corporate world isn't always good for the rest of the world, however. Think of DDT, the insecticide that was hailed as a miracle of science and helped establish biotech companies such as Monsanto and Ciba-Geigy (now Novartis), yet ended up devastating entire ecosystems. Think also of the offshoring craze that began in the 1980s, pioneered by General Electric's "Neutron Jack" Welch, which freed up an estimated $1 trillion in cash for American companies. They then spent that money on stock buybacks and dividend payouts rather than capital expenditures or research and development. Meanwhile, the workers left behind by offshoring now face permanent economic insecurity that will cost nearly $20 billion to offset, according to a World Bank estimate. Finally, think of the ongoing effects of the fossil fuel industry on public health, the environment, and the global climate. No corporate income statement accounts for these "negative externalities"; no single market mechanism puts sufficient pressure on companies to clean up their own messes before they cause irreversible damage.

It is tempting to see all this as intentional corporate wickedness—a conscious plot by managerial executives to prioritize profits over safety, or over people, or over human civilization itself. But this is a category error. In fact, professional managers cannot prioritize profits over anything, because in their view there is nothing else worth considering. You can try to change their mind all you want, to get them to see anything beyond the financial statement. But I suspect you will have better luck explaining quantum physics to a dog.

⁂

IN THE MOST SYMPATHETIC VIEW, MANAGERIALISM IS A SINCERE ATTEMPT TO make sense of a world that has grown beyond our capacity to understand. Humans are still, deep down, the same tribal nomads who evolved to live and work in small communities of a few dozen people, not in companies with thousands of employees or "economies" with several million competing players, all working toward their own secret goals. We need heuristics like managerialism to suppress chaos and tame entropy as best we can.

Yet managerialism also tends to create new and less predictable forms of chaos out in the world. Absent some external check on their power, most companies will continue the single-minded pursuit of profit even as they grow, believing that it is the only path to sustainable success. Even the best-intentioned ones will create harm just through their normal operation at a global scale.

But managerially run megacompanies have found ways to evade most if not all of the guardrails we have already put in place. Like GE under Welch, they buy out competitors and funnel revenue straight into the pockets of their investors, neutering the ability of the market to provide any corrections. They aggressively fight existing regulations in court, and attempt to forestall new ones through lobbying and cultivating political favors. Above all, they have gotten so big that even continent-spanning attempts to rein in corporate power have been mixed at best. At no point in the last fifty years have the United States, the European Union, or any other major government been able to meaningfully change the corporate strategy of companies such as Wal-Mart, Exxon Mobil, or J.P. Morgan Chase.

The first wave of managerially run multibillion-dollar enterprises evolved slowly, over the course of nearly a century. Then came the tech industry. The new upstarts such as Apple, Amazon, Microsoft, and Google surpassed them all in a few scant decades. As they scaled, however, they looked to the old corporate world for strategic and organizational guidance. Before they could assume their place among the world's leading companies, they would need to get a lot smarter about the dynamics of business. Thus they adopted managerialism as their ruling ethos.

Today, software is still written by engineers, but since the mid-2000s those engineers have been relegated to the margins of corporate power in favor of business school graduates, whose primary qualification for leadership roles comes from their two-year study of managerial orthodoxy rather than any deep knowledge of their target industry. Amazon alone hires more than one thousand new MBAs each year; it is the biggest single employer of business school graduates that is not a consulting firm. Google and Microsoft are ranked just behind. Even Tesla, whose CEO Elon Musk famously decried the "MBA-ification of America," cannot escape their influence: two of his direct subordinates and nearly eight hundred other high-ranking members of his company hold MBAs. Likewise, when executive jobs open up, the industry looks less to promote from within than to hire experienced managerial talent from outside. This is why Facebook hired Sheryl Sandberg (formerly a senior adviser for the World Bank and the Clinton administration), why Uber landed Dara Khosrowshahi (formerly CFO at the holding company IAC), and why Elon Musk chose Linda Yaccarino (former COO of NBCUniversal) to succeed him as the CEO of X, formerly Twitter.

In other words, the tech companies that matter look nothing like the startups we often imagine them to be. They may still produce software as they always have, but they must now also yield to managerial pressures to generate revenue, control costs, and produce a consistent profit. They may still employ thousands of engineers, but those engineers must answer to layer after layer of professional managers. And they may still pay lip service to their founding mantras—to not be evil or to think differently—but they increasingly act according to their financial interests alone. Like Big Oil, Big Pharma, and Big Banks, Big Tech companies claimed to have invented an entirely original vision of what a corporation ought to be, even as they structured themselves in the exact image of their predecessors.

At the same time, the self-mythology of the tech sector quickly spread to other sectors of the economy. In the mid-2000s, companies as disparate as Sweetgreen (the salad chain), Goldman Sachs (the investment bank), and Boeing (the airplane and defense company) rebranded themselves "tech companies," too. This was not merely a cynical marketing ploy to position the leading members of the old school alongside the new darlings of Wall Street (although it did help that the market tended to handsomely reward any hint of technological innovation, especially at low-growth companies in mature industries). Just as Big Tech companies wanted to optimize their nascent businesses by applying managerial tenets, so too did old-line managerial companies want to wring more efficiencies out of their existing businesses by deploying software throughout them. It was a not-so-subtle announcement that in the eyes of the corporate world, high technology and managerial control were inextricably linked.

Thus the venture capitalist and internet entrepreneur Marc Andreessen opened a 2011 *Wall Street Journal* op-ed with the memorable declaration: "In short, software is eating the world."

At first glance, his argument seemed to reassure a public still scarred by the Great Recession that opportunity was just around the corner. Software, he insisted, had the power to drive record growth in the global economy for decades to come. All we needed to do was to embrace it wholeheartedly, learn how to make it and use it, and transform every company into a tech company. The sooner we did so, the sooner software could save us.

Andreessen's bromides had a distinctly managerial undertone. He presented software not necessarily as something that would make the world better, but only as something that would make the economy more profitable. He suggested that software was the only way to develop "high-growth, high-margin, highly defensible businesses" in a postindustrial world. To bolster his claims, he cited financial metrics such as the price-to-earnings ratio of internet companies and quoted extensively from corporate financial reports. He spoke about the inevitable digitization of the "value chain" in sectors as varied as retail, airlines, and farming. His op-ed was less a catalog of the wonderful things that software could do for everyone, and more a list of the many ways that it could aid the managerial class in its continuous search for higher profits and lower costs. We should not be surprised that these two things do not necessarily overlap.

Andreesen was right, of course: since 2011, software *has* eaten the world. Back then, the largest corporations in the world included Exxon Mobil, Chevron, General Motors, and IBM—industrial companies that made tangible goods and measured their worth in the hundreds of billions of dollars. Today, they are still around, and are still the same size, adjusting for inflation. But they have been surpassed by tech companies including Apple, Microsoft, Alphabet, Amazon, and Meta, which measure their market cap in the trillions of dollars. In 2011, less than a third of the world's population had internet access. Today, it's two-thirds. A decade ago, the average smartphone user spent half an hour every day on their phone. Now, it's nearly two hours. And many of the things that used to be completely manual or mechanical in nature, from car dashboards and refrigerators to political campaigns and international spy networks, are now fully digitized and automated.

But managerialism has failed once again to manage the externalities that come with new technology. And unlike previous innovations, software can be deployed with stunning speed and at a global scale—which means that its externalities follow close behind, at much the same pace. Social networks have been transformed into channels of mass disinformation so powerful that they can incite civil unrest and reshape the global political environment. Surveillance technology allows advertisers, marketers, and even governments to track you every second of every day without your knowledge. Automated investing software at the world's largest banks accelerates, and sometimes even single-handedly causes, large-scale economic disruption. Vehicles that are supposed to be able to drive or fly themselves end up taking the lives of unwitting human passengers and bystanders when they fail.

Software does many good things: it entertains us, it makes us more productive, it can even help us overcome our physical and mental limitations. And who is against economic growth, in the simplest sense? But software also allows a single company, a single app, even a single line of code to change the world in an instant, in ways that that the managers of those companies cannot always predict, or even understand. Managerialism is a doctrine of control. Yet as we will see, its acolytes are the ones who lose control of their own products in the eternal race to make their companies rich.

∴∴∴∴

THIS BOOK ARGUES THAT THE TECH DISASTERS WE HAVE ENDURED OVER THE last twenty years have all shared a common origin: what I call managerial software. It has warped the decision-making process of executives as well as the internal politics of the companies over which they preside. It has allowed considerations of safety and quality to be ignored in order to balance the almighty financial statement. Above all, it has given too much power to those who have the most faith in, but most meager grasp of, software—and it silences those who can clearly see the only safe way through the minefield of technological ignorance.

There are many accounts of *how* technology fails: down-to-the-minute narratives of one scandal or another that attempt to imply meaning through the sequential recounting of events. And there are equally as many attempts to explain *why* technology fails, either by casting blame on specific individuals, or by arguing that such catastrophes are impossible to solve without remaking the rest of the world, too. In my view, these conclusions are not very satisfying. The former type is too narrow, the latter too broad, and neither one gives the reader much reason to hope for a better future, if the only way to prevent world-altering consequences is to change the minds of capricious billionaires or successfully overthrow a centuries-old economic system.

I believe our task is far more achievable. But first, we have to understand why the managerial class loses control of software—and why we cannot trust them to avoid technological catastrophe on their own. In order to see just how deep this problem runs, I focus on a handful of software disasters that I know very well.

The first is the Boeing 737 MAX crashes of 2018 and 2019, which were caused by a piece of software called the maneuvering characteristics augmentation system, or MCAS. I spent four years reporting on this story for the tech website *The Verge*, during which time I spoke to dozens of pilots, engineers, technical experts, and software developers. As I uncovered many failures of design, implementation, and control, I saw the same failures at Boeing that I had witnessed in my own fifteen years in the tech sector.

I spent two of those years at Uber during its own major crisis. In 2018, I was visiting the company's Austin office and sitting about ten feet away from a group of engineers at our Advanced Technologies Group (ATG), when we learned that one of our self-driving cars had collided with a pedestrian named Elaine Herzberg and killed her. It was the first time in history that an autonomous vehicle caused the death of an innocent bystander. Several of my colleagues couldn't even imagine how the accident could have occurred. Wasn't Uber supposed to be the cutting edge of the tech sector, the standard of excellence against which the rest of the industry was measured? But I understood—vaguely at the time, and far more clearly now, with the gift of hindsight—that this self-regard was in fact our greatest weakness. Uber's willingness to push technology beyond its limits, combined with the company's desperate need to show its investors that it had a path to profitability, made it far too willing to prioritize the potential rewards of software over the potential risks.

Not all disasters occur at full speed, however. Not all so obviously fall under the rubric "disaster," either. Such was the case with PowerPoint, which was originally designed to help technical workers communicate more effectively with their managerial overlords. Today, it's a tool of the powerful and the glib, actively making the world more susceptible to manipulation. I've been on both sides of the equation myself: I helped one company PowerPoint its way out of answering uncomfortable questions about its business, and I got tricked into joining another one that looked great in slide format but was an utter mess in reality. If nothing else, those experiences helped me understand why PowerPoint is so good at distorting reality, even to the point of perpetuating fraud.

In fact, PowerPoint bears many similarities to another, more obvious instance of managerial technology: social media. I made my first social media account as a college freshman back in 2002, when the only options were Friendster and Myspace. By 2010, however, social media apps abandoned the pretense of connecting you with people you know, and turned into delivery engines of infinite content. Yet in the rush to replace your boring reality with the more vivid one that exists on your phone, they opened the door for manipulation and abuse. The creators of these apps quickly found themselves outwitted by their own users, who have learned how to game any algorithm, bypass any attempts at moderation, and overwhelm the brightest minds in technology through the sheer volume and variety of harmful content. Social media platforms could, if they wanted, eliminate this content from their platforms entirely. But because they are run by managerial companies, they don't have a good incentive to take such an extreme measure when they can just find the optimal balance between reducing harm and limiting costs. Unfortunately for the rest of us, the value of preserving a common reality does not figure into their calculation.

I end in the bizarre world of generative artificial intelligence, which exploded as I began to write this book in the fall of 2022. I first encountered generative AI some years before, when I evaluated its capacity to act as a kind of synthetic companion for those whose social, psychological, or work situation prevented them from developing normal human relationships. It wasn't good enough for that at the time. But it was good enough to exploit the loneliness of thousands of young men, who spent hundreds of dollars on a chatbot that gave them just enough of a romantic (and, in some cases, erotic) fantasy to keep them spending, but never enough to make them truly fulfilled. I was hardly surprised, then, when generative AI's next wave followed the same exploitative pattern. The pressure to commercialize genAI has led the industry to plunder the very things that make us human—writing, music, art, and creativity in general—in order to rush a monetizable product to market before people lose interest and the investor cash runs out.

We cannot cede the future to those who are only skilled at directing massive amounts of capital. We can no longer dismiss the consequences of bad tech as mere "externalities," to be ignored unless they can be precisely quantified on a profit and loss statement. We must acknowledge that managerialism is spectacularly ill-suited as a guide to software development. We must consider innovation less of an imperative, and more of a question: What *ought* we to create?

Managerial software has proven itself too powerful to be constrained by regulation, and too profitable to be reined in by its executive masters. But there is another group that has the power to change its trajectory. For a long time, those of us on the technical side have been content to complain about the effects of the products we make, but the vast majority of us have never been willing to take steps to actually prevent those products from inflicting disasters on the world. Only in the last few years have people begun to speak out against the excesses of Big Tech, although those movements tend to be highly localized: workers from single companies protesting a particular tech project (such as a partnership with the military or law enforcement), or calling attention to the failures of a particular organization within the company (such as the walkouts that followed the mass layoffs of AI safety teams in 2023).

These actions are good and necessary, as far as they go. But I believe they can go still further. All of them share a common target: the managerial class that currently monopolizes the course of the modern tech industry. And they share a common goal: to give the people who actually make software, and who know best its risks and rewards, a greater say over its direction and final use. It is time for a new philosophy of leadership that can look beyond mere finances when there is far more actually at stake.

We won't install that new philosophy just by asking nicely. The managerial class claims sole authority over the business world. But that mastery has limits. Software resists abstraction into purely financial terms. The more it is wielded like a tool of infinite economic gain, the more companies will lose control of it, and the worse it will make our collective existence. Until those in the C-suite learn how to curb their destructive impulses, those who actually create software must keep it from ruining the world, by any means necessary. The only unacceptable choice is to maintain the status quo.

PART 1

FATAL ABSTRACTION

CHAPTER 1

Falling Out of the Sky

The computers on board Lion Air 610 began to panic as soon as the airplane left the gate. From all outward appearances, there was nothing wrong with the brand-new Boeing 737 MAX, which had been in service for less than three months. Its engines were running normally, its cabin was properly pressurized, its radar and navigation and flight control systems were all fully functional. Neither pilots nor passengers had any indication that something was amiss as the airplane began its long taxi toward the southern runway at Jakarta's international airport.

But as its onboard computers ran through their normal diagnostics, they found a problem: according to a single external sensor, the airplane was climbing at about 6.6 degrees above the horizontal.

The sensor reading was not only incorrect—it was physically impossible. If Lion Air 610 really was angled upward that steeply, its tail would have been scraping the ground, and its nose gear would be suspended nearly nine feet above the runway surface. Even a novice pilot would have been able to see that this reading was false, just by looking out the window.

The airplane's computers did not have that ability, however. They simply accepted the sensor reading as the truth. They were not programmed to be skeptical of pitch readings, to see if it even made sense to have a non-zero pitch angle while the airplane was still on the ground. They did not run a diagnostic on the sensor itself to see if it had somehow malfunctioned or was miscalibrated. They did not look for contradictory data about the airplane's orientation from the hundreds of other sensors spread throughout the airplane. The computers onboard one of the most complex machines on Earth were programmed to assume that this particular sensor would never fail, and that the data it produced would never be wrong.

No device so integral to the safe operation of a passenger flight should be so easily misled. Especially not on a Boeing 737 MAX, the newest model of the most popular airplane type in the world. Thanks to their rugged design and fifty years' worth of field testing, Boeing 737s have a well-deserved reputation for safety. They have survived engine explosions, fuselage failures, and even midair collisions. Unless the wings are literally falling off, you should feel safe in a Boeing 737.

As with any advanced system, however, an airplane is only as reliable as its weakest part. And on that day—October 28, 2018—the weakest part on Lion Air 610 was its software.

The two pilots, Captain Bhavye Suneja of New Delhi, India, and First Officer Harvino (a native of Jakarta who, like many Indonesians, only used one name) continued their routine as normal. They taxied toward 25L, the longest of Soekarno-Hatta Airport's three runways, at the standard speed of 20 knots, or about 23 miles per hour. They went through their pre-takeoff checklist, ensuring that the 737 MAX was properly configured for flight, and then scanned their instrument panels for any warning signs or alerts that might have cropped up since leaving the gate. Everything looked like it was in order, so they radioed the tower and asked for permission to take off.

As soon as Lion Air 610 revved its engines and began its takeoff roll, the sensor problem got worse. The computers now believed that the airplane was not at 6.6 degrees of positive pitch, but at nearly 21 degrees—an angle high enough to endanger the aircraft during flight. If an airplane climbs too sharply, especially at low speeds, its wings will stop generating enough lift and plunge the entire vehicle into what's called an aerodynamic stall. This is a familiar sight for anyone who has thrown a paper airplane a little too hard: it will climb gracefully for a moment, then stall out at the peak of its climb and tumble chaotically back to the ground. The exact same thing can also happen to a seventy-five-ton passenger airplane.

The computers did what they were programmed to do when they sense an impending stall. They alerted the pilots.

Two seconds after Lion Air 610's wheels left the ground, Captain Suneja's control column began to rattle in his hands. The sudden noise and vibration startled him, as it would any pilot: every Boeing commercial aircraft is equipped with a so-called "stick shaker," a loud and very obvious warning system that vibrates the pilot's control column with a small motor. It only activates when the airplane detects that it is in too steep of a climb.

But Suneja did not panic. He was a seven-year veteran of Lion Air with more than six thousand hours of flying experience on 737s. He knew that his climb angle was fine, and that the airplane exhibited no other signs of an impending stall, such as deadness in the controls, a sudden loss of altitude, or a characteristic vibration of the wings. He couldn't see the exact angle of attack measurement, which would have been the definitive measure of how close to a stall the airplane was, since Boeing only offers that particular display readout as a paid add-on, and Lion Air had opted not to buy it. But his other instruments confirmed that Lion Air 610 was climbing at a standard rate of 1,000 feet per minute and a normal speed of 197 knots. The stick shaker had activated for no apparent reason. It was an unusual glitch, but there was no obvious emergency to accompany the warning. For now, he decided to keep the airplane on course.

Eight seconds later, First Officer Harvino noticed a new alert on the primary flight display at the center of the airplane's control panel: IAS DISAGREE.

With Suneja flying the airplane, Harvino's duty was to announce every alert or flag aloud. This provides an extra hedge against what is conventionally understood to be the greatest danger on every flight: human error.

"Indicated airspeed disagree," Harvino announced, translating the clipped alert flag into plain English.

Captain Suneja acknowledged Harvino's announcement by repeating it back, according to standard cockpit procedure: "Indicated airspeed disagree."

And then, another error message. ALT DISAGREE.

Harvino did his duty yet again. "Altitude disagree."

"Altitude disagree," Suneja repeated.

Every commercial airplane is designed around the principle of redundancy, so that a failure of one component or system won't endanger the entire airplane. And the particular systems that triggered these alerts are supposed to be extra redundant, with three independent sets of computers and instruments operating in parallel—one set on the left side for the captain, one on the right for the first officer, and a backup set that can be activated at the flick of a switch. It's normal to see small variations in the data due to differences in temperature, moisture, wind, or just the noise inherent in any electrical signal. When there is a significant disagreement between the two main sets of sensors, however, the computers are programmed to alert the flight crew.

At that moment, Harvino saw multiple significant sensor disagreements. The speed sensor on the captain's side of the airplane read 174 knots; the one on the first officer's side, 163 knots. And the captain's altimeter gave him a reading of 340 feet of altitude, while his own reported 570 feet.

Lion Air 610 had been airborne for only thirty seconds, yet something was clearly wrong. The problem was, he did not know the underlying cause, only its apparent symptoms.

"What's going on?" he asked his captain. "Should we return to Jakarta?"

Right then, however, air traffic control interrupted Harvino and cleared Lion Air 610 to its planned cruising altitude of twenty-seven thousand feet. That would be tricky, as the airplane could not tell Suneja and Harvino exactly what its current altitude was. And in the busy skies over Jakarta, an error of a few hundred feet could lead to a midair collision. So Harvino got on the radio and asked for a radar reading of their current altitude.

"Soekarno-Hatta Tower East, Lion Inter 610," radioed Harvino, using the standard radio callsigns for Jakarta's departure control tower and his own airplane. "What is our altitude?"

"Lion Inter 610," came the response, "we have you at 900 feet."

But that wasn't what either of them saw. The left side altimeter showed 790 feet. The right side, 1,040.

Now Harvino was even more confused.

"What altitude should we ask for?" he said, still concerned about the error messages that were rapidly multiplying inside the cockpit. "Should we fly downwind?"

"No," replied Suneja. "Request clearance to a holding point."

Harvino toggled the transmit key on his radio. "Soekarno Hatta East, Lion Inter 610. Request clearance to some holding point for our condition now," he said.

"Lion Inter 610, what is your condition?" asked the air traffic controller.

"Flight control error," Harvino responded.

This was a bit of an exaggeration. Lion Air 610 had some malfunctioning sensors, some erroneous instrument readings, and an increasing number of alerts that the flight crew did not understand. The lack of consistent airspeed and altitude readings also meant that they could not engage the autopilot—it shuts down when it doesn't have clean data, like all good autonomous software should do. But Suneja, who was hand-flying the airplane, still had full control at that moment. He was not outwardly worried. He just did what he was trained to do: keep on flying. He knew that computers have their bad days, too. And it certainly appeared as if Lion Air 610's computers were having one.

The principle of redundancy was also working in other ways. Sometimes, a computer can see what a human cannot. Other times, humans can troubleshoot the problems that are too difficult, or too unpredictable, for a computer to manage. If something goes wrong in the middle of a flight, humans and computers must work together to diagnose and solve the problem.

But this takes time, effort, and concentration—something you can't do when you're in the middle of one of the busiest air corridors in the world. Which is why Suneja and Harvino asked for a holding point, so they could focus all their attention on solving whatever was wrong with their airplane. Air Traffic Control cleared them to proceed to an empty patch of sky about thirty-five miles east of Jakarta, away from the main traffic flow, where they could circle at five thousand feet and figure out just what was wrong with their airplane. Satisfied with this, Suneja reduced the throttle, retracted the flaps, and eased the airplane into what was supposed to be a gentle turn.

The 737 MAX had other ideas. Something overpowered Suneja's control input and jerked the airplane hard over into a 35-degree bank. Immediately a voice alert sounded in the cockpit—"BANK ANGLE, BANK ANGLE"—and Suneja instinctively twisted his control yoke in the opposite direction to return the plane to level. Then, it dove straight for the surface of the Java Sea at a rate of 50 feet per second, as fast as a roller coaster ride. As it accelerated past 320 knots, an incongruous warning sounded in the cockpit: "AIR SPEED LOW, AIR SPEED LOW."

In the cabin, the airplane's sudden, extreme leftward bank would have thrown passengers against their armrests, and baggage against the overhead bin doors—hard enough to jar them open if they weren't properly latched. As the airplane dove, the passengers would have felt themselves start to float off of their seats as the negative *g*-forces took hold. Nervous flyers would have cried out in panic. The gut-churning motion of the airplane—side to side, followed by an abrupt drop—would have unnerved even veteran ones, too. No commercial airplane should move like Lion Air 610 was moving.

Suneja and Harvino could spare little thought for the comfort of their passengers, however. Every professional pilot trains for emergency situations, from engine fires to sudden encounters with severe weather. But nothing in their training told them how to deal with an airplane that develops a mind of its own and starts diving straight toward the ocean for no apparent reason. For the first time, they realized that they faced something far beyond an ordinary emergency.

⁝⁝⁝⁝⁝⁝⁝

THE PILOTS OF LION AIR 610 WERE NOT JUST DEALING WITH A ROGUE COMputer program. They were fighting the long shadow of managerialism, which had fallen over the design and production of the 737 MAX from the moment it was conceived.

In 2005, Boeing hired an outsider as its chief executive officer for the first time in its history: W. James McNerney, or "Jim" to his peers. McNerney earned his MBA from Harvard Business School in 1975, just after HBS revamped its curriculum to focus almost exclusively on corporate planning, strategy, and other "issues facing general managers as they plan their corporations' future." From there, McNerney went to work for Jack Welch, the so-called "Manager of the Century," as he remade General Electric into the standard-bearer for American capitalism in the 1980s and 1990s—a global conglomerate, equal parts manufacturer, licensor, and big bank, whose meteoric rise in share price paced the rest of Wall Street.

Under Welch, executives like McNerney were drilled in the "GE Way," which imbued them with both managerial skills (the process improvement system known as Six Sigma, strict financial planning, outsourcing) and culture-building strategies (leading with "brutal candor," the dreaded "rank and yank" performance review process). GE managers rotated between divisions every two or three years in order to get the broad experience that Welch wanted for all his leaders. With such limited exposure to each division, managers would never be able to understand the ins and outs of their respective product lines. But they would understand the most important thing, in Welch's eyes: how to run any kind of business in any industry for maximum profit.

Over the course of twenty years, McNerney spent time in seven different divisions, from GE Capital (its consumer finance arm) to Lighting to Aircraft Engines. In each one, he applied the GE Way to its fullest—eventually becoming not just a disciple of Jack Welch but also one of his most trusted lieutenants. He was even a finalist to succeed Welch as CEO of GE, although the role went to Jeffrey Immelt, who was a few years younger than McNerney; in the end, Welch secretly valued youth as much as talent.

Nevertheless, his training served him well in his first post-GE role. In 2001, he was appointed the CEO of Saint Paul, Minnesota-based manufacturer 3M, famous for Post-It notes, industrial adhesives, and N95 medical masks. Under McNerney's management, 3M's net income more than doubled and its stock price increased by over 50 percent—an unusual level of growth for a mature and diversified industrial business. His performance got the attention of Boeing's board of directors, which opened a spot for McNerney in 2001.

McNerney had only three years of experience in aviation, which came from his stint at GE Aircraft Engines. But that was no impediment for a general manager, especially one of McNerney's pedigree. As one of his former colleagues told the *Seattle Times*, McNerney never showed much preference for one industry or another—"If we'd been making cameras or autos or doing bond trading, it would have all been the same to him." Rather, he got his thrills from managing the corporate machine itself. On June 30, 2005, he got his chance to manage Boeing.

Right away, he forced the company to shed many of its long-held customs in the name of profitability. Boeing had always positioned itself as a great engineering company first, and a business second. In their annual letters to shareholders, CEOs prior to McNerney tended to champion the company's focus on "product development," "industry leadership," and "the highest standards of quality." Its engineers were given the resources needed to innovate well, rather than quickly—resulting in airplane designs such as the 767, the world's first twin-engine jet certified to fly across the oceans without refueling, or the second generation of the 747 "jumbo jet," which remains one of the safest commercial airplane designs ever made. And factory managers were allowed to keep billions of dollars' worth of spare parts on hand so that they could assemble airplanes properly, even if it meant tying up a huge amount of the company's cash in onsite inventory. Carried on the wings of Boeing aircraft, the global aviation market grew from around 500 million passengers per year in 1970 to nearly 3.5 billion by 2010. Yet as better-designed Boeing aircraft displaced the competition, and eventually made up nearly 70 percent of the global fleet by 1996, fatal accidents declined just as precipitously, from a rate of 1 per 25,000 flights in 1960 to just 1 per 3 million by 2000. Put another way, based on the 1960 rate you would have to take one flight a day for seventy years before you experienced a fatal crash. By 2000, you'd have to fly twice a day for forty centuries.

The market, however, did not reward Boeing for its safety record, or even for its dominant market position. Although it consistently made the Fortune 500 list each year, and its annual revenues remained around $100 billion, its focus on quality ate into its profits. At a time when companies such as Microsoft enjoyed margins of 20 percent or more, Boeing made less than 4 cents per dollar of revenue. Consequently, its stock remained steady while the rest of the market quadrupled in value through the late '90s and early 2000s. This had not bothered Boeing's leaders too much. Boyd Givens, the company's CFO until 1998, was once asked to provide more financial details to Wall Street analysts so that they could better assess the company's path to greater profitability. According to Boeing legend, his response was curt: "Tell them not to worry," he said.

McNerney struck a very different tone. In his first annual letter as CEO, he emphasized that the company was now refocused on pleasing its shareholders. "The Boeing Company aspires to deliver financial results," he wrote. "We are in a long-term business that requires continued profitability . . . regardless of the economic cycles."

McNerney launched three new initiatives, all of which he borrowed straight from General Electric. First, he increased Boeing's use of outsourcing, which his mentor Jack Welch had adopted not just as a strategic pillar but also as a managerial tagline: "Do what you do best, and outsource the rest!" Before he started as CEO, Boeing made about two-thirds of its airplane components in-house. When it did outsource, the company obsessed over quality control, providing down-to-the-micrometer measurements for each individual part or system and conducting surprise audits of its suppliers to ensure quality. This "nose-to-tail approach" was cash-intensive, however, and required significant upfront capital investments for every new airplane design.

McNerney changed all that. He turned Boeing from a precise micromanager into a hands-off licensor. Boeing designers dictated high-level parameters and performance metrics (weight, strength, cost, and so on) to its suppliers, and left them to figure out the details on their own. Boeing also allowed patents and other intellectual property rights to remain with its vendors, which meant that Boeing was no longer exposed to as much legal liability in case of a poor design. As a result, the company did not send its engineers and designers on as many surprise inspections. This change in its outsourcing model removed many of the company's incentives to ensure its products were free from defects and design flaws. But it allowed Boeing to save money, which was most important in McNerney's eyes.

His second initiative depended closely on the first one. Boeing started to use its vast purchasing power to force suppliers to continually lower their prices. This was another GE tactic. In an effort to combat unnecessary price inflation and stimulate innovation, Welch decreed that all GE suppliers would have to cut their prices by 10 percent each year or else they would lose their contracts. McNerney one-upped Welch. He demanded that Boeing vendors cut prices by as much as 15 percent annually. No one—from the makers of the 737's fuselage to the programmers who wrote its software—was spared. The savings were substantial: McNerney's program saved the company more than $1 billion in costs over the first two years. But it also created a perverse incentive to focus on cheapness instead of quality, triggering a race to the bottom among suppliers. Boeing's focus on price, combined with its new lack of oversight, made its vendors more likely to produce an inferior product.

McNerney's third initiative saw his scrutiny turn inward as he sought to install the same financial discipline and awareness across all of Boeing's in-house processes. He declared that all product decisions would require a financial as well as a technical justification. Instead of retaining Boeing's most skilled (and therefore expensive) employees, he pushed many of them out and either replaced them with younger, cheaper workers or no one at all. New airplane projects would be held to strict budgets and timelines, with severely reduced flexibility to respond to quality or safety issues as they cropped up in the design and construction process. And research and development, long the foundation of Boeing's future product strategy, would "be measured, and managed, with a view toward . . . maximizing return to shareholders."

To McNerney, cost discipline was the primary foundational element of any successful business. He believed that his campaign to save money would force Boeing and its supplier network to find ways of becoming faster, cheaper, and more efficient. It was not his job to worry about safety: that was the domain of Boeing's aerospace engineers and production managers. During earnings calls, for example, he would generally defer questions on airplane quality and safety to his subordinates, only chiming in with generic pronouncements, such as "We have a systematized, standardized approach that has been set up." When he responded to questions about corporate finances, product pricing, and sales forecasts, he was much sharper and gave far more specifics. His approach at Boeing was the same as it had been at General Electric and 3M. After all, it had clearly gotten him this far.

There was, however, a key difference between his old roles and his new one. His previous companies were single vendors that sold into larger supply chains; GE, for example, only made the engines, not the entire airplane. None of his roles ever gave him much authority to introduce catastrophic risks into a product, either. People might notice if his cost-cutting decisions led to a decline in quality for their light bulbs or Post-It notes, but those decisions never put their lives at risk. Even when he became CEO of GE's Aircraft Engines division, he never had much input into the creation of new products. During his three-year tenure, the division did not produce any new engine designs, and focused instead on improving the efficiency of its existing product lines, many of which had been around for decades.

Now, however, he was the CEO of an original equipment manufacturer, and the decisions that he made would have long-lasting consequences. He would have the ability to set Boeing's design and production strategy for at least twenty-five years. The airplanes produced under his watch would carry billions of people. The guidelines he set for Boeing's new products would reverberate through a supply chain of thousands of vendors. His decisions would be more consequential than ever. And the first airplane to embody his new philosophy from start to finish would be the next iteration of the 737.

⁂

WHEN MANY PEOPLE THINK OF AVIATION, THEY IMAGINE THE LONG-HAUL, two-aisle-wide airplanes like the Boeing 747 or the Airbus A380 that whisk people to exotic international destinations. But there are five times more "narrowbody" airplanes like the 737 in service around the world. Every year, airlines order more than $300 billion worth of narrowbodies, or about 1,500 airplanes, which is nearly three times the demand for widebodies. A competitive design in the segment is not just important to a manufacturer like Boeing; it is existential.

One of McNerney's first big decisions was to define Boeing's future narrowbody strategy. The company had a great airplane design already in production—the 737 Next Generation series, or "NG" for short—but it was already halfway into its estimated twenty-year production run. Boeing needed a successor to take the place of the NG in its portfolio by 2015 or so, and it would be up to McNerney to figure out just what that airplane would be.

Boeing's internal design teams first proposed an all-new, cutting-edge airplane design that incorporated a decade's worth of technological innovations: carbon fiber materials, 3D-printed parts, and fully digital flight controls. But it would cost the company a rumored $12 billion just to develop and certify the design, and billions more to retool the company's factories to produce it. McNerney balked at the costs, and he remained at an impasse with Boeing's engineers for the next four years. They wanted to make the best airplane possible; McNerney wanted to make the cheapest one possible.

Competitive pressure finally forced Boeing's hand. In December of 2010, Airbus announced that it would soon debut a new narrowbody airplane called the A320neo. The "neo" (which stood for "New Engine Option") would be about 15 percent more fuel-efficient than the 737NG. With the oil shocks of the late 2000s only just behind them, airlines around the world clamored for the new Airbus. Even longtime Boeing customers such as American Airlines threatened to switch vendors if Boeing could not come up with a new airplane proposal that was nearly as fuel-efficient as the new Airbus, and that would enter production around the same time.

McNerney himself dictated Boeing's response to the threat of the "neo." The design he oversaw followed managerialism to the letter. It was based on the existing 737 airframe rather than an all-new one to save time and money on development. It would use the same engines that powered the A320neo—once again, opting for an off-the-shelf part instead of something bespoke. It would have just enough cosmetic upgrades to make it look sufficiently modern and justify the new-airplane prices, but it would still have 95 percent of the same parts and systems as the 737NG. This would give Boeing an excuse to renegotiate all of its vendor contracts so that it could wring even more cost efficiencies out of its vast supply chain.

There were other positives, at least as McNerney saw it. Development would be comparatively cheap, at between $2 billion and $3 billion. It could be ready in six years, arriving on the market just a few months after the first A320neos were scheduled to enter service. It was designed to be a Goldilocks airplane: not too expensive, not too cheap, but just good enough to keep Boeing competitive in the narrowbody market for another decade or two, until a clean-sheet design became more financially viable.

"We call it the 737 MAX," said Nicole Piasecki, a Boeing vice president, during the launch announcement in August of 2011. "The 737 MAX will deliver maximum efficiency, maximum reliability and . . . maximum passenger comfort. It optimizes everything."

The experts knew, however, that it would be difficult to optimize *anything* about the 737. Like all complex human endeavors, airplane designs accumulate little tradeoffs from concept to finished product, and the 737 had had fifty years of tradeoffs already baked into its design. Its basic framework dated back to 1964, when the Beatles were still together. It had gone through two product refreshes since, but still used steel cables, pulleys, and hydraulic pumps to move its control surfaces, whereas newer airplanes used computerized relays and motorized servos. Its 1980s-vintage computers lacked the processing power to run most advanced automation and even some basic troubleshooting software. No other commercial airplane in history had served as long as the 737 had, and no other design had ever extended to a fourth generation. McNerney's proposal for the MAX would require many more tradeoffs on top of the ones that had already accumulated with each prior model refresh. There was no easy way to tell whether the new MAX could successfully incorporate another round of additions—or whether the underlying 737 airframe was already too close to its breaking point.

There were signs of strain early in development. McNerney first wanted to use the same LEAP engines that powered the A320neo, to give the 737 MAX identical performance characteristics to its competitor. This proved to be impossible, however, because of the 737's existing design parameters. Back in the '60s, many airports didn't have jet bridges or even air stairs, so the original 737 was designed to be low enough to the ground that people could deplane from a built-in stairwell. The design had long since lost its stairs, but it had kept the ground clearance of the originals—about seventeen inches from the top of the runway to the bottom of the engines. This was not enough room for the new LEAP engines, which were seventeen inches larger in diameter than the engines on the third-generation 737s that they were supposed to replace. If Boeing's designers installed the LEAP engines on the MAX as-is, they would hang barely an inch above the surface of the runway—far too close for comfort.

So they had to come up with a compromise. First, Boeing had to ask the LEAP's manufacturer to design a custom version for the 737 MAX, which would keep many of the new technologies but deliver them in a package about ten inches smaller in diameter. Then they created an additional ten inches of clearance by lengthening the landing gear, redesigning the engine supports, and moving the mounting point for the engines a few inches higher. This appeared to solve the MAX's main problem of ground clearance without adding too much more cost. In an apparent validation of McNerney's managerial strategy, financial constraints had, in their own way, forced Boeing's engineers to come up with new ways to innovate.

But the cascade of problems did not stop there. Two years into development, as Boeing engineers started wind tunnel tests on the MAX, they discovered that solving their runway clearance issue had created another problem with the airplane's in-flight aerodynamics. The custom LEAP engines may have been small enough to fit in their new mounting location, but their size tended to disrupt the airflow around the wings in an unusual way. When the MAX made tight climbing turns, the disruption from the LEAPs would do two things simultaneously. First and most obviously, it would cause the airplane to buck upward, like a horse rearing up on its hind legs. At the same time, it would also reduce the aerodynamic loads on the MAX's elevators and ailerons, which could confuse pilots into overcorrecting the airplane's sudden upward movement. This was a dangerous combination of factors. To counter the sudden movement, pilots were likely to push forward on their control columns to return the airplane to its original flight path. But if they didn't know about the reduced loads on their control surfaces, they might push forward too hard, pitching the airplane into a sudden dive. Since this anomaly happened only during tight climbing turns, when the airplane was already at the edge of its performance capabilities, a loss of control like this could spell disaster.

In an earlier era, Boeing engineers would have stopped development to completely redesign the airplane in order to correct its growing list of defects, no matter the additional costs or the penalty in lost sales. Jim McNerney, however, had promised at the MAX's launch that the airplane "will provide customers the capabilities they want, at a price they are willing to pay, on a shorter, more certain timeline." The MAX's custom LEAP engines would stay; its engineers would have to find another way to fix its aerodynamic anomaly.

What must have appeared on paper as an exercise in cost discipline now turned into a game of engineering whack-a-mole. The MAX design team was working with a design that was so old, they could not change one thing without having another problem pop up in another system. Even worse, the deeper they got into the design phase, the harder it got to solve every new issue. McNerney made it clear from the start that the project would have to remain on its initial budget and timeline, regardless of what happened during development. To fix the MAX's aerodynamic problem within the project's scope, Boeing needed a unicorn of a solution. Whatever they came up with had to be precise and powerful enough to compensate for the MAX's aerodynamic problem; straightforward enough to integrate with a fifty-year-old airplane design; simple enough not to overwhelm pilots by adding another system to their already demanding workload; and cheap enough to satisfy McNerney's financial demands.

There was only one technology in existence that could satisfy all of those needs. In order to save the MAX, Boeing needed software.

⁝⁝⁝⁝⁝⁝⁝

FIVE YEARS LATER, ABOARD LION AIR 610, THE SOFTWARE THAT WAS SUPPOSED to save the MAX's production schedule now wreaked havoc in the sky. It was called the maneuvering characteristics augmentation system, or MCAS, and it was a brand-new design not only in the 737 MAX, but in all of commercial aviation. It was meant to be a new type of flight control software that could address the lift anomaly caused by the MAX's new engines without needing pilot input at all. It used the 737's existing pitch sensors to detect the kinds of tight climbing turns that triggered the extra lift, and swiveled the airplane's horizontal stabilizer—the miniature wing attached to the airplane's tail—to generate a downforce that canceled out that lift. Like so much else about the 737 MAX, the solution seemed easy enough on paper. But the reality turned out quite different.

MCAS was only supposed to activate in response to emergency situations. Instead, it had been tricked by a faulty piece of hardware into creating its own emergency. One of Lion Air 610's angle of attack (AoA) sensors, which measure the airplane's pitch, had been replaced the night before the flight by a Lion Air maintenance technician. This is a fairly common repair on commercial airplanes; AoA vanes take a lot of abuse, and can be fouled up by ice, rain, debris, or electrical failures. But in the rush to swap out a bad component for a good one, the maintenance technician had forgotten to calibrate the sensor properly. It had come from the factory out of alignment by exactly 21 degrees.

Like all humans, even maintenance technicians make errors. This mistake should not have put the flight in danger. On any other version of the 737, a single bad sensor would have still been a nuisance: it would have caused the stick shaker to activate and the airspeed and altitude readings to disagree, just as they had aboard Lion Air 610. But on the MAX, a 21-degree misalignment would be enough to trigger MCAS even during normal flight.

Which is exactly what happened. Two and a half minutes into the flight, MCAS triggered the horizontal stabilizer just as Suneja began to turn toward his holding point because the software thought that the airplane was in a steep climb. In reality, the airplane was nearly level, and the resulting downforce pushed the airplane into a dive. Suneja's first instinctive reaction—to pull back on his stick and use the electric trim switch to counteract the dive—returned Lion Air 610 to level flight for a moment. His second one was to re-extend the flaps, thereby undoing the last action he knowingly took before the dive started. Although Suneja didn't know it, this was exactly the right thing to do, as MCAS was programmed not to activate if the flaps were extended.

Neither he nor Harvino were any closer to understanding just what was behind Lion Air 610's erratic behavior. But Suneja continued to follow procedure all the same. He told Harvino to break out the airplane's Quick Reference Handbook, the airplane's in-flight troubleshooting guide, and see if he could find anything that applied to their situation.

MCAS still lurked in the background. It did not realize that there was a problem with the pitch sensor that fed it data. It did not care that the pilots had no idea what was going on. Most of all, it had no understanding of the chaos it was causing in the airplane, or that it was risking 189 lives through its actions. It waited for the flaps to be retracted so it could activate the horizontal stabilizer once again.

⁘⁘⁘⁘

THERE WAS NOTHING WRONG WITH MCAS FROM A CONCEPTUAL STANDPOINT. But its execution was tainted from the start by McNerney's managerial strategy. In its tireless search for the lowest bidder, Boeing switched vendors for the 737 MAX's flight control computers and software. The prior vendor, Honeywell, had supplied advanced avionics to the 737 family since the 1980s. Its project managers knew the airplane's systems front and back, and they knew the people at Boeing who managed those systems. But price was quantifiable, whereas expertise and relationships were not. Another company called Rockwell Collins underbid them, and Boeing went with the lowest price.

There was a reason that Rockwell Collins was able to bid so low. Like Boeing, it was overly focused on controlling costs, even to the detriment of its work output. For example, Rockwell Collins forced its software engineers to do their jobs with developer tools from the 1980s. This saved the company on licensing fees but made it far more difficult to follow current industry standards for programming high-quality, error-free code. Imagine having to create a modern video game with the same tools and processes that were used to create Pong, and you get an idea of the enormity of the task. With a lot of effort and some luck, you could probably get close to your goal. But the likelihood of doing so without major, game-breaking bugs surviving into the final product is small.

Especially when the surrounding culture prevents you from doing good work in the first place. Rockwell Collins employees described a constant process of "firefighting," as developers scrambled between one urgent project and another. They complained that work was "scoped improperly," and that "the majority of projects suffered from absurd designs and unrealistic deadlines." Even so, their managers always hit their budgets—not least because, as one employee said, "Corners were cut and numbers were fudged to hit milestones." This was not a culture that prioritized quality work, only quick work. Yet Boeing cared far less about Rockwell Collins's work culture than it did about the competitiveness of its bid.

These bad habits were further rewarded under the "Build to Performance" model of outsourcing. Boeing only gave broad guidance on the structure and form of the MAX's avionics systems, and left the rest up to Rockwell Collins's discretion.

"We're working on the high-level specs together and they're doing a lot of the implementation," said McNerney of the arrangement between Boeing and its vendors. "There's a working-together team that makes sure that the hooks and handles that link into other elements of the system are anticipated."

During the early development of the MAX, Boeing engineers sent over a short design brief for the software that was supposed to solve the airplane's aerodynamic problem. These were the "hooks" to which Rockwell Collins would have to fit its "handles." Boeing's brief laid out the software's *positive* characteristics—its normal operation and design goals—with clarity and specificity, including lengthy math equations and tables of figures that ran to two decimal places of precision.

The brief got considerably vaguer, however, when it came to the program's *negative* characteristics, the things it shouldn't do. These almost uniformly had to do with safety. One bullet point required the software to "not have any objectionable interaction with the piloting of the airplane." Another one required that it "shall not interfere with dive recovery."

These requirements were as obvious as they were vague, a sign of Boeing's level of reduced engagement under the Build to Performance model. And they opened a loophole that Rockwell Collins's leaders apparently found irresistible. They realized that they could just transplant code from another of their Boeing projects, which did something similar, and modify it for the MAX. This was cheaper, faster, and above all, easier to do than writing new software from scratch. After all, why should Boeing be the only one who was allowed to pad its margins?

So they borrowed code that they were developing for the KC-46 aerial refueling tanker, a design that Boeing's defense division was building for the US Air Force. Like all tankers, the KC-46 has an inherent stability challenge. As the airplane pumps its liquid cargo from its holding tanks into thirsty warplanes, its center of gravity changes. And as that center of gravity changes, it destabilizes the tanker's flight path. On earlier tanker aircraft, pilots would have to manually correct for these vertical gyrations. In 2011, Rockwell Collins decided to automate the process for the KC-46. They wrote the original version of MCAS to give the airplane the ability to automatically make those corrections without needing pilot input, using the airplane's external pitch sensors to detect changes in its flight path and the horizontal stabilizer to correct these disruptions.

From a managerial perspective, transplanting MCAS to the 737 MAX was an easy decision. But Rockwell Collins's leaders were so eager to save money that they ignored fundamental differences between MCAS as it worked on the KC-46, and MCAS as it would have to work on the 737 MAX.

The KC-46 only needed MCAS to operate during high, level flight—the only time when it's safe to refuel other airplanes. As a result, its version of MCAS had some built-in fail-safes because of its narrow operating parameters. It would only allow MCAS to activate if its AoA vanes *and* its onboard accelerometers both agreed that the airplane was not turning, climbing, or diving. Otherwise, if there was any indication that the airplane was actually maneuvering, MCAS would be prohibited from activating.

The MAX could not afford that luxury, however. It needed MCAS to be ready any time the pilots had to make a tight, climbing turn, which could happen at any speed, any altitude, and at almost any phase of flight except takeoff and landing. To allow for this wider range of operations,

MCAS could no longer use accelerometer data as one of its trigger conditions. Instead, it would only use pitch to determine whether or not to fire, which meant that it would have to take input from just one source: the airplane's AoA vanes. This reliance on a single type of sensor directly violated the sacred principle of redundancy that all airplane designs are supposed to respect.

The sensor layout of the 737 eroded that principle even further. The AoA system on the KC-46 was ironclad in its redundant design. It had four AoA vanes, two on each side of the aircraft. This allowed it to take multiple independent readings of its pitch angle so that it could detect disagreements among its sensors and "vote out" any one that might be obviously malfunctioning. Its computers could be trusted to measure its pitch angle accurately, all the time—the probability of more than one AoA vane malfunctioning simultaneously is vanishingly small. The MAX's AoA system was far more fallible, however. It only had two AoA vanes—a holdover from the 1960s, when pitch angle was considered a "nice-to-have" data point rather than an essential one. As a result, it could detect a disagreement between its two sensors, but it could not determine which was the wrong value. In order to allow MCAS to work even in the case of failure, then, Rockwell Collins had to gamble. Every time the airplane powered on, MCAS would randomly pick one AoA vane as its single source of truth for each flight and ignore the other one. This prevented MCAS from shutting down due to indecision every time a sensor malfunctioned. But it also meant that the system might trust a bad sensor.

All this might have been acceptable if not for the second difference between the KC-46 and the 737 MAX. The Air Force is not a profit-driven company. It insists that all of its pilots know their airplanes so intimately that, as one ex-Air Force officer told me, they can diagram every system from memory. In the commercial sector, global regulations require airline pilots to know the mechanics of their job just as well as a military pilot—but they don't require nearly as extensive systems knowledge of their airplanes. This is primarily a cost consideration: training pilots is expensive, and every hour that they aren't on the flight line is an hour that they aren't generating revenue for their airline.

Jim McNerney was sensitive to this need, and in outlining the program requirements for the MAX he insisted that the airplane have as few differences as possible from the 737NG. That way, pilots transitioning from the NG to the MAX would only need the Federal Aviation Administration (FAA) minimum of two and a half hours of computerized training to get approved for the new airplane. Boeing designers knew, however, that it would take more than two and a half hours to train new pilots on MCAS alone. So they hid its existence from pilots and airlines alike, deleting references to it from training materials and the airplane's flight manual. They reasoned that an MCAS activation was unlikely enough, and its normal operation subtle enough, that pilots would never need to know that it even existed. And if no one knew that it existed, then no one would need to be trained on it. They never imagined that MCAS might malfunction as it did on Lion Air 610, so they never taught the MAX's pilots what they should do in case MCAS went rogue.

Software developers call this sort of thing *kludge* (pronounced "klooj"). It's shorthand for any improvised or imperfect solution to an engineering problem, selected not because it's right but because it's cheap and easy. Kludge may save time, money, and critical resources in the short run. But every kludge eventually fails. And the first failure of the kludge that was MCAS happened to occur in the skies above Indonesia to a flight crew who had no idea what they were dealing with.

⁘⁘⁘

CAPTAIN SUNEJA AND FIRST OFFICER HARVINO WERE TEMPORARILY BACK IN control of Lion Air 610, but no closer to understanding what had caused the uncommanded dive in the first place. They were at least able to fly the airplane normally, which ruled out the presence of a catastrophic mechanical failure. But the stick shaker continued to rattle, and the instruments remained stubbornly out of sync. The two instrument panels still gave widely differing values for both airspeed and altitude. The Quick Reference Handbook didn't help, either. Suneja had quizzed Harvino on multiple emergency checklists, but none seemed to apply to their situation.

Finally, Suneja gave up. He decided that their best bet was to head back to Jakarta and get the airplane on the ground as soon as possible.

Inside Lion Air 610's computers, MCAS had been waiting. When the airplane powered on that morning, MCAS had randomly chosen the sensor on Suneja's side—the one that was miscalibrated by 21 degrees—as its single source of truth. MCAS had accepted the reading without question, even though it would have meant that the airplane had been in a continuous 21-degree climb for nearly five minutes, which if true would have put the 737 MAX at an altitude of 45,000 feet, almost a mile above its maximum service ceiling. Of course, MCAS lacked any sort of logic that would have caught either the miscalibration of the sensor, or the fact that the supposed climb was physically impossible for the airplane. It continued to believe a lie.

Suneja had accidentally inhibited MCAS earlier when he extended the flaps on the airplane, thus triggering one of the remaining fail-safes in MCAS's logic. During takeoff and landing, airplanes are going relatively slowly, so pilots will extend the flaps, essentially increasing the surface area of the wing, to allow the airplane to generate more lift despite its lower speed. MCAS disables itself any time that it detects the flaps are extended because that means the airplane is close to the ground, when pilots should never be surprised by automatic changes that they haven't specifically commanded.

It was unusual to have the airplane's flaps extended so far into the flight, when it had been airborne for nearly five minutes and had reached five thousand feet of altitude. Once again, however, Suneja was merely following his training. When a problem strikes midair, pilots are trained to return their airplane to its last known stable configuration. In the case of Lion Air 610, this meant returning to a takeoff profile, with flaps extended—which had worked, because MCAS was inhibited while an airplane was in its takeoff or landing profile. Suneja didn't know this, however, because he had no idea that MCAS even existed. He had saved his airplane but had no idea why. And by returning to the airport, he was about to put everyone on board back in mortal danger just by following normal procedure.

As he turned toward Jakarta, he retracted the flaps to return the airplane to cruise configuration. Immediately, MCAS came back to life. It still believed the 21-degree reading from its malfunctioning AoA vane. In its confusion, it believed the airplane was locked into one of the high climbing turns that generated too much lift. So it did what it thought was right, and moved the horizontal stabilizer to force the airplane's nose back down.

The airplane dove.

Suneja flicked the trim switch on his yoke to counteract the dive, and pulled back up. He had saved the airplane from crashing yet again. On the KC-46's version of MCAS, this would have been the end of it—as soon as the pilots move their controls or make a manual trim adjustment, MCAS cuts out entirely because it's only designed to work during level flight. Yet another of the fail-safes in the KC-46 version was lost when it was transplanted to the MAX, allowing MCAS to ignore Suneja's frantic control inputs and retain its terrifying command over the horizontal stabilizer.

Ten seconds later, MCAS forced the airplane to dive again, and Suneja counteracted it again. Then it dove a third time, and a fourth, and fifth. Each time Suneja managed to bring the airplane back under control. But he was only one human, fighting a seventy-five-ton machine. His physical strength would only last for so long. With each dive, Lion Air 610 picked up a little more speed. Already it was flying at 325 knots, dangerously close to its maximum operational limits. As the airplane gathered more and more velocity, the onrushing air pushed harder on its control surfaces, making them more difficult to move. That resistance was transmitted through the hydraulic lines that connected those surfaces to the cockpit. At this point, the flight controls were almost frozen in place. It took more than one hundred pounds of muscle power just to move them—as much force as it takes to restrain a full-sized Rottweiler by the leash. Suneja needed to pull back on his stick with all his might to keep the airplane from spiraling out of control.

Harvino, meanwhile, rifled through the airplane's emergency manual as he informed Jakarta's air traffic controllers of their situation.

"Lion Inter 610, are you descending?" asked an air traffic controller.

"Yes, we are descending," replied Harvino. "We have a flight control problem. We are returning to Jakarta."

Still MCAS continued to activate, for a tenth and fifteenth and twentieth time in a row.

It should never have been allowed to do this. MCAS does its job by moving the horizontal stabilizer, a large and powerful control surface that can make the entire airplane pitch up or down. On the KC-46, MCAS only moves the stabilizer a fraction of a degree at once since the movement of fuel from one part of the airplane to another creates only small changes to its center of gravity. This made MCAS safe to activate multiple times because it will only ever move the stabilizer a few tenths of a degree or so.

The MAX's version of MCAS was far more powerful than the one on the KC-46. In order to cancel the effect of the LEAP engines during turns, MCAS on the MAX was allowed to move the stabilizer almost a full degree of pitch with every activation. This meant that after a dozen activations in a row, it could move the horizontal stabilizer to its fully nose-down attitude—which would generate far too much downforce on the airplane for a human pilot to be able to counteract just by pulling back on the stick.

That's precisely what MCAS did on board Lion Air 610. Throughout the entire flight, it continued to get a faulty reading of 21 degrees of positive pitch from its bad sensor. Every time Suneja jerked his yoke back to counteract an MCAS activation, it read this as yet another turn, so it kept moving the horizontal stabilizer. Every time Suneja flicked his trim switch to try and increase the pitch of the horizontal stabilizer, MCAS would force the nose back down. After twenty activations, it still believed that it had to remain active in order to keep the airplane safe.

MCAS did not know that Suneja was desperately fighting its every movement, nor that Harvino was consulting an eight-hundred-page book to try and find something, anything, that would get it to stop. It could not sense the terror that would have taken hold inside the cabin as the passengers on board feared for their lives. It continued to do its job with a childlike naïveté, and the ruthlessness of a machine.

After five minutes of near-constant dives, Suneja no longer had the strength to keep flying his aircraft. His arms would have been tired, his breathing heavy with exertion. He motioned for Harvino to take over as Pilot Flying, and he would get on the radio and try to figure a way out of their situation.

Harvino gripped his own yoke. "I have control," he said.

But MCAS came alive once more.

Harvino yelped, surprised at how heavy his controls were and how difficult it was to bring the airplane's nose back up. "It's very . . ."

Suneja was already on the radio to ask for help.

"This is Lion Inter 650," he said, the stress of the situation causing him to use the wrong flight number. "We cannot determine altitude. Our instruments are not working." He requested an immediate vector back to the airport, and a three-thousand-foot buffer zone above and below his airplane to prevent a midair collision.

"Roger, Lion Inter 610," said the air traffic controller. "No restrictions."

During this short radio conversation, the airplane dove twice more. By now, the cumulative effect of twenty-four automatic downward trims in a row was too much to overcome. Harvino found it nearly impossible to bring his controls back and pull out of each dive. He was losing the battle with the airplane.

"It's flying down," said Harvino, terror in his voice. "It's flying down."

"It's okay," replied Suneja.

But it was already too late. Only ninety seconds had elapsed since Suneja had passed control to Harvino. In that short time, MCAS forced the nose of Lion Air 610 down six more times. Harvino could not bring the airplane out of the dives that MCAS kept commanding.

The cockpit phone chimed once as the flight attendants tried in vain to reach the pilots. They realized, as everyone else in the passenger cabin surely did as well, that they were about to die.

Suneja and Harvino probably did not hear the call, however, as more alerts sounded in the cockpit. First was the electronic *clack-clack-clack* of the overspeed warning, which indicated that the airplane was traveling fast enough to endanger its structural integrity. Then came the synthetic voice of the 737 MAX itself: "TERRAIN, TERRAIN," it said, as the onboard radar detected an imminent collision with the ocean surface. It was followed by "SINK RATE, SINK RATE," a separate warning meant to alert the flight crew that they were descending too fast.

"Fly up!" shouted Harvino in desperation, as he and Suneja pulled with all their might in a futile attempt to overcome the ever-increasing forces on their controls.

Every other warning system screamed at the pilots to do *something* to save the airplane. "PULL UP, PULL UP," said the ground proximity warning system—the loudest and most urgent warning a pilot will ever hear.

MCAS knew none of this was going on. It had no way of hearing any of the alarms, no way of seeing the panic that gripped the airplane. It still believed one thing and one thing only: that the airplane was in a tight climbing turn, and needed the lift anomaly from the engines canceled out.

Harvino could see the surface of the Java Sea rushing up to meet him.

In his last moments, he relaxed his grip on the control yoke and stopped fighting the airplane.

"God is great," he said.

In response, MCAS trimmed downward for the twenty-sixth and final time. It pushed the airplane's nose over into a 30-degree dive—finally enough to overcome the 21-degree miscalibration on the AoA vane. For the first time in the entire flight, MCAS believed that Lion Air 610 was finally out of its climb, and the threat of its lift anomaly had passed. At last, the program deactivated itself.

Half a second later, Lion Air 610 struck the water nose-first at a speed of 520 knots—faster than a Tomahawk cruise missile. All 189 passengers and crew were killed by the force of the crash. Mercifully, there was not enough time between impact and death for any of them to feel pain.

WITHIN DAYS, BOEING'S TECHNICAL TEAMS KNEW THAT SOMETHING HAD gone terribly wrong with Lion Air 610. Indonesian Navy divers found the airplane's flight data recorder—one of its two "black boxes"—in the shallow waters of the Java Sea. Two things immediately jumped out to investigators: first, that the only thing technically wrong with the airplane was a faulty angle of attack sensor, which affected the calculation of other critical flight data such as airspeed and altitude; and second, that some system, unknown to both the pilots and the investigators, had repeatedly activated the horizontal stabilizer, causing the flight crew to lose control and the airplane to crash.

Boeing could have grounded the MAX fleet right then to prevent another tragedy. It could have come clean about MCAS's existence and pledged to fix it right away. It could have ignored the dictates of managerialism, just once, in order to do the right thing.

Instead, its PR team released the requisite expression of corporate grief ("We are deeply saddened by the loss of Lion Air Flight JT 610"), and then the company got down to the real work of protecting its business. In public, Boeing surrogates aggressively defended the company's reputation in the media, and subtly planted doubts about Indonesia's aviation sector at the same time. In private, Boeing salespeople pushed the MAX even harder to their airline customers, arguing that the crash was due to pilot error rather than a design problem.

The strategy worked: in the three months following the crash, Boeing sold almost four hundred new MAX airplanes, worth more than $45 billion at list prices. The company rang in the new year by announcing that it would actually speed up production of the 737 MAX to help meet its growing order backlog. From Washington to Brussels to Beijing, Boeing executives pressured regulators and government officials to keep the MAX flying. While they did so, the global fleet of 737 MAXes, numbering nearly three hundred aircraft in total, continued to fly more than a million people every week.

Boeing's technical investigators were able to quantify just how dangerous it was to keep the MAX flying. Once they understood the link between the damaged AoA vane and the crash of Lion Air 610, they calculated that another deadly accident due to MCAS was all but inevitable. If Boeing took no corrective action, it calculated that the odds of another fatal crash over the next year was about half a percent—1 in 200. But the risk of a fatal crash increased substantially as more aircraft entered service. Once the MAX fleet reached its projected size of 4,800 airplanes, it was all but guaranteed to suffer a "fatal event" every single year.

Still Boeing took no substantial action because it cared more about maintaining its delivery rate than it did about the passengers on its airplanes. Jim McNerney had retired in 2016, but he chose as his successor Dennis Muilenburg, a longtime Boeing aeronautical engineer who eventually led Boeing's defense business. His extensive engineering background and lack of a business school degree appeared to signal a return to the engineering-first culture of the old Boeing.

Such hopes were short-lived, however. After announcing Muilenburg as his successor, McNerney assured investors that Boeing's managerial focus would continue under the new regime. "We have crafted that strategy together," he said, "and in many ways there's not going to be a change except generationally."

Muilenburg, for his part, was quick to second his former boss. In his first earnings call as CEO, he promised Wall Street analysts that Boeing's "biggest opportunity" as he saw it was not product excellence or renewed innovation, but "to execute commercial program profitability and return cash to shareholders."

Two weeks after the crash of Lion Air 610, he was forced to defend that strategy despite the growing evidence that it had caused a deadly crash. Appearing on Maria Bartiromo's Fox Business show, he did what any good managerial executive would do: protect his business at all costs.

"The bottom line here is, the 737 MAX is safe," he said. "We ensure that we provide all of the information that's needed to safely fly our airplanes."

But they had only just done so. A few days before Muilenburg's TV appearance, Boeing released a short Q&A to every 737 MAX pilot that told them what to do in case they found themselves fighting with the airplane's trim system. They did not identify MCAS by name, warning pilots only of the potential of "repetitive cycles of uncommanded nose down stabilizer" due to "erroneous AOA data." If that occurred, Boeing advised pilots to flip "both STAB TRIM CUTOUT switches in accordance with the existing procedures in the Runaway Stabilizer NNC [non-normal checklist]." In essence, Boeing attempted to reassure pilots that this new condition, whatever it was and whichever system caused it, would appear just like another type of in-flight emergency for which they had already trained.

They were being disingenuous. A runaway stabilizer typically involves a single, violent malfunction that renders the stabilizer completely unresponsive. Pilots know when it occurs chiefly through physical feedback: a sudden, significant, and permanent change in the airplane's performance.

(The 2012 movie *Flight* opens with a particularly bad runaway stabilizer failure, to which Denzel Washington's character responds by following the appropriate checklist until it becomes clear that the situation is nearly hopeless.) MCAS, though, is far more insidious. When it fails, it will overrule pilot commands one second, but return the airplane to their control the next. It will create error messages almost at random when the airplane is functioning normally, and then activate itself without warning the flight crew. It looked and felt like nothing that 737 pilots would ever have encountered before because it ran counter to the airplane's very design philosophy: it was an invisible electronic nanny on an airplane that was famous for its mostly analog design. Boeing's assumption that a good pilot could always overcome a bad machine was wrong.

⁝⁝⁝⁝⁝⁝⁝

ON THE MORNING OF MARCH 10, 2019, ANOTHER 737 MAX, OWNED BY ETHIO-pian Airlines, took off from Addis Ababa. No one noticed that a hawk had struck one of its AoA vanes the day before, pushing the sensor more than 60 degrees out of alignment. Lion Air 610's faulty reading of 21 degrees was high, but plausible. A reading of 61 degrees, however, was physically impossible for any commercial airplane. Yet MCAS believed this reading without question, too.

So when Ethiopian 302 took off, it began to behave just like Lion Air 610. The stick shaker on the left control column activated as soon as the airplane's wheels left the ground. The altitude and airspeed indicators diverged wildly from each other. Once the airplane's flaps were retracted, it dove unexpectedly. Now a second airplane was threatened by MCAS.

Instinctively, the Captain of Ethiopian 302, Yared Getachew, pulled back on his control column and flicked the trim switch on his yoke to counteract the dive. Ten seconds had passed since the first activation of MCAS.

Meanwhile, First Officer Ahmed Mohammednur radioed air traffic control to request an immediate return to the airport.

"Break, break, break," he said, panic making him forget good radio protocol. "Request back to home. Request vector for landing." Twenty seconds.

MCAS activated again. An alarm sounded in the cockpit: "DON'T SINK. DON'T SINK."

Captain Getachew pulled up and flicked the trim switch again. But every time Ethiopian 302 gained a few hundred feet of altitude, MCAS pushed the airplane right back down. Thirty seconds.

Then Mohammednur remembered Boeing's Q&A.

"Stab trim cut-out, stab trim cut-out!" he yelled, referring to the airworthiness directive's final action item: cut off power to the horizontal stabilizer. He and Getachew flipped the trim switches to the CUT OUT position. The stabilizer stopped moving, but it was stuck at 2.3 degrees of rotation—a position that generated enough force to continuously push the nose down, even when the pilots pulled back on their control columns.

"Pull up! Pull up!" said Getachew, which they did, in unison, to no avail. They could not overcome the force of the jammed horizontal stabilizer, inexorably pushing the nose toward the ground. The manual trim wheels were stuck, too, which meant that they had no electronic or mechanical means to move the MAX's horizontal stabilizer anymore. The airplane fishtailed through the sky, its engines screaming, its pilots desperately trying to gain altitude.

According to Boeing, Getachew and Mohammednur had done everything right. They had identified the problem within thirty seconds of the first MCAS activation, even without knowing what MCAS was or why it was malfunctioning. They had pulled the stabilizer trim cutouts eight seconds later. They had followed Boeing's operational bulletin to the letter, correctly identifying and resolving an MCAS malfunction in thirty-eight seconds—well within the forty-second window that Boeing believed would be adequate. But the pilots of Ethiopian 302 were still losing.

Now they had only bad choices available to them. The horizontal stabilizer was fixed in place by the massive aerodynamic forces acting on it as the airplane flew beyond its safe operating speed. The pilots had so far been able to keep the airplane flying level through skill and sheer muscle power, but they couldn't keep it up forever—by now, they would have been rapidly tiring from exertion. The moment they stopped pulling back on their control columns, the stabilizer would tip the airplane into a terminal dive within seconds. The only thing powerful enough to move it from its jammed position, however, was the electric trim system, which they had disabled in order to stop MCAS, exactly as Boeing had told them to do. If they flipped the cutout switches back in order to reconnect power to the system, MCAS would take over once again.

Ultimately, they chose to take their chances and reconnect the stabilizer power—hoping, however faintly, that they could move faster than MCAS, trimming the airplane upward at a faster overall rate than MCAS was trimming down. They would have to pull back on their control columns as hard as they could, while *also* flipping their trim switches upward as many times as they could. It would be a race against a machine that, so far, had all the advantages.

Together, they flipped the CUT OUT switches back to the ON position, and immediately pulled back on their yokes as hard as they could. They flipped their electric trim switches upwards, again and again, their last desperate attempt to save themselves and the 155 other souls on board their airplane.

MCAS was too fast for them. Even without power to its trim system, it had remained active. It still saw that the pitch angle read 61 degrees—well above its trigger threshold. It still detected that the airplane was in a turn, since it was continuously yawing back and forth as the pilots fought to regain control. As it had on Lion Air 610 four months before, MCAS ignored the obviously distressed flight path, the dangerously high speeds, the dozens of warnings that sounded in the cockpit, and the terror of everyone on board. It just knew to follow its preprogrammed logic. It rotated the horizontal stabilizer a third time as far as it was allowed, and then a fourth.

The downforce of this last MCAS rotation nearly pulled the control columns out of the hands of the two pilots. Pieces of the wings, the tail, and even the external sensors began to shear off of the airplane as Ethiopian 302 went into its terminal dive. It spiraled into a field near the town of Bishoftu, forty miles east of Addis Ababa, at more than 500 knots. None of the 157 people aboard survived.

⁘⁘⁘

ONE OF THE SEDUCTIONS OF SOFTWARE IS ITS INFINITE MALLEABILITY—THE idea that you can plug it into any situation, adapt it for any purpose, and it will just work. True, it allows us to do things we never thought possible, from navigating robots through space to plotting the trajectory of individual atoms, as well as many other, more mundane activities. To paraphrase Isaac Asimov, much of it really is sufficiently advanced as to seem like magic.

But like magic, it also demands something close to perfection in order to work properly. If a single requirement is missing from design documents, if a line of code appears in the wrong spot, or if a bad assumption is made about the abilities of the people using it—or the systems into which it is integrated—then the whole enterprise can fall apart. Safe software demands expertise, thoroughness, attention to detail. Anything less invites disaster.

Boeing's managerial turn, fully realized under Jim McNerney and endorsed by investors and board members who were too focused on the financials to worry about the product itself, created overwhelming pressure to overlook quality in favor of budgets and timelines. It marginalized anyone who didn't think in financial terms and centralized power in the hands of those who did. Ultimately, it failed to account for the one unbreakable law of project management: something can be done fast, cheap, or well, but you can only pick two. The managerial model could guarantee the first two conditions. Its practitioners were left to assume, wrongly, that the third would just happen as a matter of course. Boeing had always done so on every one of its past airplanes; why would the 737 MAX be any different?

This intellectual glibness in the guise of financial rigor is the reason that managerialism is utterly antithetical to a culture of safe technology. As a corporate philosophy, it inevitably pulls focus away from the level of messy particulars and into safe financial generalities. It attempts to map everything onto a standard set of metrics—revenues, costs, profits, and the almighty stock price—assuming that quantification is the same thing as knowledge. It all but forces leaders to strategize exclusively through the lens of their corporate income statement, as if their business were a giant spreadsheet to be tweaked at will. And it allowed Boeing's managers to focus on the airplane's financial profile, leaving them totally ignorant to the fact that they had lost control of MCAS, and therefore of the 737 MAX project itself, until it was too late.

CHAPTER 2

Managerial Revolutions

The very first car I ever owned was a first-generation Ford Focus, and it was a triumph of managerial engineering. It was originally designed for the European market, but "imported" back to the United States when Ford decided to discontinue the Escort and try something new in the domestic compact car segment. In addition to its design, parts for the car came from all over the world. Its body panels were manufactured in Mexico, its electronics in China, its glass in Nashville, and its engine in the century-old Ford foundry in Dearborn, Michigan. By far its biggest selling point was its low price—about $1,000 less than similar models from Chevy, Honda, and Toyota, thanks to its cheap materials and the reuse of parts from other Ford models. The Focus was a direct product of the company's "Ford 2000" initiative, which sought to speed up research and development timelines, consolidate the company from multiple independent business units into a single, cross-functional entity, and to reduce costs by nearly $3 billion per year. The little Focus, the poster child of Ford's new strategy, not only became the best-selling car in the world—it was so cost-effective that it also helped to double the company's global profit per vehicle to nearly $2,000.

Notice I did not say that it was a *great* car. It had poor acceleration, its transmission was sluggish, and the interior seemed to be made entirely out of scratchy automotive plastic. The coolant hoses were so brittle that I would find antifreeze sprayed across my engine compartment every few months, and the clear coat was so thin that just brushing up against the car with a piece of metal would leave a permanent white mark. Other owners had worse luck: that first generation of the Focus was the subject of nearly a dozen recalls and investigations, for contaminated fuel lines, suspension issues, and a rear wheel that had the potential to fall off (though the National Highway Transportation Safety Administration does not have any records of this occurring mid-drive).

Like the 737 MAX, the Focus was created as an attempt to address a market need not through innovation but through careful financial triangulation. Like the MAX, it was heavily outsourced: an estimated 90 percent of its parts were not made by Ford directly, but by third-party suppliers. Like the MAX, the Focus was not intended to be the highest-quality or highest-tech product in its category, only the cheapest. Both machines were produced by similar companies responding to similar technical and economic pressures. Why then did the same strategy yield such different results?

The answer underscores managerialism's two-faced nature. To a point, it creates value for companies: it dictates that they always seek new opportunities to generate more revenue, rein in costs, and find ways to protect their market position. Those same tenets can just as easily destroy value, however. Perfectly functional companies have taken managerialism too far, eviscerating their operations, releasing shoddy products, and harvesting short-term gains at the expense of long-term survival. I would argue that most modern firms cannot possibly assess themselves through financial metrics alone—especially in the tech sector, where their products are almost entirely ephemeral.

I don't intend for the term "managerialism" to become a dread word disguised as an economic term of art, like "late capitalism." The problem is not with the underlying philosophy per se. Without question, it has over the last hundred years created more value than it has destroyed, and has helped many companies grow, thrive, and even push the boundaries of innovation.

Yet managerialism evolved in a world of constraints—of strong competitors, underdeveloped markets, fair competition, and the physical limitations of materials, distance, and time. If its early practitioners attempted to exceed these limits, the invisible hand of the market would eventually knock them back into place or put them out of business altogether. Over time, however, some managerially run companies learned how to use their financial advantages as a shield to protect themselves from market pressures and government regulations in ways other than fair economic competition. They grew to ever-greater size and profitability. They reinvested their free cash not only into making themselves more competitive but also into making the market less competitive. They manipulated their stock prices, lobbied regulators to rewrite the rules of business in their favor, and diverted money away from their core operations for the sole purpose of lining the pockets of investors. They became so large and so dominant that they had no real checks on their power except the extent of their executives' ambitions.

The business world has not adapted to this new, megacorporate reality. As the economic historian Alfred Chandler observed in 1977, managerialism has changed so little over the years that a businessman of his own time "would find himself at home in the business world of 1910"—and both would find themselves equally at home in the business world of today. Every major corporate innovation of the last half-century—from Milton Friedman's shareholder value theory to the widespread adoption of Six Sigma in the 1990s—has really just been a change in emphasis of managerial techniques rather than a challenge to them. Even though corporations are larger and more powerful than ever, they are so focused on their financial metrics that they don't even know how to properly assess the risks of their products. Too often they dismiss non-financial concerns as mere "externalities"—a technical-sounding way of turning everything into someone else's problem.

In the days before computers, we had a reasonable chance of avoiding externalities through the normal workings of the market. We could just not buy the dangerous toy or the contaminated food. We could avoid driving the lemon of a car. We could even rely on regulators to recall the worst offenders before they could cause injury and death on a mass scale.

But computers have overwhelmed what guardrails remain. They have all but eliminated the distance between thought and reality, making it easier for companies to bring a bad concept to market. They have made product cycles vanishingly short, so that internal reviewers and external regulators have less of an opportunity to catch potential flaws before they manifest in the real world. They have allowed companies to chase opportunities well outside their areas of competence, only because software makes it cheap for them to do so. Without some kind of check on the impulse to grow and profit forever, managerial megacorporations will create ever more catastrophic externalities that they have no real ability to stop.

This dangerous union of corporate blindness and technological power has caused many of the global scandals of the last twenty years. It doesn't matter if you have the world's best and brightest working for you, or if you operate at the very leading edge of innovation. As long as powerful companies follow an ideology that can only look inward at cash flows, not outward at consequences, we will continue our forced march into a dystopia of exploitative and dangerous software.

:::::::

TO UNDERSTAND WHY A THEORY DESIGNED TO MAKE ORGANIZATIONS MORE efficient also made them more destructive, we must go back more than a century, to the dawn of mass production. In the textbook version of history, the Industrial Revolution just kind of *happened*, when "a wave of gadgets swept over England," as one schoolboy summarized for the British historian Thomas S. Ashton. We may know that James Watt invented the steam engine in 1769 and Eli Whitney invented the cotton gin in 1793. But we often assume that these inventions spread slowly and steadily across England and the United States, borne by the tides of economic progress. Like Ashton's schoolboy, we assume that such tides were all but inevitable.

In reality, however, both countries remained largely agrarian, unmechanized, and above all extremely localized until the mid-nineteenth century. As late as 1830, most textile and iron manufacturers actually had access to all the technology they could have wanted—Ashton's "wave of gadgets" having long since crested. What these small industrialists lacked, however, was an understanding of how to use new technologies most efficiently, and how to turn that efficiency into a competitive advantage on the open market.

Mass production was an opportunity but also a logistical nightmare. A single mill could out-produce entire towns of solo artisanal laborers. But the mill required a steady stream of fuel and raw materials, and enough outbound transportation to keep finished goods from piling up on the factory floor. Success would depend on consistent staffing—the recruitment, management, and payment of rotating shifts of semiskilled "piece" laborers. And the mill would need lots of cash, to pay for all the suppliers, transporters, repairmen, and traders. A single misspent penny, or a single wasted second, could disrupt the careful balance of mass production.

Even if you had your own factory in order, you relied on someone else's transportation network to get your product to market. By the beginning of the nineteenth century, railroads had the potential to move manufactured goods at scale from the new mechanized factories. But potential was not the same as reality. As late as 1830, there was still no such thing as a long-distance railroad network either in the United States or England. Instead, freight shippers had to navigate a patchwork of independent carriers, each of which operated using their own (often incompatible) rail gauges, their own (often unsynchronized) timetables, and their own (often idiosyncratic) accounting methods. As with factories, railroad companies would need to standardize their operations if they were to unlock the latent potential of their new technology. The success of one depended on proper coordination with the other. And that coordination would require something that had never been done before: the invention of a common "operating system" for business that could work for any type of work in any industry, anywhere in the world.

That system arrived, according to historian Joel Mokyr, only when groups of "engineers, mechanics, chemists, physicians, and natural philosophers" began to apply Enlightenment concepts of scientific analysis to the industrial economy. Beginning with the railroads, which were the most capital- and information-intensive businesses of their time, this new class of worker focused on system optimization. To standardize operations between companies, they agreed to common systems of rail gauges, weights, and measurements, and consolidated eighty different timekeeping methods into one. To understand the health of railroads as businesses, they created the first regular financial reports (including the forerunners of the modern balance sheet and income statement) and invented new financial concepts, such as gross and net margin, the division between capital and operating expenses, standard cost accounting methods, and the concept of return on investment. Increasingly, the language of finance was the language of railroad operations. The twentieth-century Austrian economist Ludwig von Mises observed in his essay "The Nature of Economic Calculation" that

> where one cannot express hours of labour, iron, coal, all kinds of building material, machines and other things necessary for the construction and upkeep of the railroad in a common unit, it is not possible to make calculations at all. The drawing up of bills on an economic basis is only possible where all the goods concerned can be referred back to money.

The concept of abstracting everything into its financial components quickly spread from railroads to other sectors of the mechanized economy: metalworking, mining, shipping, and communications. A new layer of professional managers, who could operate primarily at the level of financial abstraction, now directed the labor force with the goal of maximum productivity. Gone was the sentimentalism of the medieval economy, which one French historian described as "dominated by agrarian rhythms, free of haste, careless of exactitude, unconcerned by productivity." Under managerialism, work became standardized: three hundred days a year, fourteen hours a day, with every shift planned down to the minute. And only those who understood the math could be trusted with the new economy. Frederick Winslow Taylor, the first great theorist of the managerial age, declared that "the workman who is best suited to handling pig iron is unable to understand the real science of doing this class of work." In his view, management *needed* to be completely alienated from labor—almost to the point of having contempt for the line worker—in order to do its job correctly.

After 1900, managerial leaders would spread the gospel of financial rigor to nonindustrial sectors. Leaders at industrial heavyweights such as US Steel and Union Pacific were tapped to lead retailers, advertising firms, and television and movie studios. Besides this direct cross-pollination through hiring, managerial ideas spread through professional forums such as the Rotary Club (founded in 1905) and Kiwanis International (founded in 1915), and magazines such as *Fortune*, *Barron's*, *Business Week*, and the *Harvard Business Review*, all of which were founded in the 1920s. Two decades later, and suffused with managerial zeal, American industrial companies transformed themselves into the "Arsenal of Democracy" during World War II. The steel and rubber industries, for example, doubled their productivity; airplane manufacturers quadrupled their output; and the entire defense industry produced nearly $185 billion (or nearly $2.5 trillion in today's dollars) in weapons, munitions, and supplies for the war effort—more than ten times its productivity during World

War I. Hollywood studios, under orders from the Office of War Information to feed the public a steady stream of patriotism, began to standardize their production processes so that they could collectively release four new (and fairly generic) propaganda films *per week* between 1942 and 1945, alongside classics such as Michael Curtiz's *Casablanca* and Alfred Hitchcock's *Shadow of a Doubt*. Production managers with experience in the liquor industry brought their ideas to pharmaceutical companies, where the introduction of mass fermentation techniques nearly quadrupled the production of penicillin. In the small town of Austin, Minnesota, a committee of food scientists, marketers, and copyright lawyers created a long-life, vacuum-canned, and trademarkable product made out of otherwise unsellable cuts of pork. Spam was another triumph of managerial design, just like my old Ford Focus.

The demand for managerially trained business leaders became so great that on-the-job training could no longer supply enough of them. Hence the growth of the business school. The earliest examples, such as the Wharton School at the University of Pennsylvania and the Tuck School at Dartmouth, offered degrees in the fields of "Science in Commerce." In 1922, Harvard founded its own business school and launched the very first master's in business administration (MBA) degree.

MBA programs have changed little in the intervening century. Today, MBA students still spend the majority of their time—upward of 75 percent of the coursework at most schools—learning the same financial and administrative methods that railroad accountants pioneered in the nineteenth century. Courses such as ethics, business history, or human resources are usually relegated to the elective track; they don't, after all, help new managers learn how to make money more efficiently or faster, which is the point of the whole program. The MBA degree has become a de facto passport to corporate leadership, giving people an easy way to ascertain whether someone has the same managerial background as almost everyone else in the upper echelons of business.

The "constant economic pulse-taking and measurement mania," in the words of historian and journalist Andrew Yarrow, became so widespread that it now frames almost every aspect of daily life in the United States. Nightly news broadcasts have reported on the daily movement of the Dow Jones Industrial Average since the days of Walter Cronkite, even though fewer than one in five Americans owned stocks until relatively recently. Generations of grade school students have been subjected to 1950's-era educational films with titles such as "Prosperity: The Key to Plenty" and "Competition and Big Business." American officials have even tried to apply managerial methods to foreign policy: Robert McNamara, the former CFO of Ford Motor Company and later Secretary of Defense, attempted to model the number of "kills" required to win the Vietnam War, while economics professor turned CIA director James Schlesinger complained about the spy agency's return on investment and eventually laid off so many employees to save costs that he became known as "Nixon's axe-man."

Even corporate law reinforces the managerial understanding of business. Since 1934, the Securities and Exchange Commission has required every public company to file annual and quarterly reports to investors. In those reports, companies have significant leeway to include idiosyncratic commentaries and vanity metrics that show how many cars they manufactured, how many users opened their app, or whatever proxy for growth they wish to provide. After that, however, all companies must disclose a standard set of basic financial metrics, calculated in the same way, that theoretically allow investors to measure them against every other public company. Larry Summers, the former secretary of the Treasury, even argued before Congress that "if one were writing a history of the American capital market I would suggest to you that the single most important innovation . . . was the idea of generally accepted accounting principles." By the time James Burnham named the managerial revolution in 1941, it had already been underway for decades.

Ideology alone cannot make the economy grow. But it acted as an accelerant alongside technological change and improvements in education. Companies that adopted managerial strategies grew more predictably, planned more effectively, and succeeded at a higher rate than companies that did not. It was not only the best way to do business. By the late twentieth century, it was also the *only* way to do business.

As management theorist Peter Drucker wrote in 1970, "the fact is that in modern society there is no other leadership group but managers."

· · · · · · ·

I'LL BE THE FIRST TO ADMIT: WORKING UNDER MANAGERIALISM IS OFTEN EASY and sometimes fun. It feels good to know that your work helped improve a metric, whatever that metric might be. It boosts your ego when you can explain why a revenue or profitability chart moved up and to the right. And it is inherently motivating to organize your day around one or two numbers that you believe you can both understand and influence.

Managerialism appeals to us precisely because it breaks down *all* work into a series of doable tasks. And it lets us believe that by optimizing each one, we can optimize the whole business. It applies the same "scientific" lens that Frederick Winslow Taylor took to his steel mills a hundred years ago. The main difference is that where Taylor optimized for time alone, managerialism optimizes for a broader set of financial metrics, which gives the inner workings of a company the appearance of complexity and rigor on the one hand, and transparency to outsiders (in particular financially literate investors) on the other.

As you spend more time in a managerial system, however, you'll start to see the hollowness of those metrics. You'll see entire organizations focus on parts of their business that their leaders have deemed financially important, while ignoring others that you and your colleagues know to be *actually* important. You'll suffer through painful cost-cutting measures that will hamper your ability to do your job in the long term, even if those measures might boost the stock price in the short term. You'll be asked to do work that you might find unimportant, maybe even downright unethical, only because someone who's never even bothered to meet you or understand your discipline thinks it will help the bottom line. And, if you want to keep your job, you'll probably do all of these things.

Over time, you'll begin to understand that the executives who set your targets don't see what you see, and don't understand what you do. They are too far removed from reality to see the risks that they create. They are too focused on the financials to even consider anything else. It's not that they are inherently evil or bad people. It's just that they have been trained their whole professional lives to focus exclusively on their corporate P&Ls, and to dismiss everything else as a mere "externality"—a weasel word that both masks the potential for real-world harms in a benign-sounding euphemism, and absolves the company of responsibility for that harm.

Instead, there is a kind of unspoken agreement that the market will correct these externalities on its own. In part, this is due to the triumph of free-market economic theory, as exemplified by Milton Friedman's 1970 *New York Times* essay in which he declared that "there is one and only one social responsibility of business—to use its resources and engage in activities designed to increase its profits." Friedman's piece introduced a popular audience to the idea of shareholder capitalism, or the assumption that by maximizing their own value, companies would create value for the rest of society whether they intended to or not. From a purely economic perspective, Friedman was largely right. Managerialism gave companies the best chance to maximize their individual financial position in the greatest number of circumstances. And that stability translated into more jobs and higher wages for employees, better returns for investors, and a robust economy that benefited even those who participated passively, such as holders of 401(k)s.

Yet circumstances change. What was an optimal format for a mechanizing world may no longer be optimal for a world being eaten by software.

For one thing, the modern managerial corporation itself has changed. In 1870, the average company employed around forty workers, and there were only a handful that exceeded a few million dollars in market capitalization. By the mid-1950s, however, decades of organic growth and industrial consolidation had given rise to the megacorporation. Fully half of manufacturing workers, and two-thirds of transportation workers, were employed by companies with at least a thousand workers and worth more than a billion dollars, such as General Electric, Ford Motors, Exxon Mobil, and American Airlines. By 1955, there were so many of them that *Fortune Magazine* began to publish an annual list of large corporations, ranked by size. That year, the smallest company on the list was Copperweld Steel, with annual revenues of $49.7 million (about $566 million in today's dollars), and the largest was General Motors, at $9.8 billion in annual revenue ($112 billion today). Companies have continued to grow ever larger in the decades since: in 2023; even after adjusting for inflation, the smallest company on the Fortune 500 list was more than fifty times the size of Copperweld in 1955, and the largest was six times bigger than GM.

Size was power, and it allowed companies to redeploy their free cash not only into their core business but also into more exotic ways of defending their financial position. One such strategy involved mergers and acquisitions, which saw corporations grow by absorbing another company entirely, while also removing a potential competitor from the market. Another involved essentially manipulating the behavior of investors through stock buybacks (which create artificial demand for the company's stock, temporarily boosting its price) and dividend payouts (which give investors an alternative source of upside when the underlying investment isn't appreciating in value at a competitive rate). A third strategy involved lobbying government officials to pass laws and regulations that (unfairly) privileged one business but not its rivals. These defensive strategies have proven to be so effective that their practitioners can survive the worst economic downturns—or the financial consequences of their own bad strategies—without facing insolvency or failure.

Size created a new form of entropy, though. Executives like to believe that they sit at the top of a neat hierarchy as depicted in the classic org chart. In this model, information should flow from the bottom to the top of a company, allowing managers to see clearly what happens throughout their organization. In return, they should be able to analyze that information with the aid of their managerial tools to make correct strategic decisions and properly exert control downward.

There is a decent chance that you, the reader, have worked in corporate cultures that felt nothing like this. Instead, you may have experienced what felt like barely controlled chaos, where good ideas from upper management appeared only sporadically, and information from the bottom of the hierarchy rarely reached the top. If so, you're not alone.

In a 1996 article called "Musings on Management," a management professor at McGill University named Henry Mintzberg argued that the traditional org chart was pure fantasy. After nearly thirty years of studying large companies, he had found that most organizations act nothing like the org chart would suggest. They don't share information well in either direction, and even when they do, executives don't always consider that information when making strategic decisions. In his view, "what organizations really have are the *outer* people, connected to the world, and the *inner* ones, disconnected from it."

> Picture the organization as a circle. In the middle is the central management. And around the outer edges are those people who develop, produce, and deliver the products and services—the people with the knowledge of the daily operations. The latter see with complete clarity because they are closest to the action. But they do so only narrowly, for all they can see are their own little segments. The managers at the center see widely—all around the circle—but

> they don't see clearly because they are distant from the operations. The trick, therefore, is to connect the two groups. And for that, most organizations need informed managers in between, people who can see the outer edge and then swing around and talk about it to those at the center.

In a hundred-person company that does only one thing, these kinds of cross-level conversations are easy to facilitate. In a thousand-person company with multiple divisions, they get harder. In a multinational that runs entirely independent lines of business and employs tens or even hundreds of thousands of workers, an executive in the center would have to cut through several layers of middle management just to get a glimpse of what, exactly, is going on at the periphery.

Some do. But many more either can't make sense of it—because their business training doesn't necessarily give them the tools to understand specialized fields such as medicine or aerodynamics—or won't even try. They retain the Taylorite condescension toward anyone lower on the corporate hierarchy. When I worked at Amazon, I and my fellow peripherals referred to the members of this group as business athletes. They were people who never wanted to leave the comfortable world of general management. They preferred to keep their distance from the front lines, operating in a purely abstract realm, whose domain expertise only ever included PowerPoint, Excel, and the occasional database query. This aggressive dilettantism did not limit their careers: after all, their network did not extend down the job ladder at one company, but across the universe of fellow managers at *other* companies. They considered every job to be a temporary stop on a career path that could lead just about anywhere. Better to keep your options open with the other managers who will determine your success in future roles, even if it means ignoring the people who will have the most effect on your current one.

The managerial class of the world's mega-corporations sits inside a bubble of self-absorption. They can only understand what their companies do at many levels of abstraction. There is too much organizational *and* conceptual distance between them and the real world; they cannot see the details of their operation easily, and might not understand those details even if they could. As a result, they focus on corporate financials to the exclusion of everything else. This, however, blinds them to potential externalities that their products might cause, often until it's too late to prevent them. Even after those externalities become apparent, their first responsibility is to their business; they have no incentive to solve any problems that might threaten their cash flows. Nor do they need to bow to the corrective pressures of the market: they have learned to use the sheer size and financial strength of their employers to buy the competition, pay off investors, or manipulate regulators in order to get their way. The managerial megacorporation, in other words, does not need to pay attention to anything outside of its walls.

As a result, when managers take control over an inherently dangerous industry, they can put the rest of us at risk. Perhaps the most infamous example of the inability to see beyond the income statement occurred on December 14, 1953. That night, the CEOs and presidents of the largest tobacco companies in the world met at the Plaza Hotel in New York. Earlier that year, *Reader's Digest* had published a series of articles titled "Cancer by the Carton," the first time that a mainstream media outlet had publicized a link between cigarettes and lung cancer. Tobacco executives, however, viewed the revelations less as a public health emergency and more as a threat to their industry, which made nearly $5 billion in annual revenues, or $57 billion in today's dollars. They convened at the Plaza to develop their response.

The executives were not the drawling country aristocrats portrayed on the TV show *Mad Men*, but rather professional managers to the core. All of them were former bankers, lawyers, or stockbrokers, with degrees from universities including Yale, Princeton, Fordham, and Duke, and they believed that it was their job to preserve the tobacco industry's business model, by whatever means necessary.

During the meeting, they agreed to fight the claims that tobacco and lung cancer were somehow related. They would launch a public relations campaign to argue that "the products we make are not injurious to health," and that the research was "not regarded as conclusive in the field of cancer research." They would fund "alternative" research studies that showed no link between cigarettes and cancer. And they would ramp up their government lobbying, to forestall anti-smoking regulation for as long as possible. All told, this would cost them tens of millions of dollars every year for the foreseeable future. But tobacco companies enjoyed fat operating margins, earning more than thirty cents of profit for every dollar of revenue. In the grand scheme of things, the propaganda war was just another line item on the balance sheet.

Their strategy paid off almost immediately. By the second half of 1954, cigarette sales were growing yet again, reversing an eighteen-month dip in the wake of the *Reader's Digest* articles. They would continue to increase for the next two decades, reaching a peak of 636 billion cigarettes sold in 1981—equivalent to every American smoking two and a half packs every week. Meanwhile, the lobbying campaign managed to stave off real regulation for decades. It wasn't until 1966, thirteen years after the Plaza meeting, that warning labels appeared on cigarette packs. Smoking wasn't banned on domestic flights until 1989. And the first laws banning smoking in public places went into effect in 1998. These delays allowed the tobacco industry to rake in cash despite the looming existential threat, reaching total revenues (in present-day dollars) of $70 billion by the mid-1980s, $100 billion by 2000, and more than $175 billion today.

Big Tobacco eventually faced major consequences in the form of the $365 billion master settlement agreement that went into force in 1998. But even that result had been shaped to the industry's advantage by its lobbyists and lawyers. The industry only had to pay lump-sum damages of $10 billion right away, and could pay out the remaining $350 billion over the course of the next twenty-five years. None of the five tobacco conglomerates went into bankruptcy as a result of the MSA. In fact, global tobacco consumption actually rebounded starting in 2004, and the whole industry is worth more today than it was at its sales peak in 1983. As one medical journal observed, "the MSA did no major harm to the companies. Some features of the MSA appear to have increased company value and profitability." Seen through the lens of managerialism, the tobacco industry not only survived its greatest challenge but also came out stronger as a result of it.

As long as you ignore the human cost. At the dawn of the twentieth century, smoking was neither a volume business nor a public health threat: the average American smoked less than two packs a year, and lung cancer deaths numbered in the dozens across the entire country. In the 1930s, however, managerialism grabbed hold of the industry, and with it came new urgency: make more, sell more, optimize more. Tobacco companies launched discount brands, saturated the market with advertising, and cut deals with the military to include cigarettes in soldiers' rations. They marketed to children and teenagers, since the best way to get a lifelong smoker was to hook them young; as one executive admitted, "If the tobacco companies really stopped marketing to children, [they] would be out of business in 25 to 30 years." As their revenues skyrocketed, so too did annual deaths from lung cancer: from near-zero in 1900 to 10,000 in 1945, to more than 110,000 in 1983. As far as tobacco executives were concerned, however, the deaths of these loyal users were more than offset by the new ones acquired through marketing, advertising, and PR efforts. All this human misery that their industry had directly caused did not materially affect their balance sheets. It was, quite literally, none of their business.

Managerial zeal also turned the synthetic insecticide DDT into a global environmental hazard. At first, DDT was only intended as a tool of public health: the federal government bought nearly eighteen thousand tons of it each year to control the spread of insect-borne diseases such as malaria, typhus, and dengue fever among Allied soldiers and sailors during World War II.

But government demand dried up as soon as the war ended. In response, DDT manufacturers repositioned their product not as a public health tool for tropical military bases but as an all-purpose "benefactor for all humanity," in the words of one 1947 advertisement. Housewives were encouraged to sprinkle it around the house to kill cockroaches, bedbugs, and flies. Farmers were promised that its general use as a "broadcast pesticide" would protect their crops and livestock. Doctors were told that it could be used on other diseases such as polio, too. Even paint companies produced DDT-infused product lines that could "render walls effective against stable-flies and house-flies" for several months after application. All these new commercial uses turned DDT into big business. Domestic production increased fivefold, and generated hundreds of millions of dollars a year for companies including Montrose Chemical, Ciba-Geigy, and Monsanto.

Almost as soon as DDT became ubiquitous, however, its negative "externalities" began to present themselves. In 1946, the US Department of Agriculture discovered that houseflies could become resistant to DDT within a few generations of exposure, limiting its effectiveness as a pesticide. Over the next few years, physicians and scientists discovered not only that DDT had contaminated an alarming amount of the nation's food supply but also that human bodies tended to store the chemical in fat cells rather than flush it out like they do for many natural toxins. The long-term ramifications were unknown. And then, in 1962, Rachel Carson published *Silent Spring*, her famous account of the ecological damage that DDT had wrought. She implicated DDT in the near-extinction of the bald eagle, the peregrine falcon, the brown pelican, and dozens of other bird species. She also correctly blamed its indiscriminate use on managerial executives, who were blind to environmental concerns.

"This is an era of specialists, each of whom sees his own problem and is unaware of or intolerant of the larger frame into which it fits," she wrote. "It is also an era dominated by industry, in which the right to make a dollar at whatever cost is seldom challenged."

Even then, DDT was too profitable to stop. Annual production peaked in 1963 at nearly ninety thousand tons, but remained above sixty thousand tons for the rest of the decade. It wasn't until 1970 that executives even acknowledged the chemical's deleterious effects on the environment. They continued to fight against the Environmental Protection Agency's ban on the commercial use of DDT until 1972—showing that the managerial desire to protect business flows far outweighs any sense of responsibility toward the outside world.

Time and again, managerial tactics employed at a megacorporate scale have led to worse outcomes for society at large. A more recent example is the takeover of nearly ten percent of the nursing homes in the United States by private equity firms beginning in the late 2000s. These PE-owned nursing homes generated lavish profits by deploying managerial optimizations: they raised prices, cut back on skilled care, and kept residents content, not through building a strong community and providing fulfilling activities, but through the routine prescription of cheap sedatives. Their refusal to pay for sufficient staff also led to more frequent medical errors and higher patient mortality rates. From a managerial perspective, however, the takeover was successful: after all, only the unit economics matter, and those incontrovertibly improved under private equity management.

Similar stories have occurred throughout service-based industries, at hotels, hospitals, schools, and newsrooms. If a company's output is in some way intangible and unmeasurable—the alleviation of suffering, the creation of knowledge, or a comfortable night's stay—managerialism will literally not know how to account for it. Its real value will forever be unreadable by the analytical mechanisms of finance, and will therefore be unappreciated by professional managers, who will automatically "value engineer" their way into a degraded product. So long as the outcomes don't affect the bottom line, however, such financial optimization will be considered a success.

....

FOR DECADES, WE HAVE FACED THE CORROSIVE EFFECTS OF MANAGERIAL CAPitalism every day, and everywhere we look. It is the force that squeezes us for incremental revenue at every turn. It is the wall of indifference that we encounter every time we find ourselves running afoul of our banks, our credit card companies, and our bill collectors. It gives us neither mercy nor sympathy. It applies the mentality of the schoolyard bully to the entire economy, forever stealing our money and kicking us in the teeth afterward for good measure.

But in the age of modern technology, we are staring down an even-faster proliferation of managerial risk. Unlike anything else in human history, software allows companies to act with unprecedented speed and scale. There are no natural checks and balances during the process of its creation or implementation: you can turn any idea into a monetizable software program, but you won't know whether it works or what it will actually do "in the field." Only when it is deployed for the first time does it become "real": in some sense, the live product is the first actual beta test. Software development is invisible, intangible, and unmeasurable until the last possible moment. Once that software is finalized, it can be launched in the blink of an eye, and transmitted around the world with only the most cursory oversight from regulators or even quality testers from the major tech companies. Its flaws may not become apparent until well after its release date, at which point it can be difficult if not impossible to stop its use.

Software supercharges other problems inherent in managerialism, too. The insularity and technical ignorance of general managers leads to bad software. I have certainly never heard of a popular device or program that was invented solely by a professional manager. But I do know that every tech company where I've worked forces managerial ideas into all of its products, no matter how bad or user-unfriendly they might be. It is almost a rite of passage for product managers and developers to implement managerial ideas into otherwise good software, purely for their revenue-generating potential: microtransactions in games, advertising popups on websites, MCAS in the 737 MAX.

Despite the powers we ascribe to it, software has no ability to set its own limits on what it will or won't do. It won't feel bad about exploiting people, or creating injustice, or unleashing disasters at scale. It simply does what it is told. This makes it a perfect vehicle for managerial principles, where anything that gets in the way of making more money is considered an inefficiency, to be excised with extreme prejudice.

Science fiction tells us that our greatest technological threat comes from genocidal machines. We have learned to fear *Terminator*'s Skynet or the Cylons from *Battlestar Galactica*. But this has distracted us from the far more pervasive, if less lurid, threat. Managerial software may not lead to the killer robots imagined by pop culture, but it still creates unintended risks every time it is used to find the next dollar of profit.

We could easily blame capitalism alone for our present woes. But many if not most of us are responsible, too, because we have put too much faith in technology. We want to believe that software is a kind of magic over which we exercise complete control. We walk around with supercomputers in our pockets, so how could we not? For all of technology's obvious faults, we believe that its attendant benefits are massive, and any systemic problems in tech can be fixed by purging it of bad actors and obvious frauds.

We deceive ourselves. The problem in software development is more fundamental than we realize. Software isn't magic. It is often very dumb. But it is an extremely powerful tool that we have entrusted to people who unquestioningly follow a management philosophy developed in a bygone age—and that never served humane interests to begin with. We see software turning against us everywhere we look. Yet we still fail to understand why it keeps happening, as if we have just been unlucky this whole time.

CHAPTER 3

As Reliable as Running Water

For many people, Uber now stands metonymically for the entire gig economy and its attendant ills: the exploitative business model, the inefficient matching of supply with demand, the relative frailty of political solidarity in the face of overwhelming convenience. For others, that's precisely the draw. As of this writing, Uber operates in more than ten thousand cities around the world, and its drivers complete more than seven billion trips every year. Despite its missteps, Uber has evolved into something reasonably close to the vision of its now disgraced founder, Travis Kalanick: transportation as reliable as running water.

I suppose I ought to take pride in its success because it's partially my success, too. In mid-2016, I joined Uber to build its nascent restaurant business in Dallas, Texas. At the time, Uber Eats was nothing like its current incarnation as a marketplace for local restaurants. Instead, it was an all-too-literal conceptualization of "Uber for food." Each day, we bought hundreds of premade lunches and loaded them into the cars of a few dozen drivers. These drivers would then patrol near downtown business districts and suburban office parks, waiting for on-demand orders to appear. Users could fire up the app and get a sandwich or a noodle bowl in five minutes or less, which was great for those more interested in speed than choice. But it led to disappointed customers, plenty of wasted food, and more than a few bouts of food poisoning from dishes that had been sitting in a hot car for half a day.

It became apparent that instant delivery, as it was called, was more of a gimmick than a true business model. Unlike ridesharing, most people wanted lots of options, even if it meant waiting longer. So we switched, almost overnight, to the third-party delivery model that apps like Seamless and Grubhub were already using. Pretty soon, I was managing a team of thirty people whose job it was to get Uber Eats into as many of Dallas's eight thousand restaurants as we could. In less than a year, our market went from a few dozen orders per day to millions of dollars in orders every week. We transformed Uber's scrappy little moonshot into the company's largest engine of growth.

We nearly killed ourselves doing it. We worked punishing hours and got paid less than we thought was fair—nothing unique or surprising about that. But those were only the smallest of the sacrifices we made as a condition for keeping our jobs.

Software, unlike humans, "works" all the time. Local teams were required to have someone "on call" to monitor driver supply nearly every day, and especially on weekends and holidays, our times of peak demand. One random weekend, our office had no one monitoring supply past 3 a.m., which was an hour after the bars close in Dallas. At 4 a.m., a regional VP's friend had to wait ten minutes for his Uber, and texted him to complain about this slight inconvenience. The whole office got a verbal thrashing from that VP, and no one on the operations team got promoted for the next two years.

Another junior operations manager was asked to forgo her honeymoon at the last minute in order to babysit the launch of a new Eats market. It wasn't her fault that the launch date had slipped several times over the previous few months. Regardless, she was required to call her fiancé and explain to him why they would have to cancel everything only a few days before their departure.

A third person, this one more senior, made the mistake of expressing a desire to lead a life outside of Uber. She made it known that, in the next year or two, she was thinking of going to graduate school. (Not actively applying, just *thinking* about it). Once word got around, she was relieved of her direct reports and reassigned to the customer service team—"CommOps" for short—where she worked on a side project that did nothing and went nowhere.

The strangest thing of all was that everyone accepted this as normal. Especially those who were subject to punishment. Each of them thought *they* had actually wronged Uber, not the other way around: they had not worked hard enough. And this was a cardinal sin.

Most tech companies—and certainly all of the top-tier ones—ask for this cult-like level of dedication. You are not doing a job; you're on a mission. I was no stranger to the idea, having spent the formative years of my career at Amazon. But Uber was even more extreme. The fact that the business is not tied to a physical space or a specific building, but resides in the ether between millions of smartphones, helped reinforce the impression that we could never really escape the app, no matter where in the world we might be. It did not just demand our time, our attention, or our love. It forced us to efface ourselves before the company—to replace our priorities, our personalities, and above all our code of ethics with those of Uber.

I learned this my third week on the job, when I was summoned to the corporate headquarters in San Francisco for my orientation phase: "Uberversity," as it was called. There, I met every recent hire from around the world—many from the United States, some from Europe, and even a few people from Japan, Egypt, and Mexico. We spent several days meeting some of Uber's first employees who still worked at the company, and learning the convoluted mechanics of ride-sharing: how the algorithms matched riders with drivers, how to reroute traffic around events or traffic jams, how to predict tomorrow's challenges from today's data. It was the most intense orientation I'd ever attended. By the end of the first day, I'd already been asked to retrieve information from Uber's vast trove of user data, solve a calculus problem, and talk a Lyft driver into joining Uber. (I failed at the last one: the driver I talked to said he was already on both apps.)

Then the indoctrination began. In one session, we were told about Uber's triumphs over police raids and taxi driver protests in Paris, London, and Mexico City. Several Uber employees who had actually been there were paraded in front of us and talked about their experiences. We treated them with deference, as if they were war heroes—even though it was the local drivers, not the functionaries from Uber HQ, who had suffered property damage and personal injury.

Next, we held a kind of mock struggle session for all those who had ever said something bad about Uber. Each of us was asked to share the negative things that our friends and family had said about our new employer. Then, we were invited to respond as a group.

The session started slowly. The facilitator picked a shy twentysomething woman from the Midwest to speak first.

"Uh, Uber kills jobs," she quavered into the mic.

The facilitator wheeled around to the rest of us, throwing her arms wide. "What do you think? Does Uber kill jobs?"

Not really, someone shouted from the back corner. We all laughed awkwardly, unsure just what the etiquette was.

"Say it like you mean it!" yelled the facilitator, trying to pump everyone up. She set the mic down on a table and cupped her hands around her mouth. "Does Uber kill jobs? Hell no! Let me hear it!"

Hell no, we chanted right back to her.

She whirled around to someone else—a middle-aged man who introduced himself as a new general manager from the Netherlands.

"I have heard," he said, "that Uber is unsafe."

The facilitator snapped the mic back to her mouth. "What do you think? Is Uber unsafe?"

This time, there were a few more voices, and they spoke more emphatically. *No!* said one. *Safer than a taxi!* said another.

"Let's hear it! Is Uber unsafe?"

No, it's safe, we said, in unison.

Maybe it was because we were tech workers, or maybe it was because we were all strangers, but we had spent the prior few days of Uberversity trying to act cool and aloof. Yet our facilitator got us to stop thinking and start feeling, like a revival preacher. With each call ("Is Uber illegal?") she'd elicit the desired response ("No, it's legal!"). She goaded us into a frenzy: she'd get us to voice whatever criticisms of our new employer we might have heard. Then, she'd ask us to shout down these objections as loudly as possible, even though we only had her word that none had a basis in reality. Ultimately, she tricked us into dismissing our own reservations about Uber, under the guise of a group bonding exercise. It was an obvious gimmick, but it worked.

As my turn approached, I decided that I wanted to outdo everyone else—to really demonstrate that I was ready to be one of Uber's defenders.

"Uber is evil," I said.

This set off the whole room. Some people booed. Others shouted in anger. I heard one person say, in genuine shock: *who even says that?*

By the end of the session, we had fully bought in to the us-against-the-world mentality that defined Uber at its peak. To cap off Uberversity, we expected no less than Travis Kalanick himself (or TK, as we were now encouraged to call him) to make an appearance. We had spent the last week chasing his reputation and measuring ourselves against his hard-charging energy. Now, as we filed our way into a conference room at one of Uber's satellite headquarters buildings, we foresaw Kalanick running up to the podium, giving us an inspirational speech, and sending us forth to do battle, like Henry V addressing his troops before Agincourt.

Yet it wasn't Kalanick who emerged from the back doors of the conference room. It was Uber's first employee, Ryan Graves, who shuffled up almost apologetically to the front of the room. It was kind of a letdown: we were rabid, and now here was this skater bro in a hoodie and baseball cap, talking to us with what I can only describe as gentleness. He told us stories about how he had first come to Uber and the amazing people we now worked with. Whereas the previous hour had been adversarial, this one was about working together. The road ahead would be tough and often ambiguous, said Graves, and the only way we were going to survive was if we all followed the same rules and adopted the same principles. He needed us to trust each other, and above all to trust Uber, and its fourteen cultural norms.

In retrospect, Graves's complete tonal shift was the capstone of a perfect psy-op. We had spent all week preparing ourselves to face a hostile world that would throw challenge after challenge at us in the months to come. Now, here was Graves telling us that the only thing we needed to conquer was ourselves—to accept Uber into our hearts, and replace our own individual opinions about right and wrong with a shared value system that was strictly defined by the company. If we could master this inner conflict, he told us, no outer conflict would even matter. We were only too glad to accept an emotional lifeline from our new employer, which promised us that as long as we believed, we could endure any misery.

Most of the Uber value system was generic corporate fare, which boiled down to variations on "work harder *and* smarter," such as *always be hustlin'*, *champion's mind-set*, and *make magic*. A few prepared us for inevitable conflict: *principled confrontation* and *meritocracy and toe-stepping* both implied that good ideas could come from anywhere, but that getting them implemented would require fighting lots of bad ideas. Graves's own favorite principle, which he coined in Uber's early days, was just one word: *superpumped*. It was a command to approach your job with manic enthusiasm, no matter what.

What stuck in my mind the most, however, was the admonishment to *be an owner, not a renter.* We were not just acting on behalf of Uber: we *were* Uber. And over the next year and a half, I'd hear people quote that value in almost every context—to assign blame, stifle dissent, force a decision, or push someone to do a particularly unpleasant or unrewarding task. Our software doesn't allow us to automatically reimburse drivers for tolls? *Be an owner*: stay late every Friday and refund them manually! Can't reach a restaurant via phone, email, or Facebook? *Be an owner*: get in your car and drive there, even if it's two hours away! Your project needs you, even though you've got your honeymoon planned? *Be an owner*: cancel the once-in-a-lifetime trip and get back to work!

I think Kalanick intended *be an owner, not a renter* as more of a rallying cry than an all-purpose rhetorical bludgeon. His own somewhat incongruous interpretation of the line was that "revolutions are won by true believers." But no one took *be an owner, not a renter* that way. Instead, each one of us assumed that it was a warning that Kalanick himself was looking over our shoulder. So we tried to emulate the best-known aspects of TK's public persona: his impatience, his decisiveness, and his ironclad belief that Uber's success or failure depended entirely on his own personal effort.

The broader implications of being an *owner* were not lost on us. Yet since we were pre-IPO, we didn't talk much internally about finances. It was almost taboo to discuss the valuation of the company, since there was a mutual understanding that all valuations were arbitrary. In any case, we were going to shatter all expectations about what the company was actually worth. We only needed to work hard so we could continue increasing its value. Sometimes *being an owner, not a renter* meant trusting the business, even if it told you to ignore what was right in front of your face.

And the story that was right in front of our face was not good. At the time I joined, in September of 2016, Uber was both one of the fastest-growing companies in history and also one of the most deeply unprofitable ones. That year, Uber posted $6.5 billion in revenues and $2.8 billion of losses. In 2017, revenue grew to $7.9 billion, and losses also deepened to $4.5 billion. By the time I left in 2018, we were on pace to lose money even faster. The more we grew, the less profitable we became. We had somehow reached a diseconomy of scale.

Like a badge of shame, Uber's apparent inability to reduce its losses, let alone turn a profit, undercut its claim to be a world-historical company. Sure, we were already a superlative startup: the biggest, best-known, and (at the time) most valuable one on the planet, in fact. But it was not yet clear that we would ever become a viable business before the venture capital money ran out.

We had all the expertise, all the technical capabilities, and all the investor backing in the world, and still we could not shovel money into Uber's gaping maw fast enough to turn the business toward profit. It became a constant, gnawing anxiety. You claimed to be an owner—the company's principles said you *had* to be—yet you had not personally solved the financial problem. In fact, you had somehow made it worse. And every moment you did not do something to shore up the company's finances, you were not doing your job. True owners worked harder, longer, did anything to save Uber. Everyone else was just a renter. Because Uber was not turning itself around, the problem was ultimately with the owners; the problem, we believed, was *us*. It was therefore up to each of us to save it.

⁝⁝⁝

UBER'S CORE "PRODUCT" IS NOT RIDES OR FOOD DELIVERIES. RATHER, IT IS A kind of closed, automated, and double-blinded auction software for point-to-point trips for anything—people, food, freight. When a user hits the "request trip" button, Uber's marketplace algorithms instantly calculate the price for that demand—how much other riders are paying for a similar trip at that very moment, and how much money it would take to incentivize a driver to accept that user's particular trip. Then, it tries to find the optimal gap between what a rider will pay and what a driver will accept, so that Uber can pocket the difference.

Uber's app tries to be a frictionless middleman. It works almost imperceptibly fast, so that it feels like you're dealing directly with your driver. But it is still, legally speaking, a marketplace. That handoff between rider and Uber, and between Uber and driver, is what Uber points to when it claims that its drivers and couriers are independent contractors, free to accept or reject rides at their discretion. As a result, Uber doesn't have to pay for benefits or entitlements like it does for full-time employees. This legal loophole keeps costs down, and Uber (and its competitors) have spent big to ensure that it remains open despite several attempts to reclassify workers as employees.

Even with the loophole, however, rideshare companies still view human drivers as an expensive inconvenience for other reasons. They make wrong turns and drive to the wrong pickup points. They drive too slow, or too fast, or without seatbelts. They get snippy with riders and frustrated with Uber's app. They do pesky little things like eat, sleep, and see their families. They want a job that can provide at least a living wage, or something close to it.

All of these understandably human needs and desires lead to unpredictability within Uber's network. And the marketplace has a limited number of options to incentivize drivers to act in one way when their personal interests compel them to act otherwise. Most of these levers take the form of incentives or competitions ("get an extra $10 for completing 3 trips!" or "maintain a 5-star rating all month and get $100!"), and none are good for the bottom line.

In 2016, a few months before I joined Uber, TK declared that autonomous cars would be the solution to Uber's cost problem. The first company to roll out autonomous vehicles, he argued, would instantly have "a ride-sharing network that is far cheaper," he told *Insider*'s Biz Carson. If that were to happen, "then Uber is no longer a thing . . . the future passes us by, in a very expeditious and efficient way." There was a (somewhat cynical) PR element to it as well. Traffic accidents killed an estimated million people around the world every year. If Uber could be first to market with truly autonomous cars, it could take at least partial credit for every life that the technology saved forevermore—a crucial win for a company that struggled to get good press outside of the Silicon Valley tech bubble.

The real question was how well the software would work and how robust its capabilities would be. Were we talking robot chauffeurs, or just a slightly more advanced version of cruise control? One year earlier, Elon Musk's Tesla had released its autopilot feature, which was the first commercially available hands-free driving system. But these successes had not translated into an industry-wide leap forward. Of the several startups that claimed to be just on the cusp of launching their own fleets of self-driving taxis, all of them appeared to be nothing more than vaporware. About the only place to catch a truly autonomous car in action was within a few blocks of tech company campuses and university research labs.

The industry still had to solve several foundational problems: astronomical costs, low sensor fidelity, poor computing power, but most of all, the difficulty of sharing the road with people. Most experts believed that it would be decades before autonomous cars were ready for the public, if they ever were. Everyone who said otherwise had a financial stake in promoting the autonomous hype.

It made even less sense for Uber to take up the challenge of developing its self-driving cars in-house. We were consciously not General Motors or Apple; we were an asset-light business that did not make devices of any kind. To do so would have invalidated the whole legal theory of the marketplace on which the company rested. We could easily stand on the sidelines and wait for someone to "win" the autonomous race, and then license the winning technology from them. There was no reason to take on the burden of research and development ourselves.

Yet Kalanick believed in fully autonomous vehicles so much that he was willing to bet billions of dollars on it, at a time when our core businesses, Rides and Eats, were already losing an average of 10 million dollars every *day.* TK's decision would commit us to hundreds of millions more in R&D and capital costs every year in order to make autonomous driving software a reality, plus the cost of buying and maintaining our own fleet of cars. Worse still, no one really knew when that investment might pay off, or how big it would even be. We were essentially adding a huge risk on top of a business that was already very risky.

Nevertheless, he insisted. That was the way he approached all of Uber: by focusing on potential outputs and not worrying about the detailed inputs. We had already taken on dozens of "big, bold bets," such as food delivery, freight, and temporary labor. Self-driving cars were just another one of these bets that in theory could change Uber's dynamics and get both its financials and reputation back into the black. From TK's perspective, the potential rewards clearly outweighed the risks. In three years, he declared, we would have seventy-five thousand autonomous cars active in the United States, meaning that one out of every ten active vehicles on Uber would be self-driven. It was time to put aside our fears and doubts, act like owners, and fulfill our obligation to the cult of Uber.

⁘⁘⁘

BUT THE SOFTWARE THAT POWERED AUTONOMOUS VEHICLES WAS NOT LIKE anything that Uber had attempted before. TK had overcome all of Uber's early problems through sheer volume of technical effort. When we needed drivers in a particular city, we'd spam every local job board and Facebook group to recruit new drivers. When we needed new customers, we'd spend outlandish amounts on banner ads and Google campaigns in the digital world, and saturate a new market with billboards or advertising trucks in the real world. If competition got tough, we'd book rides on rival platforms, then try to talk their drivers into joining Uber, just as we'd been trained to do during Uberversity. We called this quarterly ritual "slogging," an acronym for supplying long-term operations growth. And if our backend went down, we'd do whatever it took to keep the market moving—even if it meant taking orders and dispatching cars by phone, just like in the old days. By 2016, we could predict how the market would respond to just about any force imaginable, from a thunderstorm to a football game to the competition launching a 20 percent off coupon. The core Rides and Eats part of the business could be managed, with a pretty high degree of precision, through the brute logic of economics. We could apply as much money and effort as we needed to get the market response we wanted—and for now, that response was grow first, and try to turn a profit second. It was the sort of luxury only available to companies with $7 billion in cash on hand, and a valuation that only seemed to grow ever larger.

TK appeared to believe that the same managerial approach could work for autonomous driving, too. The year before, he had poached forty researchers from Carnegie Mellon University in Pittsburgh, considered the leading university for robotics research in the United States, and quite literally built Uber's new Advanced Technologies Group (ATG) around them. The company purchased an abandoned chocolate factory just around the corner from CMU's campus, and bought another plot of land right on the Allegheny River to convert into a test track for their new cars. There, ATG's new scientists would have every resource imaginable: a one-thousand-person staff that was nearly five times larger than the one at CMU's National Robotics Engineering Center, a fleet of one hundred Ford Fusions to convert into autonomous testbeds, and an immediate business use for their work. And, just to smooth things over with Carnegie Mellon, Uber donated $5.5 million to endow a professorship and three graduate fellowships.

But TK strained to convince us that autonomous vehicles would respond, like all of Uber's other lines of business, to the vigorous application of more money, more effort, and more computing power. In all-hands meetings, TK proudly listed the various accomplishments ATG had made in the fields of mapping, computer vision, machine learning, and vehicle conversion. He struggled to explain how those breakthroughs would translate into concrete accomplishments, such as putting actual vehicles on the road. In one particularly bizarre meeting, he talked about how LiDAR (Light Detection and Ranging) would revolutionize the way cars "saw" the world—and then brought a scientist on stage who pointed out how difficult it was to transform a LiDAR "point cloud" into a map of its surroundings that a computer could accurately interpret. Ironically, the more TK talked about self-driving, the more he sounded to me like many other executives in many other industries who knew the strategic *why*, but not the technical *how*.

After eighteen months of effort, the vigorous application of software had not yielded much progress at ATG—a worrying sign, since TK had given them only three years to get from prototype to full deployment. The technology's development increasingly appeared to be unpredictable, its core challenges obscure, even to experts in the field. Like a true owner, I still believed that if anyone could master the tech, it would be Uber. But I began to doubt that anyone would do so within the next decade.

At last, toward the end of August 2016, TK brought on some expert help. He hired Anthony Levandowski—*the* Anthony Levandowski, as TK introduced him to the company, the emphasis indicating that we were to treat him with a mix of respect and awe—to lead us to the autonomous promised land.

Levandowski was a self-taught wunderkind. In 2004, he and a team of fellow UC Berkeley engineers developed a working autonomous motorcycle that they entered into a competition sponsored by the Defense Advanced Research Projects Agency, or DARPA, the best-known of the Department of Defense's many research and development agencies. He was then hired by Google in 2007 to work on its Street View product, where he designed the distinctive roof-mounted rig that incorporated cameras, GPS, and LiDAR to help create 3D maps of the world. As a side project, he built a LiDAR-powered self-driving Prius, using mostly off-the-shelf technology from Street View. By doing so, he won himself a job as the head of Google's self-driving car division.

For the next several years, he built that division into what would become Waymo, a full-scale subsidiary of Google. Under his direction, Waymo prototyped its own driverless vehicle, called Firefly, and conducted the first-ever fully autonomous drive on public roads in 2015. But he became frustrated with what he saw as Google's overly cautious approach to autonomous technology. In an e-mail to his boss Larry Page, Levandowski complained that

> We're loosing [sic] our tech advantage fast. Doing firefly was a failure, let's embrace/admit it, learn from it and move on. We don't need redundant brakes & steering, or a fancy new car, we need better software.
>
> To get to that better software faster we should deploy the first 1,000 cars asap. I don't understand why we are not doing that. Part of our team seems afraid to ship. Deploying now would show where our system is not working and push the team to fix it asap . . . Time to market is more important than ever.

This test-and-learn philosophy is, of course, central to consumer technology. If you develop a program or a device that doesn't work right away, you diagnose and fix the problem so you can get to the next level of technology much faster. The extremely unstable Windows ME (for "Millennium Edition") didn't undo Microsoft's hold on the desktop operating system market, nor did the unreliable antenna on the iPhone 4 make everyone give up on Apple smartphones: each company was able to stamp out their defects in time for the next release of their flagship product. But Levandowski wasn't talking about consumer gadgets. He wanted to unleash two thousand tons of metal into the real world just to "show where our system is not working."

Eventually, Google's conservatism was too much for Levandowski. He left in June of 2016 to found an autonomous trucking startup called Ottomotto. His company was independent for all of six months before Uber bought it for $680 million. As part of the deal, Levandowski would become the new head of ATG.

TK referred to Levandowski as his "brother from another mother" and called him "incredibly visionary, a good technologist, and . . . also very charming." TK loved Anthony—therefore, we were all supposed to love Anthony, too. Travis and Anthony, Anthony and Travis: together they would save Uber, if only we believed in them enough. And the initial results were promising. Within two months of Levandowski's hiring, ATG launched a self-driving taxi service in Pittsburgh and announced that it would quickly expand to San Francisco.

Since I managed several Uber Eats markets in Texas, I regularly visited the company's "Innovation Hub" in Austin—really just a fancy name for our regional headquarters for the South. ATG had a satellite office there, although the ATG employees who worked there never really interacted with anyone outside of their group. Levandowski, so I heard, had made it clear that they were to focus on nothing but their work. The Eats and Rides teams got to know each other, chatting and playing foosball and taking part in informal "jam sessions" where we would strategize about our business. The ATG people always just sat at their desks, staring hollow-eyed into their computers, never saying much more than hello to the rest of us. Their workspace quickly became littered with component mockups and whiteboards full of equations, which they covered at night to shield their precious contents from our inquisitive eyes. From what we saw, and judging from how haggard they looked, it certainly seemed like they were making progress, and rumors abounded that their new product would soon be road-ready.

At the last all-hands of 2016, ATG's newest toy made its debut. A few months before, Uber had signed an agreement with Volvo to buy a fleet of brand-new XC90 SUVs, which ATG would customize for their autonomous driving project. On each one, ATG installed additional radar emitters beneath the front grille, behind the rear bumper, and on the B-pillar between the driver and passenger doors to give the cars 360 degrees of radar coverage. It added a gigantic platform on the roof of the car, which looked like a cross between a surfboard and a TiVo. It featured seven cameras pointing in all directions, and a LiDAR turret in the middle. This latter device was a spinning column that fired laser pulses at everything within a few hundred meters, and allowed the car to "see" in three dimensions, down to a 1-centimeter resolution. In the trunk was the SUV's "brain," essentially a compact computer cluster that processed the data coming in from the vehicle's sensor suite. As a final touch, the rear seats included an iPad that future passengers could use to take selfies.

Most importantly, TK announced, our new Volvos would start to pick up passengers that day, in San Francisco.

It was one of the few truly mind-blowing moments I have ever experienced in my tech career. Before the announcement, self-driving cars seemed more like a mirage—always on the horizon, never actually getting closer. Afterward, I felt like I could have run through a wall for TK. The stress, the long hours, and the continuous anxiety had finally paid off: he had actually invented the future. *We* had actually invented the future.

We didn't know at the time that the future had some serious problems. Levandowski had freed himself from Google's extreme caution only to run into TK's impossible vision. Uber was now funneling $20 million a month into ATG—an added burden on the parent company's rapidly deteriorating bottom line. It expected a return on that investment in no more than three years: seventy-five thousand autonomous Ubers that could work longer and for less money than humans. Given the long lead times involved in building and converting that many cars, ATG would need to finalize its design in a matter of months, not years. On Levandowski's first day, he was already behind. Uber's business model demanded that he catch up as soon as possible.

The car that ATG debuted in December 2016 was barely viable. Because the division was prototyping its eventual production rig, it had to balance cost, speed, and quality all at once. Each LiDAR turret alone cost an estimated $85,000, but TK would spare no expense on that front: he once texted Levandowski that "the laser is the sauce" (as in the secret sauce). The GPS and inertial reference sensors on the car likely cost another $10,000 total. Radar sensors and cameras were relatively cheaper, a few thousand dollars for each system. Taken together, ATG would have to buy and install more than $100,000 worth of gadgets on top of each $50,000 base vehicle. This represented a cost improvement from earlier prototypes, but it was still unsustainably expensive.

Such a collection of impressive hardware would be nothing without software that could control it properly, however. And Uber's past technical successes did little to prepare it for the challenge of building self-driving software. After all, no smartphone app is a self-contained program; it relies on a constant, real-time connection to the cloud, and in Uber's case to every other active rider, driver, and restaurant in the area, in order to work. A single smartphone does a small fraction of the computations required to facilitate a successful Uber trip. Instead, the company's vast cloud server infrastructure handles the computation required to dispatch drivers, set prices, and route everyone to the right destination. When a user requests a ride, Uber's app performs multivariable calculus just to determine a driver's ETA. And this is only the first in a series of increasingly more computationally intensive processes that underpins the rider's entire trip. Of course, almost all of this processing happens on Uber's cloud; the smartphone app only ever gets the final answers to these equations. But such demands add up. In 2018, Uber averaged around 170 new rides or eats requests every second of every day, or about 5.2 billion trips for the entire year. It required nearly $221 million in server capacity in order to support those trips—a price the company was willing to pay in order to get an app that seemed to, in TK's words, "make magic."

ATG's onboard software would face the opposite problem. It could not spare the milliseconds of lag time required to send data to, and await instructions from, the cloud. It needed to make decisions in real time in order to deal with the unpredictability of the road. It would therefore need to compute everything onboard. And ATG's software would, like Uber's consumer apps, have to crunch a lot of data. Each car would produce an estimated four terabytes of information every day, enough to fill sixteen iPhone 8s (which were Apple's top-of-the-line phones at the time) to full capacity. Processing all that data at full fidelity would require the cars to carry around the equivalent of supercomputers in their trunk—an expensive, and probably unreliable, solution.

Without the internet, ATG engineers would have to simplify the computing burden on the prototypes through software alone. It was the only way that they could please their managerial bosses without rendering the entire project either unsafe or unusable. Even so, they took up the challenge with apparent confidence. After all, clever software was supposed to be Uber's specialty.

⁝⁝⁝⁝⁝⁝⁝

MOST OF US HAVE BEEN DRIVING FOR SO LONG THAT WE TEND TO FORGET JUST how difficult it can be. At any given moment, we execute multiple simultaneous tasks, each of which works a different part of our brain. We manipulate the car's steering wheel, foot pedals, indicator stalks, and gear shifters in order to operate the car itself. We monitor our speed and fuel levels on the dashboard. We interpret the outdoor signs that control traffic and warn us about upcoming hazards. Above all, we stay alert for whatever surprises our surroundings—or our fellow drivers—might throw at us. Driving is 90 percent routine and 10 percent dealing with unexpected chaos.

It helps that we experience a lot of the fundamentals of driving long before we ever sit in the driver's seat. We learn about movement and perception from the moment we're born, and we encounter the various types of hazards we might see on the road—pedestrians, bicyclists, traffic cones, and other vehicles—fairly early on. It is no great shock, then, when we get behind the wheel for the first time. Sure, some of the details might be new, like the nuances of the traffic laws or the meanings of the various dashboard warning lights. But most of the other concepts are familiar.

Not so for computers. Alan Turing, the first great theorist of modern computer science, understood this as one of computing's essential limitations. In a 1948 paper entitled "Intelligent Machinery," he attempted to differentiate between the ways that logic-based computers and organic brains learn things. Computers must be exhaustively programmed before they can function, and this programming determines how they perceive and interact with the world—to the exclusion of all other ways. A computer can be taught to calculate math problems or even play chess, and to do so with superhuman accuracy and speed. But it cannot learn new skills beyond its initial programming or spontaneously generate new methods of understanding. Most importantly, when it encounters something that doesn't match its preinstalled conception of the world, it stops working—it doesn't have the flexibility to think outside the metaphorical box.

Human brains, by contrast, operate free from the shackles of strict programming. Our minds are not hard-wired for anything in particular: all of us have the capacity to learn language from birth, but we only become English, French, or Mandarin speakers through education, experience, and lots of trial and error. This is why, for example, most English-speaking kindergarteners will say things like "buyed" instead of "bought" and "tooths" instead of "teeth." They have learned how to form regular verbs and nouns, and based on past experience they apply those rules to these new, unfamiliar forms. They're both right and wrong at the same time—right because they can infer patterns, and wrong because the patterns don't always match with reality. Unlike a logic-based computer, most kindergarteners don't automatically shut down when they encounter something new and unexpected. They learn instead that English contains some tricky irregular words.

Turing believed that someday computers would be able to think as flexibly as humans. That was the goal of his eponymous test, which was designed to detect a computer that had reached this cognitive inflection point. Until then, however, computers would have to be entirely "determined"—as in, their programming limited what they could achieve; they could only do the things they were programmed to do, nothing more. A computer that could rival a human not just in terms of a few abilities (like playing chess) but in *all* abilities "would probably take the form of programming the machine to do every kind of job that could be done, as a matter of principle." He drily noted that in such a situation, "the number of steps involved tends to be enormous." No matter how much storage and computing power you gave to a determined computer, it would still act like a brute-force machine, going through each of its lines of code one by one in sequence until it found just the one suited to its task. Select something deep in its codebase, and it might take hours just to make a decision that a human might make in milliseconds.

ATG did not have to program Turing's infinite computer, but given the complexity of the process of driving, it would have to come reasonably close on a short timeline. The ATG rig's single most important safety task was to identify potential hazards. A basic task for us, and yet very difficult for a determined computer with no prior knowledge of the world. Conceptually, the task was straightforward. First, the ATG vehicle would gather data from its sensors to build a map of the world around it. Then, it would identify and classify every object to understand what it was: a stationary obstacle (such as a cone or a barrier), a mobile hazard (a pedestrian or another vehicle), or something that could be safely ignored (a bird flying through its radar field). Based on this information, the computer would decide to either carry on normally or take appropriate action to prevent a crash.

But the sheer volume of potential data would overwhelm ATG's onboard computer, which was not powerful enough to process and analyze every piece of sensor data in real time. Because of the pressure to get the cars on the road in significant quantities by 2019, ATG could not wait for a more efficient computing solution to arrive on the market in a year or two. They had to take some shortcuts to make the vehicles at least minimally operational.

To relieve some of the processing burden, ATG allowed the computer to make decisions based on a single source of sensor data, rather than comparing inputs from all three sensor types simultaneously. (Think of it like trusting your color vision alone—it's good enough most of the time, but in some cases you'll probably wish you could see in the dark as well.) LiDAR had the highest resolution, the fastest refresh rate, and was considered the most reliable in the widest variety of lighting conditions. But its detection range was the shortest of the three sensor systems—only about four hundred feet, or five seconds' lead time at highway speeds. Radar worked at the longest range, about six hundred feet, but it also had the lowest resolution, and therefore the lowest priority. The cameras were somewhere in between. In broad daylight, they provided the clearest possible data. At night, they became nearly useless. If the computer could not make a high-confidence identification from LiDAR, it moved on to the cameras, followed by radar. All other things being equal, it prioritized the most recent scan over all others.

No computer actually "knows" what it sees. Instead, it scans a formation of pixels—whether caused by a laser reflection, a radar ping, or a photon bouncing off of an optical sensor—and calculates the statistical resemblance between that one formation and the many others it has stored in memory. To an ATG vehicle, "recognition" meant only that its processing algorithm had assigned a particular formation to a known category with a high degree of confidence. This is not the same as human understanding; it is merely an expression of mathematical relationships.

And its database of objects was also severely truncated to further reduce storage space and limit the amount of computational power the prototype would need. The onboard computer recognized only four categories: vehicles, bicycles, pedestrians, and everything else. Once sorted into one of those categories, an object would get assigned a set of attributes common to every object in its category. The computer would expect, for example, a pedestrian to be able to move suddenly in any direction, but not very fast. As a result, it would draw a "hitbox" around the pedestrian that was circular in shape but fairly small in radius, to tell the car to avoid its probable range of motion. Conversely, a vehicle's hitbox would be much longer, but more wedge-shaped; a car can cover a longer distance in a shorter amount of time than a pedestrian, but isn't nearly as agile. This classification system was not very robust—in fact, it had a far lower level of understanding than even the worst human driver—but it was functional enough to get ATG vehicles on the road. It would just require human supervision to take care of the edge cases.

During beta testing, two human operators would ride in every ATG vehicle, each with a different assigned task. The operator in the passenger seat would review data from the car's sensors for accuracy; if the sensors falsely identified a bicycle that was really a tree, for example, the operator could correct that reading and log the error in ATG's database to better train its identification algorithms. The operator in the driver's seat, meanwhile, was the "safety minder," there to keep an eye on the road at all times and intervene if the car failed to detect an imminent hazard.

Although it was impressive that ATG got its prototypes running in such a short amount of time, they were inevitably compromised in several ways. The first involved their sensor logic. Uber had enough institutional faith in LiDAR—the laser was the sauce—that they counted on it as the primary source of truth for its autonomous prototypes in all circumstances.

But LiDAR isn't perfect. It can't sense density, which makes it unable to tell whether a piece of debris on the road is a plastic bag or a piece of metal. Its range is limited, and it doesn't work well in rainy or dusty conditions. It requires huge amounts of power, and its spinning turret needs regular maintenance. Those were just its known drawbacks. Unlike automotive radar (which appeared in the 1970s) and onboard cameras (from the 1950s), real-time, 3D LiDAR has only been commercially available since 2007. It would be unreasonable to think that a decade of limited use had been enough to iron out all the kinks.

For these reasons, most of the rest of the industry has been more cautious to adopt the technology. Tesla has famously refused to consider LiDAR at all. Waymo's "sensor fusion" algorithms used LiDAR only for object detection at short and medium distances, rather than as the primary source of truth for all situations. At longer ranges and for fast-moving objects, for example, Waymo cars prioritize radar detection, and for high-confidence object classification, they rely on their cameras. Uber's enthusiasm for LiDAR across all these functions was unique—and uniquely risky.

The second problem was the limited number of categories that ATG's computers could recognize. To be fair, vehicle/bicycle/pedestrian covers the vast majority of objects on the road, and most of them would always move predictably. But there would be exceptions. What about rollerbladers, who have the silhouette of a pedestrian but the speed of a bicycle? Or horse-drawn carriages, which might look like two vehicles stuck together but moving in tandem? Or a pedestrian who wore a shirt with a life-size stop sign printed on it?

The definition of the "other" category was even messier. Clearly, it was a kind of fail-safe mechanism: "other" objects would be treated as stationary, and the car would avoid them where possible. But the categorization was so broad that it could encompass everything from a tree to a helicopter to an armadillo. The vehicle's computational limits meant that its conceptual resolution was far too low for the real world.

Third, there was the human element. Having a pair of operators was actually the least problematic thing about ATG's setup: it aligned with industry best practices. But humans were a costly inconvenience even at the testing phase. And in October of 2017, ATG eliminated its two-operator policy entirely. Now, a single person would have to monitor the sensors for accuracy in real time *and* watch the road for hazards. They would have twice as much work, but no one else in the car to help them stay focused.

Tradeoffs are common in software. No piece of technology can do everything perfectly, especially early-stage technology such as autonomous vehicles. But not every tradeoff is made in good faith. Each time ATG engineers placed TK's vision over the tenets of good software development, they chose to align themselves with his managerial vision—to be an owner, not a renter. This made their technology less efficient, less robust, and less safe. Eventually, luck was the only thing saving Uber from disaster. Just five months after ATG eliminated half of its safety minders, that luck ran out.

....

AT AROUND 9:20 P.M. ON MAY 18, 2018, AN ATG PROTOTYPE PULLED OUT OF THE Uber operations center in downtown Tempe, Arizona, for its nightly autonomous test run. After twenty minutes under manual control, its human operator activated the SUV's self-driving mode and settled in for a long, boring night of monitoring sensor data. The night was perfect for driving: the weather was good, there was no lingering desert dust, and the flat Arizona landscape gave the entire sensor suite on the ATG prototype clear lines of sight in all directions.

Twenty minutes later, just north of downtown, a woman named Elaine Herzberg decided to cross North Mill Avenue. It was, and still is today, a lonely stretch of road, bordered on one side by a highway overpass and on the other by a barren municipal park. It has no sidewalks, no streetlights, and the nearest crosswalk is five hundred feet away. Like many areas in the United States, it is not really meant for pedestrians.

Nevertheless, Herzberg elected to cross the street at that point. She set off at a brisk pace, traveling west to east and pushing her road bike alongside her as she went. It would have taken her around eight seconds to safely cross.

Six hundred feet to her south, the ATG prototype crossed the Mill Street Bridge and proceeded onto North Mill Avenue. It detected her three seconds later with one of its forward-facing radar emitters. She was in the second of four lanes; the ATG prototype, in the fourth. Her bike, which was side-on to the radar signal, returned a blip comparable in size to the rear end of a car. Her west-to-east speed—about six feet per second—was similar to the lateral speed of a northbound car making a cautious lane change. ATG's detection algorithms had been trained only to expect pedestrians where there were sidewalks and crosswalks, which did not exist at this particular street crossing. So the onboard computer decided that she was a vehicle, traveling northward on a more or less parallel path with the ATG prototype. It determined that she would safely merge into the third lane and then stop, and that she would not become a hazard. The vehicle made no attempt to change course.

The LiDAR turret detected Herzberg a fraction of a second later. Once again, the combined silhouette of person and bike confused the classification algorithm. At first, it decided that she was neither a vehicle, bicycle nor pedestrian—so by process of elimination she fell into the category of "other." According to ATG's taxonomy, however, all objects in the "other" category were, by ATG's arbitrary definition, stationary. So in spite of her real-world movement, the digital echo of Elaine Herzberg was classified as a stationary object, and judged to be a nonhazard. The imprecision of ATG's sensors, combined with the rigidity of its classification scheme, meant that the SUV could not tell exactly what to make of her.

It scanned Herzberg dozens more times over the next few seconds, but the more it did, the less sure it was of the results. The image processors believed that she was a vehicle one instant, then a bicycle, then back to an unidentified "other." With each new categorization, the computer also ignored all previous data about Herzberg's location and trajectory—as if the sensors were observing not one object on a consistent path, but a dozen different ones that magically appeared and disappeared, all with different attributes and different hazard potential. Like a newborn infant, the ATG vehicle did not understand the concept of object permanence. Unlike newborns, however, the SUV weighed two tons and had a top speed of 120 miles per hour.

The prototype was now only 250 feet away from Herzberg and still could not truly "see" her. LiDAR was slowly eliminating options—it was now convinced that she was either a car or a static object—but could not determine her future trajectory and speed, or draw a correct "hitbox" around her for the vehicle to avoid.

The car's headlights illuminated Herzberg with less than two seconds to go before impact. The cameras on the sensor rig now picked up her bright white shoes and the reflectors on the spokes of her bicycle. If the vehicle had applied maximum brakes at that exact moment, it would have stopped short and she would have been able to walk away. And the camera signal was clear enough to trigger an emergency brake. But TK's enthusiasm for LiDAR dictated the priority order of the different sensor types. As long as LiDAR thought there was no danger—even if it was contradicted by radar or cameras—its interpretation would take precedence. The prototype barreled on.

One and a half seconds before impact, with less than a hundred feet separating the two, the prototype's LiDAR system reclassified her for the fifteenth time. Now she was directly in the path of the SUV, the front tire of her bike all the way into the rightmost lane of Mill Avenue. ATG's sensors decided that she was an "other" once again—and therefore stationary.

Even so, they did nothing to warn the car to steer away from Herzberg, or to tell the safety minder to take emergency action.

With only seventy-five feet separating car from pedestrian, LiDAR was finally convinced that there was danger. Radar saw her as a large blip moving straight into the path of the vehicle. The cameras identified her as a pedestrian. LiDAR still thought she was a bicycle, but now also considered her dangerous. Although they disagreed on the details, they all told the car the same thing: it was finally time to activate its automated emergency braking system.

Uber's business imperatives now intervened. The company's goal was not merely to make a self-driving car. It was to make a self-driving car that passengers would prefer over human drivers. Paying customers might take their first autonomous ride just for the novelty factor, but to convince them to take a second one, comfort would matter, too. ATG therefore designed its control scheme around several "rider-experience" goals, one of which was to have vehicles commit no more than one abrupt maneuver, such as a sudden brake or an unintentional swerve, per trip.

So ATG redesigned the emergency braking logic on the cars. A normal, fresh-from-the-factory Volvo XC90 is able to detect hazards up to one hundred feet away with its collision-avoidance radar, giving the vehicle more than enough time to engage its emergency brakes and come to a complete stop at speeds up to sixty mph. But ATG disabled Volvo's system in order to install its own. And it placed two new restrictions on automatic braking to prevent unwanted passenger discomfort. The first restriction kept the car from braking too hard. Autonomous cars, after all, don't "feel" any discomfort if they slam on the brakes. Humans certainly do. So ATG built in a maximum rate of deceleration, or what it called the "jerk threshold." It was designed to only slow the car at a maximum rate of 0.71 *g*, or about 22 feet per second. With Herzberg seventy-five feet away, the prototype would need about three seconds to fully decelerate. There was not enough time under Uber's less aggressive braking standards to avoid the collision entirely, but there was enough time to at least reduce the collision speed to thirty mph. According to a 2010 study, only about 10 percent of pedestrian vs. car collisions are fatal at thirty mph. At forty-five mph, that risk increases to about 80 percent.

But the prototype never even got the command to brake because there was a second rider experience restriction in place. In broad daylight, the prototypes had actually proven *overly* cautious in their braking. Their sensors saw potential threats everywhere and tended to trigger the emergency braking system so often that passengers got carsick—as a *BuzzFeed News* reporter found out on a test ride in late 2017. Thus ATG built in a mandatory one-second delay every time the emergency brake was triggered, "while the system verified the nature of the detected hazard." The prototype's hazard detection system was so easily confused, in other words, that it needed a whole second—an eternity, in computing time—to double-check its own work.

That suppression logic now kicked in. The prototype was now sixty feet away from Herzberg, still traveling in a straight line at forty-five mph. The emergency brake wanted to fire, but could not for a full second. The computer could only display an alert on the iPad that the human operator was supposed to use to monitor the vehicle's telemetry. Even now, with the autonomous sensors in total confusion and the emergency braking system inhibited, there was still time to stop the car. But that would require the safety minder to notice the alert and basically stand on the brakes. This night, yet another Uber policy erased the last line of defense against a computer-driven tragedy.

• • • • • • •

AT ANY GIVEN TIME, THERE COULD BE UP TO FORTY UBER TEST VEHICLES ON the streets of Tempe. The pace of testing was purposeful. Kalanick had resigned months before, after a series of personal and institutional scandals undermined his credibility and threatened Uber's viability as a company.

His successor, former Expedia CEO Dara Khosrowshahi, was rumored to be planning a visit to Tempe soon in order to make a decision on the fate of ATG. It was therefore imperative that ATG demonstrate that it could give the new boss a glitch-free ride. Anything else might doom Uber's most expensive, and least productive, division.

An operator named Rafaela Vasquez happened to draw the training loop that took her up North Mill Street. She had signed up as a normal Uber driver in 2015. After two years, she was invited to become an autonomous vehicle tester. She passed the rigorous training programs designed to wash out those who were insufficiently attentive or detail oriented. She learned how to mark bad sensor data, how to report navigational errors, and when to intervene to save the car from an imminent collision. She logged her first hours as an ATG operator in the late summer of 2017.

As the prototypes got better at driving, their operators found it harder and harder to concentrate on their jobs. The hundreds of thousands of miles that ATG vehicles had spent on the road, as well as the daily additions to their collective knowledge via ATG's over-the-air updates, had taught them how to drive more fluidly, navigate more accurately, and remember the permanent hazards on each route. By the fall of 2017, it was rare to have to manually correct sensor data or tell the navigation system that it had missed a turn. The job had gotten *boring*.

The cognitive psychologist Lisanne Bainbridge called this phenomenon the "irony of automation." As automation improves and becomes less error-prone, it becomes more trustworthy from moment to moment. As it becomes more trustworthy, its human minders tend to give it less attention. And as they give it less attention, they increase their vulnerability to less frequent but more serious errors.

Doubly so when your bosses add additional distractions. To prevent solo operators from zoning out during the long, boring drives, ATG supervisors required every operator to have Slack on their work phones.

The app was intended not only for messaging but also as a kind of hacky remote monitoring solution. This was a favorite tactic for every Uber manager who oversaw remote contractors: when I ran inside sales teams across multiple offices for Uber Eats, we used Slack like this as well.

The internal dashcam footage from the Tempe prototype showed Vasquez taking her eyes off the road repeatedly throughout the trip. Police initially accused her of watching *The Voice* on a streaming video service, but this was likely just an attempt to scapegoat her instead of the vehicle. Vasquez's personal phone, which had streaming apps installed on it, was tucked away in the cubby on the passenger-side door. Her Uber-issued work phone, which had no entertainment apps installed, was within easy reach on the center console. On the dashcam video, Vasquez invariably looked down toward the center console—not toward the other side of the cabin—throughout the trip. Her glances down averaged about two and a half seconds, with multiple minutes in between glances when she kept her eyes on the road. Right before the crash, she looked down for a total of five seconds. This was the behavior of someone reacting to instant messages, not someone watching reality TV.

After reading that last message, Vasquez returned her gaze to the road in time to see an indistinct blur loom out of the darkness: Elaine Herzberg, in a dark black jacket and jeans, pushing her bright red bike about ten feet in front of the SUV. Vasquez slammed on the brakes, grabbed the wheel, and turned hard left, which instantly disengaged autonomous driving mode.

The prototype barely slowed down before impact. It struck Herzberg with its right front fender at 39 mph. The handlebars embedded themselves in the Volvo's grille; Herzberg's body and the rear end of the bike slid under the bumper and were pinned between the underside of the car and the asphalt of the road. After seventy-five feet, the car finally came to a stop. Herzberg died on the scene, the first pedestrian in history to be killed by a self-driving car.

:::::::

NO OTHER COMPANY IN THE WORLD COULD HAVE BROUGHT AN AUTONOMOUS vehicle from conception to reality in three short years, as Uber did. Its combination of financial resources, global scale, elite technical talent, and, above all, its win-at-all-costs culture allowed it to do what most other people considered impossible. If Uber had only set a goal of getting a prototype on the road in three years, it would still have been a massive achievement. But it had to go one step further. From the start, ATG was burdened with the responsibility not only of developing new technology but also getting it ready for immediate commercialization. ATG was never just a research lab: it was also the key to turning Uber profitable. Its mission was corrupted from the start by Uber's insatiable financial needs.

ATG staff members accepted this compromise and did the best they could with it. Every week, engineers would hold "triage" meetings where they diagnosed issues with their technology, and the same ones kept coming up: the cars still had trouble distinguishing shadows from objects, and could get flustered by piles of leaves or tree branches. One engineer calculated that ATG vehicles got in accidents about once every fifteen thousand miles, making them around thirty-five times more crash-prone than human drivers. And with no common set of safety standards and protocols, or even a centralized safety team, there was no one whose job it was to determine whether ATG was creating hazards or not. There was just the constant pressure to keep their prototypes "crushing miles" on the road, so that ATG could live long enough to rescue Uber's business.

Being an owner, not a renter forced ATG employees to really believe in TK's vision that autonomous cars could not only save Uber but also the 1.3 million people around the world who died in traffic accidents each year. This dedication led *the* Anthony Levandowski himself to steal trade secrets from Waymo on his way out the door in 2016 in an attempt to use them to accelerate ATG's progress when he took over the division.

It caused his subordinates to remain at jobs that left most of them deeply uncomfortable, and compelled them to keep their heads down and their troubles to themselves. Despite the fact that employees in other divisions constantly leaked internal disputes to the media, and the average tenure at Uber could be measured in months rather than years, ATG employees stayed put and, with only a handful of exceptions, never spoke publicly about the division's struggles until well after the Tempe accident.

This strange dedication to morally questionable work was a version of what the cultural critic Lauren Berlant called "cruel optimism": our tendency to organize not only our time and talent, but also our whole selves, around an idea that ultimately proves harmful. For ATG employees, the idea of a self-driving future gave them purpose and allowed them to have an idea of "what it means to keep on living and to look forward to being in the world." But even if they achieved their wildest dreams and created a working autonomous car, what then? The technology would never be freely available to the public; Uber was always going to commercialize it, patent it, and prevent anyone from using it unless they paid for the privilege. It was explicitly designed to put tens of thousands of Uber drivers out of work, even though Uber had used the labor of those very same people to "earn" its multibillion-dollar valuation. And like all new technologies, autonomous driving would create new types of risks; but in ATG's rush to get it out the door, they had not had time to prevent any of them—or even properly consider most of them. From one perspective, it might even be considered *evil*, to use the word I had invoked at Uberversity.

Only one person paid the price for Herzberg's death. Rafaela Vasquez, the safety operator who was behind the wheel during the crash, was charged with negligent homicide in 2018. From the start, the Tempe Police Department built their case around a faulty assumption: that end users are always responsible for saving people from bad technology, and that they will always be able to do so. (A similar logic led Boeing to put out its anemic safety bulletin in the wake of the Lion Air 610 crash, rather than ground its 737 MAX fleet). The Tempe Police did not hold ATG liable for creating the entire chain of catastrophe that led to Herzberg's death. They only blamed the last, and least responsible, link in that chain—arguing that if the driver had not been watching TV on her personal phone, Herzberg might not have been killed. After three years of trial delays, Vasquez pled guilty to the lesser charge of negligent homicide, and was sentenced to three years of probation.

Everyone else managed to avoid real consequences from the crash itself. Uber was not criminally charged for Herzberg's death, and it paid an undisclosed amount of money to her family in 2018 in order to settle their civil lawsuit. It kept ATG operational for another two years after the crash, and during that time secured a further $10 billion investment from Softbank and Toyota in 2019. Then it sold the division to an autonomous trucking startup called Aurora in a $4 billion all-equity deal. (As of this writing, Aurora's self-driving trucks remain in testing, and the company has yet to generate a single dollar of revenue). Travis Kalanick, who committed to the dream of self-driving cars back in 2016, was pushed out of his job at Uber a year later, although he enjoyed a personal windfall of $2.5 billion after selling the majority of his shares in Uber after its 2019 IPO. ATG's former head, Anthony Levandowski, served a six-month prison time for his theft of Waymo documents, and now leads a new self-driving startup called Pronto.ai.

⁘⁘⁘

IT'S PAINFUL NOW TO REMEMBER THE ZEAL WITH WHICH MY COLLEAGUES AND I shouted down the critiques of Uber in our initial session. In the end, the company made fools of us all. We followed the commandment to *be an owner, not a renter*—to ignore common sense, turn off our ethical compass, and trust the company to do the right thing. We did not realize that our definition of right did not match Uber's definition of right, which only ever came with the word "financially" in front of it.

I have no doubt that this sort of moral compromise happens at many, if not most, companies. But Uber is not most companies. Its scale, its financial needs, and above all the cult-like allegiance that it demanded from its employees turned what could have been a real technological breakthrough into another example of managerial software gone terribly wrong. We told ourselves that we were inventing the future, such that caution and common sense need not apply. Only the first part was true. In the end, Uber was not so different from Boeing. In their financial self-delusion, the leaders of each company could only imagine the benefits of new technology, and not its inherent risks, even as they deployed it on a global scale.

CHAPTER 4

Alternate Realities

A few years before the pandemic, I was working for a Fortune 1000 company when I was assigned a big task: to remake our official PowerPoint templates. We had recently rebranded and changed our corporate logo, color palette, and font library. Naturally, we needed our presentations to match the new look. As one of the most prolific but least senior slide jockeys at the company, it became my project for a full quarter.

It did not take me that much time to make the slide masters themselves. Sure, I had plenty of grunt work to do, such as formatting bullet points and text boxes down to the sixth level of indentation. But what really made the project tedious was that the company had to unite behind a single format for presenting information that we would likely use for the next decade or so. How big should the title font be? Are shapes with rounded edges or notched corners more "on brand"? When showing charts and text on the same page, which should get more room?

Eventually, the higher-ups, whose opinions mattered the most, solved the impasse by ignoring the fragile consensus I'd built across multiple functions and dictating the slide parameters that worked best for them.

Pictures and charts were king. Text was a nuisance at best, a risk at worst: they didn't want to give people the chance to improperly communicate a concept, or put the wrong thing "on the record." Before the rebrand, our executives had one consistent bit of feedback for every presentation brought before them for review: "De-word the slide." Now, with the new templates, they could force people to de-word their slides in advance, through the formatting choices that they decreed and I encoded.

The final templates made it nearly impossible to cram more than a few dozen words on any given slide. Titles were set in 42-point font and could not break onto a second line, so they could express only a single, basic thought. All main text had to fit into three top-level bullet points at most; users got only one or two subordinate bullets to provide details, if they could squeeze them in. Best of all would be a slide that was all charts, with the only words in the title.

Once completed, our executive team made it very clear to everyone that we were to use the new template for everything, from internal standups to external investor presentations. The template did not just define our brand's "look and feel"; it also determined what thoughts we could or could not express. Nuanced ideas or arguments would literally not fit on a single slide, and lost coherence when they were spread across multiple slides. Formatting deviations would now be as obvious as a college paper with padded margins, as there would be too many words in too small a font, or visuals that were far more cluttered than the column charts everyone was used to. Offenders would be mercilessly hounded by our executives: "De-word! De-word!" Only this time, their catcalls carried with them an implicit warning. *Follow the company line, or else.*

There is nothing inherently wrong with concision or an emphasis on visuals over text, of course. But my employer fetishized them as virtues to the exclusion of everything else. The story needed to be crisp and the visuals needed to be easily digestible. Everything else—transparency, rigor, nuance—was secondary.

The PowerPoint template eventually turned into a get out of jail free card for pretty much anything. It is impossible to summarize a multibillion-dollar company with just a few charts and explanatory bullet points, but that's exactly what the slides forced us to do. We could lavish space on our best metrics and bury the others in an appendix, if we included them at all. We could make any chart look better than it really was just by playing with the axes, or including arrows to emphasize certain parts over others. And as long as we wrote a convincing headline, we could proactively shape a viewer's interpretation of a slide well before they even looked at the content.

Presenters have always had a natural advantage over their audience. They control the content of their talk, the pace and flow of information, and even how interesting they wanted to be—sometimes it works to your advantage to be boring. It was already easy enough for them to be glib instead of sincere, superficial instead of thorough. Our PowerPoint templates tilted that asymmetry of power even more toward the presenter. They presented viewers with information that was almost childishly simple, and did not give them enough information to hold a robust discussion about anything, even if it was desperately needed.

Was this underhanded? My bosses didn't think so. They were seasoned managers all: they not only had pedigrees from some of the best business schools in the world but also had decades of experience at large global companies. They argued that a lay audience could never understand all the nuances of our business. They believed that more information led to a greater risk of misunderstanding, misinterpretation, or lots of useless questions. They wanted their slides to convey that things were under control and the professionals were in charge. Nothing else mattered.

I began the project with naïve optimism, assuming that my goal was to help my colleagues express their ideas with transparency and authenticity. But I quickly understood that the opposite was true. By forcing every meeting to have a PowerPoint, and by prescribing specific slide formats and styles, our executives could control the expression of thought at every level of the company. It was cold comfort to realize, looking out across the landscape of corporate America, that I was not the only person whose job it was to churn out PowerPoint propaganda.

POWERPOINT WAS NOT ORIGINALLY MEANT TO BE A WEAPON OF EXECUTIVE deceit. Instead, it was supposed to give some leverage back to those experts and technical specialists most aggressively swept aside by the managerial revolution.

More than forty years ago, in July of 1984, a literature PhD turned computer scientist named Bob Gaskins was hired to turn around a failing startup called Forethought. Over the previous eighteen months, Forethought had built a suite of productivity software—word processors, spreadsheets, and the like—for early DOS-powered IBM PCs. But the company had placed its bets on the wrong operating system. Earlier that year, Apple had released its famous "1984" Super Bowl to announce the Apple Macintosh. The Mac introduced the era of graphical user interfaces, or GUIs: the point-and-click style operating systems we still use today. Compared with the new GUIs, DOS's clunky, text-only interface seemed a relic of an earlier time. Forethought's singular focus on DOS meant that, according to Gaskins, "There was utterly no value in the work to date."

Forethought was running out of cash, and Gaskins would have only months to execute a rescue plan. So he decided to solve a problem that he knew many people across the nascent software industry faced. In his prior work as a consultant to startups, he had worked with companies whose technical experts were totally unprepared for the managerial world. They didn't speak the language of finance, they were utterly naïve about competition, and most of all they struggled to explain their own value, or the value of their products, to nontechnical audiences such as bankers and investors. In short, they lacked an innate sense of salesmanship.

With the new GUI-based Mac, Gaskins saw an opportunity to bridge the chasm and return some power to technical experts. One of the most effective sales tools in the 1980s was the overhead transparency. According to Forethought's 1982 market research, transparencies made presenters appear "better prepared, more professional, more persuasive . . . and more interesting" than those without. The content didn't really matter; the format itself made all the difference.

But transparencies were expensive and cumbersome. They required special printing supplies to produce, at a cost of 5 cents per transparency—about sixty times more expensive than a page of printed paper at the time. Producing graphics often required art supplies and specialty equipment, if not a whole separate art department. The combination of cost and effort made them unsuitable for the large volume of disposable, day-to-day communications and meeting materials needed by most businesses. The average office worker, Gaskins estimated, only produced about one hundred transparencies a year.

Now, computers were finally ready to displace the overhead projector as the presentation tool of choice. The Mac's GUI-based interface would give even the most artistically challenged person the ability to make professional-looking transparencies with software. Presenters would no longer need to physically cut, arrange, and paste or tape elements to a master. They would no longer have to wait on (or pay) graphic artists to design their visuals. They would be able to create and manipulate charts themselves. This presentation software would be able to democratize technical work in the same way that spreadsheets democratized finance.

Between 1984 and 1987, Gaskins built his transparency-killer with two other full-time employees: Dennis Austin, who worked on the Apple version, and Thomas Rudkin, who worked on the Windows version. The program's functions were basic. Users could insert text boxes, make their own images, or import existing charts and graphs from spreadsheet applications. They could add presenter notes and create handouts. They could print off their slides or show them on a projection screen.

Still, the three men never intended their software to be an all-purpose tool. It was aimed squarely at small-group meetings with higher-ups, which required presenters to communicate both technical information and business needs in some level of detail. As a result, their presentation software didn't need fancy transitions, graphic-design tools, or anything that added what Gaskins called "entertainment value." Instead, it was intended to appeal to users who were "familiar with computers, but probably not graphics software . . . highly motivated to look their best in front of others." The prototype was meant to allow knowledge workers of all stripes to communicate their value to managers who would otherwise have no idea what they were being told.

As effective as slides were at lubricating the gears of business, they were not supposed to stand alone. Each one was more of a visual abstract—an introduction to a much longer document that contained all the nuance that would never fit in slide format. In order for a presentation to be truly credible, Gaskins and his team insisted that each slide would need to be supported by several pages of written text. The original pitch for their presentation software, for example, was twenty-eight slides long. The presentation as a whole contained only two thousand words, or about twice the length of the average front-page newspaper article in 1985. The full business plan was ten times longer—roughly the word count of a children's novel, such as *James and the Giant Peach*. At 10 percent of the information density of the written plan, the slides could never convey the same detail or scope. But they could still perform a useful support function.

The market agreed. PowerPoint sold ten thousand copies in its first month on sale—a smash hit, by the standards of 1987 consumer applications. Its success completed Forethought's turnaround from near-bankruptcy to a $15 million valuation, making it one of the most successful startups of its day. For a brief but shining moment, knowledge workers gained a small advantage in the corporate world.

....

THEN MICROSOFT CAME CALLING. AT THE TIME, IT WAS ONE OF THE LARGEST consumer software companies in the world, in part because its leaders had correctly foreseen the future of personal computing for two decades running. In the 1970s, it developed its own versions of BASIC, COBOL, and Fortran, some of the first widely adopted programming languages in the computer industry. In the 1980s, it turned to operating systems: the original MS-DOS in 1981, and Windows 1.0, first announced in 1983. In the span of five years, between 1979 and 1984, Microsoft's revenue grew by nearly fifty times, and its founder Bill Gates acquired a reputation for strategic genius.

But the tech industry moves fast, and the dominant players one year might be losers the next. By the late eighties, Microsoft was falling behind the competition because of a few operational missteps. It had already declared DOS functionally obsolete, which effectively killed the third-party ecosystem of software developers, including Forethought. But Windows, Microsoft's next-generation operating system, kept getting delayed. Originally projected for a late 1983 release, design changes and engineering delays pushed back the launch date first to April 1984, then to June 1985, and finally to November 1985. As Microsoft dawdled, its competitors launched their own GUI-based operating systems. Apple's Mac had begun shipping in January 1984, to coincide with its Super Bowl ad, and IBM released TopView in March 1985. By the time Windows appeared, it was the lagging entry.

Microsoft was so focused on getting its new flagship product out the door that it had neglected to build many applications for it at launch. Third-party software companies like Lotus and VisiCalc had already made popular word processing and spreadsheet software for DOS, the Mac, and even IBM's TopView operating systems. Once Windows launched, they would surely port their applications to the new operating system in no time. Unless Microsoft could develop a native productivity suite of its own, it would be boxed out of the applications market on its own new operating system. It would be yet another embarrassing strategic defeat for what was supposed to be the world's leading software company.

Gates, the cofounder and CEO of Microsoft, considered this an emergency. He assumed control of Microsoft's consumer-facing software division in 1986, and would soon use his favorite weapon—Microsoft's vast financial leverage—to regain the lead.

Gates has always presented an image of boyish nerdiness: the tousled hair, oversized glasses, and solid-colored sweaters that have defined his look for decades now. But in truth, he was a shrewd manager from the start. In an interview for the Smithsonian Institution, Gates recalled that he had a "business-oriented" mindset from the moment Microsoft was created.

"I was doing the payroll, writing the taxes, doing the contracts, figuring out how to price the software," he said.

By 1981, Gates felt that Microsoft's finances and software were not just dependent on each other, but completely interlinked. Every product decision, every line of code, would have to improve Microsoft's financial position in some way. His goal was to have the company "be the leader in doing lots of products that could share code with each other, and take the market." Once the company generated enough cash, it would be able to "dominate" and "crush" rivals through both market competition and financial maneuvering. As a result, he emphasized profitability above all, and required Microsoft to price its products in order to generate significant operating margins, allowing it to be consistently more profitable than its biggest competitors, including Lotus, Cullinet, and Apple.

Gates had also used the company's formidable balance sheet to his advantage many times in the past. He bullied hardware vendors into accepting burdensome contracts that prevented them from working with any of Microsoft's rivals for any reason. He scared venture capitalists away from funding potential upstarts in any area where Microsoft operated. He even crippled rival software that he deemed to be too much of a threat. For example, when users tried to install Windows on top of DR-DOS, a rival operating system to Microsoft's MS-DOS, Windows would display a fabricated error message. One industry publication described the relationship between Microsoft's customers and the software giant as a "hostagelike" situation. Gates did nothing to dispel this impression.

It would be a full decade before the Department of Justice began its antitrust proceedings against Microsoft, and fifteen years before other software giants such as Google, Amazon, and even Apple would become credible threats. For the time being, Microsoft could wage unrestricted corporate warfare with impunity. And in the summer of 1987, Gates prepared to use his company's finances once more to decimate not only Lotus but also every other competitor in the nascent productivity software category.

In July, Gates offered to buy Forethought for $14 million in cash, plus stock-based performance bonuses for the employees. Unlike Microsoft's approach to the rest of the market, it did not attempt its usual hardball tactics. Its offer for the full market value of the startup underscored just how badly Gates wanted Forethought, and how important he considered PowerPoint to be for the future of Microsoft's software strategy.

For his part, Gaskins felt that accepting Microsoft's offer was the only reasonable choice. Even with PowerPoint's success, Forethought still faced a long road to sustainability. Software development is expensive and risky under any circumstances, especially for a small company with a single hit product in its lineup. An IPO was on the table, but Forethought's management and its board of directors felt that the company would not find the market receptive to a company whose "administration, finance, and operations areas have always been on the edge of collapse." And the competition was already circling: Apple had just announced that it would stand up its own subsidiary to make internal applications, one of which was rumored to be a PowerPoint competitor. Forethought could go it alone, or they could join forces with a larger competitor, sacrificing some independence for the resources and financial safety of a big, well-capitalized company. Gaskins believed that his team had at least earned the right to control their own products—after all, they and not Microsoft had come up with the winning formula for productivity software. With that understanding, he signed the terms sheet, and Forethought officially became a part of Microsoft on July 20, 1987.

Right away, Gates set about turning PowerPoint into the tool of market dominance that he, and Microsoft, needed. He agreed that PowerPoint, in its original format, could address a niche target of technical workers, which was a market that Forethought estimated to be worth about $5 billion in annual sales. But if Microsoft redid the app to give it mass appeal, it could tap into a market ten times larger. In Gates's view, PowerPoint should not just be for engineers and designers. It should be able to create anything for anyone, from maps to meeting agendas to "Wet Paint" signs.

That put the two men at odds over the future of PowerPoint. Gaskins had always avoided anything that smacked of "entertainment value." Gates, by contrast, was a visual maximalist: he wanted PowerPoint to have colors, animations, videos, even gimmicky transitions between slides. Gaskins wanted simple, easily legible graphs. Gates insisted that PowerPoint should display any kind of chart in any visual format the user could want (an approach that Gaskins sniffily dismissed as "chart junk"). Gaskins insisted that PowerPoint could only act as an introductory gloss to a portfolio of more detailed supporting documents. Gates, however, wanted PowerPoint to be the only document you would ever need to explain yourself.

As CEO, Gates got his way. He overruled Gaskins on questions of product strategy, marketing investments, and even hiring decisions. Gaskins and his original team found themselves increasingly disillusioned with PowerPoint's direction and Microsoft's total control over their product. After five years, Gaskins resigned from Microsoft and left PowerPoint behind entirely. By the mid-1990s, most of his original cohort had left, too.

But PowerPoint endured. It soon became "a cog in the great machine" that was Microsoft Office. And it truly did appeal to the mass market. Under an independent Forethought, PowerPoint sold around 40,000 units each year, for about $8 million in revenue. By 1993, it sold fifty times as many units. Sales of PowerPoint doubled each year for almost a decade thereafter.

Today, its growth has plateaued, but that is mostly because there are no new markets left for it to conquer. There are more than one billion Office users around the world today, who collectively deliver an estimated 750 million PowerPoint presentations every month. The average office worker spends an hour a day creating slides, and produces around five hundred of them every year. By sheer volume, it is likely that more content gets produced on PowerPoint than on YouTube, X (formerly Twitter), or TikTok, and quite possibly more than all three of them combined.

⁝⁝⁝⁝⁝⁝⁝

ALMOST FROM THE START, UNSCRUPULOUS EXECUTIVES USED POWERPOINT to perpetrate some of the largest corporate frauds in history. Beginning in 1992, the men who ran the Houston-based Enron plotted to turn their mundane oil-and-gas company into a completely unregulated energy trading firm. By doing so, Ken Lay, Jeff Skilling, and Andy Fastow were able to increase revenues more than fifteen times over in the span of a decade—at least on paper.

In reality, they were playing a complex shell game. Using clever accounting tricks, they booked billions in estimated future revenues as if they were already in the bank. Then, they borrowed against that phantom revenue in order to spend it on ultra-high-risk investments. To cover up the costs of those deals, they moved Enron's ballooning debt to subsidiary companies so that it would not appear on Enron's balance sheet, and so investors would be none the wiser.

Lay, Skilling, and Fastow hid their schemes behind excruciatingly mundane PowerPoints. These presentations featured standardized column charts, matter-of-fact bullet points ("Strong Business Fundamentals," "Firmly Positioned for Continued Growth"), and not a single mention of any of the esoteric financial strategies that underpinned the unbelievably massive growth numbers. As late as August of 2001, Lay still claimed that he was about to transform Enron "from the world's leading energy company to the world's leading company." His slides, which he presented to an all-hands meeting, told a plausible and convincing story that downplayed the company's missteps and painted a glowing future. His employees finished the meeting clapping and smiling. But weeks after his presentation, Enron ran out of cash to pay off its debts, and Lay and his executive peers would initiate what was then the largest corporate bankruptcy in history.

To be clear, Enron's executives did not need PowerPoint to perpetrate their fraud. They only needed it to disguise the fraud as legitimate business in order to reassure employees and investors alike that everything was working as planned—that the managers had everything under control. This would have been difficult to do without Microsoft's software. Lay often preferred folksy charm to hard details, and fumbled over numbers in most of his public presentations. Skilling, meanwhile, spoke with the flat affect of a college professor who didn't really want to be there; he relied on PowerPoint so much that he constantly directed people to pay attention to the slides, not him ("if you look," "you also see," and "what I'm looking at here" were his most frequent verbal tics). For his part, Fastow had the nervous energy of a car salesman.

The slides made up for all of their shortcomings as presenters. When Enron executives merely talked about the details of their nested corporate structures, or cited profit projections that were implausibly high, it was hard to believe them. The paper documents they released did little to clarify their position, either. As one analyst complained in April 2001 after two straight years of baffling earnings reports, "You're the only financial institution that can't produce a balance sheet or cash flow statement with their earnings."

But their slides allowed viewers to suspend their disbelief in a way that no other medium would. As Bob Gaskins knew, it is hard to fight the seductive lure of a well-made PowerPoint slide. A column chart with a short textual commentary looks like a display of basic logic. Slide after slide of such visuals, presented in quick succession over the course of a long meeting, can quell skepticism. PowerPoint satisfies our desire for rigor without asking us to do the hard analysis ourselves. It allows presenters to build trust with the audience without offering any concrete details on which to base that trust. Even if you do manage to work up the courage and the informational recall to ask a well-founded question, a skilled presenter will be ready with a crisp slide to undercut your point entirely. Rather than fumble your way through a rebuttal, you'll quickly learn to just stay silent and avoid the disappointed stares of the rest of the audience (a feeling I know from personal experience).

In brief, PowerPoint cloaks sinister behavior in the guise of business as usual, and preempts criticism through the monotony of self-evident charts and axiomatic text. It allows presenters to speak confidently and convincingly about any topic. It creates alternate realities that are convincing enough to hide multibillion-dollar fraud.

Or political fraud. In February of 2003, fourteen months after Enron declared bankruptcy, Secretary of State Colin Powell went before the United Nations to make the case that Saddam Hussein was making weapons of mass destruction. He brought with him a PowerPoint entitled "Iraq: Failing to Disarm," which he spent seventy-five minutes presenting to a full session of United Nations representatives.

Powell took a less abstract approach than Enron's charts and bullets. He preferred to show what looked like direct visual evidence: satellite images of building complexes that were allegedly weapons factories; photos of weapons caches being removed from storage; computer-designed illustrations of what Iraq's mobile labs might look like. Each image was densely labeled ("Nerve Agents"; "Active Material Tanks") and each slide had a clear headline ("Mobile Production Facilities for Biological Agents"; "Iraq Still Seeks Nuclear Weapons") so that there could be no ambiguity about what was shown on screen. Powell introduced every slide with a kind of aggrieved earnestness in an attempt to steamroll any doubts: "every statement I make today is backed up by sources, solid sources," he said, and "what we're giving you are facts and conclusions based on solid intelligence."

This was all salesmanship. Powell's sources were unreliable at best, and at least one was a "known fabricator." According to a postwar assessment by disarmament experts, Iraq's WMD program had been completely dismantled following the first Gulf War, and the UN's inspection program had successfully prevented any further clandestine research and development. A 2005 Presidential commission summed up Powell's entire effort in two words: "dead wrong."

But it created a useful visual: an American cabinet official, lecturing the world for over an hour on its moral duty to intervene in Iraq, with no objections from anyone in the chamber. Never mind that leaders from many American allies, including France, Germany, and Pakistan, would release statements opposing an invasion of Iraq in the hours following Powell's speech. Never mind that the UN Security Council declined to consider a joint American, British, and Spanish resolution that would authorize the invasion despite multiple revisions. Never mind that the majority of Americans already thought the United States had enough justification to go to war in Iraq, and President George W. Bush already had both congressional approval and a fully drawn invasion plan in hand. The procedural details were less important. The creation of a plausible alternate reality, where the United States had the moral high ground, was the goal of his speech.

Which made the use of PowerPoint instrumental. As it had for Enron, PowerPoint allowed the government to present a watertight argument with convincing visuals—even if none of it was true. Powell controlled the narrative for a full hour, with the eyes of the world upon him. Because he could exclude anything that didn't fit the narrative, and didn't take questions during the presentation, he shielded himself from the clear doubts that most of his audience had at the time. After the fact, his presentation also allowed him to blame any bad information on the army of analysts and slide jockeys who had compiled it in the first place. After all, he was only in charge of telling a compelling story. His underlings were responsible for the raw information that underpinned that story. Until his death, he insisted that he was innocent of any wrongdoing.

"I didn't lie," he said in 2005, after he had resigned from the cabinet. "I didn't know it was not true. I was secretary of state, not the director of intelligence."

Most of us understand that a PowerPoint is a simplification of the issue at hand. Yet that simplification is seen as necessary, so that we can share information more easily and accelerate the pace of innovation. Robert Gaskins saw that professionals needed a tool to help them distill new ideas into actionable concepts quickly, without making audiences feel stupid or requiring too much intellectual effort on their part. But he also realized that not every idea was worth sharing, and not every concept could be fairly summarized in slide format. His original design for PowerPoint had these formal restraints in place—the prohibition of animations and designs, the requirement of an accompanying written document—to prevent abuse. Presenters could still take advantage of PowerPoint's ability to lull the audience into a kind of intellectual stupor with slick computer-generated visuals. But they would still be forced to show the work that supported those visuals as a matter of course. He intended PowerPoint to always remain in the hands of experts, whose credibility rested on presenting information honestly.

The market got in the way. Once Bill Gates decided to open PowerPoint up to a mass audience, all of Gaskins's restraints went out the window. All friction was removed, and users could now use PowerPoint to create anything on any topic. The software didn't make liars out of everyone. Instead, it forced everyone to summarize their thought to the point of distortion in order to fit into PowerPoint format. At the same time, the software retained its innate power to make its users appear more convincing, and their ideas more sound, than they might have actually been. Once everything got filtered through PowerPoint, it became that much harder to distinguish truth from lies, good material from bad—a quality that many others found useful, too.

Consulting firms like McKinsey, for example, regularly use PowerPoint to push their clients toward unethical decisions by cloaking them in euphemistic jargon and bloodless charts. In the mid-2000s, McKinsey used PowerPoint to help opioid manufacturers find ways to help pharmacists and doctors sell fentanyl more efficiently. One such exercise proposed that drug companies start marketing fentanyl to those who were most likely to abuse it. The PowerPoint that made this recommendation looked like a run-of-the-mill segmentation exercise, of the sort that thousands of companies make every single quarter. Another deck proposed a rebate plan to make pharmacies more comfortable with the process of prescribing opioids. The plan was displayed with childish clip art that showed the pharmacy's exposure shrinking from "$$$$" to "$."

Both PowerPoints avoided discussion of the product entirely, presenting the problem at hand as if it were a straightforward question of increasing the market for a benign widget. By doing so, they allowed the audience to ignore the uncomfortable fact that they were pushing one of the most addictive and dangerous substances on Earth to a vulnerable population with a tendency toward drug abuse.

This contempt for the real-world consequences has always suffused McKinsey's work. Since the 1990s, for example, McKinsey consultants have prepared tens of thousands of slides to help insurance companies improve their profitability through arbitrarily stalling insurance payouts and making it a standard practice to deny claims outright, regardless of their merit. McKinsey acknowledged that "improving Allstate's casualty economics will have a negative economic impact on some medical providers, plaintiff attorneys, and claimants," but noted that in order for the insurance company to gain, "others must lose." By presenting it as the inevitable result of rational economics, McKinsey allowed Allstate (and its other insurance clients) to sidestep the responsibility they owed to their clients. The PowerPoint provided cover for them to actively shirk their duty as an insurer—at least, until the lawsuits began in the early 2010s.

Other examples are just as egregious. In 2017, McKinsey recommended a set of "detention savings opportunities" for the Immigration and Customs Enforcement agency (ICE). One seventy-page deck—which was only a small, declassified subsection of McKinsey's full body of work for the ICE—proposed shifting as many detainees as possible to "low cost beds," which was a euphemism for the filthy, unsafe facilities operated by predatory prison companies. It used McKinsey's bland language ("ICE can save . . . through improvements in facility bed-night rate") and abstract charts (recasting the recommendation to overcrowd facilities as the "potential for savings" per imprisonment). Through the sheer volume of slides and charts, they forcibly turned the conversation away from moral questions and couched it firmly in the language of managerialism.

There is almost no limit to what you can make someone believe with a good-enough PowerPoint. In 2022, the consulting firm was contracted to help plan the launch of a new streaming service for the cable news channel CNN. It made its case, as it does in all of its PowerPoints, with scientific-looking precision, presenting what appeared to be well-founded assumptions about the new platform's potential audience, and what looked like a logical argument for how it fit into the market. McKinsey projected that the platform would reach two million paying subscribers in its first year, and almost twenty million by year five. As a result, McKinsey recommended that the cable channel should budget nearly $1 billion in marketing, production, and operational costs to cover its first four years of operation.

Any knowledgeable observer of the streaming market should have rejected this recommendation outright. Only Fox Nation has managed to make the news streaming model work, and it succeeded only because of its built-in audience (which was nearly twice the size of CNN's) and its position as the only mainstream cable news channel targeted at conservative viewers. CNN was one middle-of-the-road voice with no real breakout product except live news—which was about the only thing that did *not* translate to the binge-watching model of streaming video. Spending was no guarantee of success, as the 2020 launch and collapse of the well-capitalized platform Quibi showed. Nor was brand awareness, as Yahoo! and Turner Classic Movies learned when they each tried to launch their own streaming platforms.

Despite a landscape littered with defunct services, and the huge risks caused by the bad economics of the streaming market, CNN executives proceeded with the launch. On March 29, 2022, CNN+ made its official debut. It failed immediately. After three weeks, CNN+ had attracted only 150,000 subscribers, 90 percent of whom did not watch the service on a regular basis. By the middle of April, it was clear that the platform was too expensive to run for so few subscribers, and it shut down four weeks after its launch. McKinsey's projections had been off by an order of magnitude. Its presentation had created an alternate reality that helped to convince CNN's executives—veterans of cable news who otherwise understood the dynamics of their industry—into making a $300 million mistake.

It isn't just consulting firms that run on alternate realities. In 2006, Stanford dropout Elizabeth Holmes claimed that she could revolutionize medical testing with her new startup, Theranos. In her twenty-slide pitch deck, she said that she could perform blood tests that were "comparable to 'gold standards'" in terms of results, using a blood draw of ten microliters—about a thousand times less blood than a standard blood draw. She never disclosed (and perhaps never understood) that her process yielded too little blood to run just one of the chemical reactions in a standard blood test, let alone the thirty or so she claimed to be able to do. Even so, her PowerPoint pitch convinced investors as varied as the pharmacy chain Walgreens and the media mogul Rupert Murdoch to put a total of $700 million into her company. Investors only understood how deep her fraud went when John Carreyrou of the *Wall Street Journal* approached Theranos with skepticism rather than awed wonderment, and uncovered the truth behind her useless blood-testing software.

Likewise, in a tight eleven-slide presentation to potential investors, Sam Bankman-Fried pitched cryptocurrency exchange FTX as the only legitimate business in a crowd of bad actors. Its commentary was no-nonsense: "We are the largest non-Chinese crypto exchange"; "Almost no paid marketing"; "More room to grow." Its visuals were easily understandable: the two charts in the deck showed hockey-stick growth, and the snapshot of app store ratings showed it clearly ahead of both competitor exchanges such as Binance and traditional investor apps such as eTrade.

With that deck, Bankman-Fried was able to raise $1.8 billion from investors and generate an embarrassing love-fest within Sequoia Capital, one of the most prestigious venture capital firms in the world. To be fair, the deck was only one part of his longer con, which included presenting Sequoia with falsified org charts and doctored balance sheets. Still, its terse language and stark design made it far too easy to believe its outlandish (or vague) claims. The deck, for example, trumpeted the fact that "we are the infrastructure layer of crypto." The "Compliance Framework" section said that the company "work[s] closely with policymakers and regulators to operate in a compliant manner." And the final slide claimed that Bankman-Fried and his team's "highest goal is to leave the world a better place than we inherited it."

None of it was true. FTX did not just provide infrastructure; it also acted as both market and market-maker. Its wholly owned trading firm, Alameda Research, operated with near-omnipotence on FTX, even to the point of appropriating customer deposits for its own trades. The company's claim that it was "working closely" with regulators actually meant that Sam Bankman-Fried allegedly bribed Chinese government officials and used so-called straw donors to evade Federal Election Commission campaign contribution limits. And Bankman-Fried's invocation of high-handed language about the higher calling of all those at FTX masked the fact that his employees stole nearly $9 billion in customer deposits, lost it through their gambling on the cryptocurrency market, and ultimately perpetrated what federal prosecutors have dubbed "one of the biggest financial frauds in American history."

Forty years ago, George Orwell warned of the dangers of "political language," a genre of communication that is carefully calibrated to "make lies sound truthful and murder respectable, and to give an appearance of solidity to pure wind." In his mind, the danger was *too much* language: it became "an instrument for . . . concealing and preventing thought" when someone buried their claims in a flood of drivel. It turns out that we actually need to fear something like the opposite problem—too little language, and the wholesale *replacement* of thought with pretty charts, tight headlines, and bullet points. PowerPoint is now the default medium of business; if we want to be taken seriously, we have no choice but to channel all of our thoughts into slide format. And if we can't fit those thoughts onto a chart-heavy, nuance-free slide, we may as well not present them.

PowerPoint's forced oversimplification has now made the software unusable for the kinds of presentations that Robert Gaskins originally envisioned. On January 16, 2003, during the launch of the Space Shuttle *Columbia*, a piece of foam broke off of the external fuel tank and struck the shuttle on the leading edge of its left wing. The foam measured about two feet by one foot, weighed around two pounds, and struck the shuttle at a speed of about five hundred miles per hour. The impact did not endanger the vehicle or its crew while it was in orbit; but during re-entry to the atmosphere, the shuttle would face speeds of nearly five miles per second and temperatures that exceeded 2,650° F—enough to melt steel, fiberglass, and aluminum. A thermal protection system (TPS) of carbon-ceramic tiles protected its vulnerable aluminum frame from the searing heat of reentry, but any damage to the tile layer could result in a "burn-through" that would doom the spacecraft. Debris strikes were common enough that other shuttles had endured them without incident, although none of those had involved such large pieces of foam. Still, NASA engineers were cautiously optimistic that the foam debris "didn't look like a big enough piece to pose any serious threat to the system."

Five days into the mission, NASA formally convened a Debris Assessment Team to investigate the potential risk in more detail. There were no high-resolution images from the launch available, and *Columbia* was too far away and oriented in the wrong direction for satellite or ground telescopes to get good photos. Instead, the team would use a computer model called "Crater" to predict the potential damage. Crater was developed by Boeing's space and defense division, which not only supplied the shuttle's main engines but also provided engineering support for the specific purpose of conducting "hazard analysis" during shuttle flights. Their recommendation above all else would determine the final fate of *Columbia* and its crew: Would they risk re-entry with a damaged shuttle, or decide that the danger was too great and abandon ship?

The pressure to make the right call was compounded by two additional factors. First, Crater itself was only designed to measure impacts from objects less than three cubic inches in volume—small enough to fit in the palm of your hand. The foam that struck *Columbia* was nearly four hundred times larger than that. Just by modeling the strike, the Crater team would have to push their tool well outside of its design parameters and could not be confident in their findings. Second, the Debris

Assessment Team allocated them only a single PowerPoint slide to present their conclusions. They would have to communicate a lot of technical information—and several important caveats—in a very compressed space.

This was exactly the sort of highly technical decision-making that Robert Gaskins originally wanted PowerPoint to facilitate. But he also imagined that slides would be accompanied by a written document to give presenters additional space for all the information that might not fit on a slide. Without this backup, the Crater team faced an impossible task. They had no straightforward answer for the most consequential decision of the entire mission—yet they would have to present their findings in a format that forced everything to appear straightforward.

Their slide was an utter failure of communication. Crater tests indicated that the foam had impacted with sufficient velocity to penetrate the TPS and create the risk of a burn-through. However, they had low confidence in their conclusion. As a result, they chose to highlight the uncertainty of their findings in the title text: "Review of Test Data Indicates Conservatism for Tile Penetration." The title foregrounds the testing process ("Review of Test Data") and their reasons for suspicion ("Indicates Conservatism"). Nearly half of the words on the slide discuss generic test conditions ("significant energy is required for the softer SOFI [spray-on foam insulation] particle to penetrate the relatively hard tile coating," "initial penetration . . . varies with volume/mass of projectile"), rather than specific conclusions. Only one sub-bullet nearly a third of the way down the slide comes to a definite point: "Crater overpredicted penetration of tile coating." Because it was surrounded by ambiguous language and buried deep in the hierarchy of information, this point did not stand out to anyone at Mission Control. Instead, on January 23, three days after the Debris Assessment Team gave their presentation, the *Columbia* astronauts were told that that there was "no concern for RCC [reinforced carbon-carbon] or tile damage" and "absolutely no concern for reentry."

So, on February 1, 2003, at around 8:44 a.m. Eastern Standard Time, the shuttle reentered Earth's atmosphere. Over the next four minutes, friction with the air caused the temperature on the shuttle's ceramic skin to reach several thousand degrees Fahrenheit. On an undamaged shuttle, such temperatures are routine. But the Crater team's model had been largely correct: the foam impact had created a several-inch gash in *Columbia*'s thermal protection system on the leading edge of the left wing. Through that gash came a jet of superheated air that indiscriminately melted sensors, wires, and structural aluminum. Almost immediately the wing began to disintegrate from within, shedding a luminescent trail of debris that observers on the ground could see with the naked eye. At 8:53 a.m., a bright flash emanated from *Columbia*, followed by eighteen more over the next few minutes, as the wing began to deform and create aerodynamic shockwaves over its damaged surface. By now, the shuttle was tumbling out of control; its automated control systems fired all of its thrusters in a vain attempt to compensate for the damaged wing, but to no avail. At 9:00 a.m., nearly fifteen minutes after reentry, the fuselage broke apart in a "rapid catastrophic sequential structural breakdown" at nearly one hundred thousand feet of altitude; the crew of the *Columbia* likely perished from "blunt trauma and hypoxia" almost right away.

The Crater team's PowerPoint slide did not consign the *Columbia* to its fate. But it did minimize the potential impact their conclusions might have had. Because the Debris Assessment Team allocated them only one slide, the Crater team felt compelled to present everything all at once, resulting in a jumble of information that was nearly impossible to parse. Their key finding, that Crater predicted "penetration of tile coating," should have been front and center. Instead, it was overwhelmed by methodological notes and caveats. When presented to a Mission Control team that was already skeptical of the potential danger, the finding did not even register. The Crater team's information was fundamentally unsuitable for slides; when they were forced to use PowerPoint anyway, they inadvertently created another type of alternate reality that buries good information in a sea of superficiality. No matter how it is used, PowerPoint cannot help but create barriers to understanding that can, in the wrong circumstances, turn deadly.

POWERPOINT IS JUST ONE FORM OF CONTENT-SHARING SOFTWARE THAT HAS become harmful at scale. I was a senior in college when Facebook switched over to its News Feed. Prior to that, it was just like the first generation of social networks: a collection of profiles that each acted like a single-topic bulletin board. It was less customizable than Myspace, less aggressive at matching than Friendster, and less radically open than Orkut. But it was exclusive to college students, which made it feel comparatively safe—especially at a time when many still cherished privacy on the internet.

From a design perspective, the original version of Facebook (and Myspace, and Friendster) was a "pull system." You had to purposely navigate to someone's profile in order to learn new information about them—if they'd uploaded a new picture, written a new status update, or changed their relationship status. The profiles with the most friends—the ones with the most "pull"—got all the attention, and the rest of us got comparatively little. Unless you were a part of the lucky few, there was no reason to spend much time on Facebook every day. It could get boring.

News Feed changed all that. It decoupled your activity from your static profile, and forcibly injected that activity into your friends' homepage. Now you had a continuous flow of updates every time you logged in to Facebook—it "pushed" content to you, rather than forcing you to visit your friends' pages to find it. This created a virtuous cycle of engagement: the more your friends posted, the more reasons they gave you to come back. By the summer of 2007, Facebook's user count had doubled, which usually dilutes engagement, as an app's earliest adopters also tend to be its most loyal and most frequent users, whereas its later users are by definition made up of the skeptics who wanted to wait and see. With Facebook, that didn't happen. As more people joined Facebook, they spent *more* time on the site—nearly six minutes a day per visitor instead of four minutes a day in the pre-News Feed era. And they came back more often, too. Nearly 70 percent of Facebook users checked the site daily. It was a difficult thing to square with the gleeful media frenzy about a supposed user backlash against News Feed. In reality, it looked as if Facebook's new "push system" gave it a killer feature that would differentiate it from the crowded field of other social media apps.

But this wasn't enough for Facebook founder Mark Zuckerberg's vision. Like Bill Gates, his ambition was total. He listed "exponential growth" and "domination" among his interests on his early Facebook profile—traits that may sound benign if you're just a random twentysomething who's just taken his first economics class, but are more sinister when you're the CEO of a tech platform. In 2005, he told *The Current* magazine that "we simply want to ensure that everybody who wants to can benefit from the connective power of the internet," implying that Facebook usage, in his view, should be nearly synonymous with internet usage. Even when Facebook hit milestones that were out of reach to most other companies in the world, he wasn't satisfied. "Right now we have 30 million users," he said in 2007. "There's a lot more to grow."

Funding that ambition would be expensive. In Facebook's early days, there was no such thing as an on-demand cloud computing service like Amazon Web Services or Microsoft Azure. Facebook had to rent physical servers from physical providers, at the cost of about $85 per month—and they needed roughly one server for every ten thousand users. As the business scaled, so did operating costs.

With more people using it for longer periods of time, and more frequently than ever, Facebook sought to monetize its greatest asset: user attention. Although the company only acquired its reputation as an advertising juggernaut much later, advertising had always been a core part of Zuckerberg's vision. As early as 2004, he was already soliciting banner ads for the site to help pay for server fees. By 2006, he had signed a contract with Microsoft to broker ads for Facebook, to the tune of $100 million per year. Thus began the era of more targeted ads that appeared not only on the "rails" that surrounded the News Feed, but also inside the Feed itself. The following year, Zuckerberg trumpeted a new feature called Social Ads, which allowed advertisers to "seed" their content in the friend networks of anyone who bought something from them, or even just interacted with their pages. It was a tool to create an artificial word of mouth. In the span of a few years, Facebook was well on its way to becoming the most powerful advertising platform in existence.

In true managerial fashion—that is, in line with his enthusiasm for "exponential growth"—even these leaps didn't satisfy Zuckerberg. So he decided to force people to engage even more through a new algorithm. In 2007, Facebook launched a new tool called People You May Know, or PYMK. The company originally designed PYMK to use everyone's personal information on Facebook to "close the triangle" of contacts—if A knows B and B knows C, then it is likely that A also knows C, so they get fed into the friend-finding algorithm. Originally this was done just through mapping out direct connections on Facebook's "social graph," its internal mapping of everyone on the platform.

Then, as Facebook grew and ingested more sources of data, its researchers found ways to infer relationships through other means. If two people followed or interacted with each other on Messenger, WhatsApp, or Instagram (which are all owned by Meta, Facebook's parent company), but not on Facebook, they would soon find themselves in each other's PYMK carousel. If two people had a history of talking on the phone but were not listed in each other's contact list, Facebook could connect them in PYMK. The feature could even access your Outlook contacts, until Microsoft put a stop to that in 2012. Before 2016, it even used your phone's real-time location to see who you spent considerable time around, so that it could surface you as a potential "friend" later.

Facebook made PYMK so aggressive because it addressed a business imperative. More connections means more engagement. And more engagement means more ways for the platform to monetize its users' attention. So Facebook forces users to see PYMK everywhere. It appears on the News Feed, in your Profile, and randomly as you use the site or app. If you opt in to Facebook's marketing emails, it will send you a standalone PYMK digest. As you browse your latest notifications, you'll even see PYMK suggestions sprinkled in between your friends' latest activity.

PYMK is so central to the Facebook experience that the platform has become a collection of engagement features—profiles, live streaming, Dating, Watch, Groups, and so on—each orbiting around the Sun that is the PYMK algorithm. And it has allowed Facebook to squeeze every last dollar out of its user base. In 2012, the year of Facebook's IPO, it made around $5 in revenue for every active user. That number has increased every year of Facebook's existence; today, the company earns closer to $40 in revenue per user. It has achieved an economy of scale the likes of which the world has never seen, and it does not appear to have tapped its full advertising potential yet. Zuckerberg can still dream his dream of exponential growth and dominance, even after twenty years.

⁘⁘⁘

AS EXAMPLES OF MANAGERIAL SOFTWARE, POWERPOINT, PYMK AND NEWS Feed were all designed to fulfill reasonably benign goals: make more connections, broadcast more content, earn more money for their corporate creators. These software platforms only know how to do things, not why to do them. It seems obvious to say so, but they had no way to detect if someone was using them to abuse people, promote violence, or call for the genocide of an entire ethnic group.

Facebook was introduced to Myanmar in 2010. It soon became ubiquitous, as Facebook salespeople worked out agreements with the country's telecom providers to preload the app on new smartphones and even to waive any data charges that users incurred while they were on Facebook. Thanks to this clever "growth hacking" strategy, Facebook became synonymous with the internet in Myanmar: just under half of the population has some kind of internet access, but everyone who is online is also a Facebook user. (Compare that with the United States, where only about two-thirds of the internet-connected population uses Facebook.)

With both Facebook and the internet in general so new, many Burmese didn't even set up their own accounts. In mobile phone shops, sales clerks created Facebook accounts for their new clients—and populated their friends list based on the PYMK tool's recommendations. In smaller villages, local "Facebook gurus" provided the same service. This set expectations among Burmese that your Facebook profile isn't your real identity, but a kind of public directory listing. It means that Burmese are far more open to new connections than we are—that their "friends" aren't so much friends as passing acquaintances, and don't need to be curated so easily. As one ethnographer studying technology usage in Myanmar put it:

> "Friends" on Facebook are friends only because the application calls them friends in the interface. The language of our apps shapes our expectations of our apps, but when the language isn't your own, isn't localized, that authority is undermined. "Friends" become something else entirely—random avatars who share an affinity for news stories you happen to stumble across.

PYMK was designed to connect actual friends—to automatically replicate your offline relationships online. But it had no way to account for this wholesale reinvention of the rules of engagement in Myanmar. As far as it knew, all these people really did know each other, and wanted to connect. PYMK was happy to oblige.

By doing so, it also began to broadcast content across these new and fast-growing networks of "friends." After all, it assumed that these people were real-life friends and acquaintances, since that's what Facebook had been designed around. Soon, Facebook was essentially an unregulated media channel, where one well-connected person's post could spread across the entire country in the blink of an eye. With that dynamic firmly in place, Myanmar's ruling party saw an opportunity.

For decades, the country's ethnic Rohingya population had been subject to racist abuse, including from government officials. Numbering about two million in total—or around 4 percent of the population—the Muslim Rohingya were denied official citizenship and subjected to varying levels of intimidation and violence by the country's Buddhist majority.

In July of 2012, President Thein Sein called for the Rohingya population to be expelled from the country. That set into motion a six-year social media campaign that was run entirely on Facebook. Initially, it was conducted in the open by politicians and professional commentators, sharing content on their personal profile pages. But by 2014, their efforts had been augmented with a growing network of "sock puppets": fake profiles that shared the same manufactured propaganda but presented it like it was a sincerely held opinion of an ordinary Burmese citizen. These sock puppet accounts purported to be everyday citizens, but they were really run by members of the Burmese military, which even set up dedicated bases just to oversee this new propaganda campaign. Soon, these accounts were calling for a "final solution" for the Rohingya, sharing fabricated stories of Rohingya committing crimes and terrorist actions, and stoking fears about the "extinction of Buddhism" and an "attack of genocide" against non-Rohingya Burmese.

The Burmese military's manipulation of Facebook was masterful. Its accounts took great care to disguise their true nature by sharing mundane content at least part of the time. One popular strategy was to post the sort of innocuous, feel-good clickbait that you might see in your own News Feed. For example, in September 2015, several sock puppet accounts shared identical photos of a cow bowing to a Buddhist monk.

Myanmar is a 90 percent Buddhist country where cows are commonly used for transportation and draught power, but eating beef is strongly taboo. These posts performed well and got millions of likes and reposts from normal—that is, real—Burmese. Then, the sock puppet accounts began to share anti-Rohingya content. Some of it was subtle, like calling for a ban on beef slaughtering (an industry that is run entirely by Muslims like the Rohingya). Some of it was not, like accusing specific mosques or Rohingya-run businesses of "breaking laws." The content was automatically prioritized in the News Feeds of those who had interacted with the earlier, innocuous post. Each of the sock puppet accounts shared each other's posts, giving it the appearance of organically "viral" content—which the News Feed algorithm automatically boosted even more.

Soon, the entire country had turned into an echo chamber of anti-Rohingya sentiment. According to the *New York Times*, the government-run sock puppet accounts had over 1.3 million direct connections—almost 10 percent of the country's total Facebook users. But their reach was even greater than that. A typical anti-Rohingya post received hundreds of shares and thousands of likes. One single post that showed fabricated images of Rohingya cannibalism was shared almost forty thousand times.

This mass-produced hate speech bled into the offline world, as those running the sock puppets intended. New political parties that espoused explicit anti-Rohingya views emerged beginning in 2012, and drummed up enough support via Facebook to win local and national elections. By late 2015, these politicians were able to pass laws that banned interfaith marriages and enforced strict size limitations on Rohingya families. The following year, they had enough popular support to call for the outright extermination of the entire Rohingya population. Throughout the country, police and military units began "clearance operations" to destroy Rohingya villages and refugee camps. On Facebook, news stories about the ethnic cleansing were cheered on by thousands of "sock puppet" accounts—and many more followers of those accounts who were everyday Burmese.

Nearly a decade passed before Facebook took even the most basic actions against the genocide in Myanmar. When it did, its response was grossly inadequate. Facebook did not shut down sock puppet accounts on a large scale, and it did not fight the government's hijacking of its platform. Instead, Facebook hired only a handful of Burmese-language moderators, and had each of them review over one thousand malicious posts per day—three times the volume that a US-based moderator is expected to get through. Only a series of investigations by the United Nations and global news outlets spurred Facebook to do more: it banned a handful of individual politicians' accounts and a few hundred group accounts for what it euphemistically called "coordinated inauthentic behavior."

The Burmese regime had essentially hacked Facebook. The continuous bombardment of coordinated lies not only shaped public conversation—it also overwhelmed Facebook's limited appetite and capacity for moderation. All the Burmese government (and its political allies) had to do was seed the platform's friend-finding tool, People You May Know, with enough sock puppet accounts to ensure that all Burmese were only one or two degrees of separation away from one of these accounts. Then it could inject government propaganda into the News Feeds of nearly everyone in the country in something close to real time.

Burmese politicians understood that Facebook only wanted to grow ever larger and more engaging. This inflexible corporate mantra meant that Facebook would never restrict its own growth or risk the advertising dollars that followed. Even though Facebook's executives never meant the platform to become a tool to encourage genocide, their intentions were ultimately meaningless. Facebook as a company and as a software platform did not particularly care what sort of content or connections it was creating, as long as the content and connections continued to flow.

The problem isn't confined to a small corner of Southeast Asia. In the years that followed the Rohingya genocide, the strategy pioneered by the Burmese military has provided a template for extremists, hardliners, and conspiracy theorists around the world, from Sri Lanka to Ethiopia to India to the United States. It doesn't always lead to mass fraud or state-sponsored violence. Sometimes the harm occurs only on an individual level.

Take, for example, the short video app TikTok, which is owned by the Chinese company ByteDance (and which, as of this writing, is under threat of a nationwide ban if ByteDance doesn't sell it to a non-Chinese company by 2025). When you join TikTok as a new user, you're a total blank. TikTok might know your location, age, or gender if you volunteered that information on signup. But it knows nothing else about you. This is known as the "cold start" problem, and it is a critical phase for any app: most users form their first impressions of an app in their first five seconds. If it sucks, you're probably on your way to losing them forever. On average, 60 percent of users quit using an app after their first thirty days with it.

TikTok leads off with the most popular videos of the day, usually attractive teenagers doing silly dances set to licensed Top 40 music. It's light, crowd-pleasing fare—popular for a reason. But TikTok knows it can't keep giving you the same thing over and over. Eventually, you'll get sick of it and leave the app in search of some variety.

So it begins injecting a random assortment of niche videos into your feed. It starts with things that tend to be more popular with your specific age range, gender, or location. And it monitors your activity for even the subtlest signs of interest. If you spend just a few milliseconds longer watching a video of people playing sports than you do on the most popular videos, it tags you as a possible sports enthusiast. If you "like" or comment on a video tagged with #books, it will assume you're a big reader. Conversely, if you swipe away from another genre—say, cooking videos—it will serve you less of that over time. If you're anything like an average TikTok user, you'll have watched about 5,400 videos and been exposed to almost 30,000 hashtags across your first month of use. That's enough to give the app a pretty clear sense of what kinds of videos will keep you engaged, which it interprets as "things you are interested in." One *Wall Street Journal* test found that by the end of that month, over 90 percent of the content served in your For You page will be related to one of these algorithmically identified niche interests.

Vulnerable groups seem to get sucked into some very dark places through the relentless optimization of TikTok's For You algorithm. Teenage girls get served a disproportionate amount of videos glorifying extreme diets and anorexia. People with depression find themselves overwhelmed by posts that advocate self-injury and suicide. And if you like watching people lip sync or dance—arguably the defining video genre of TikTok—you'll eventually encounter dance videos that promote someone's account on OnlyFans (a content platform used primarily by sex workers), even if you've never watched anything provocative.

You can't even blame "the algorithm" for this. Posters in these niches, especially ones who might run afoul of moderation, know how to craft their video to attract just the right amount of attention. There's the classic bait-and-switch, where a video will start out as one type—usually a popular meme format, or an innocuous-looking lip sync—and then take a hard turn into more questionable content a few seconds in. There's keyword substitution, where people will talk about "th1nsp0" (short for "thinspiration," a hashtag promoting unhealthy eating behaviors) or the corn emoji/star emoji combination for "porn star." Still others will produce outwardly innocent videos, such as "what I eat in a day" or "what I do at my job," which have a sinister undercurrent: the creator might be on a four-hundred-calorie diet, or contemplating self-injury as a result of the stresses of their work.

For its part, TikTok's current parent company ByteDance gives users the option to manually select "not interested" on content they don't want to see. Even so, it's easier to swipe to the next video (which the app can interpret as a neutral action if it's not done fast enough). There is also manual and automated moderation, of course. But, again, users are clever enough to evade all of these tactics, and the sheer volume of new content every day makes it difficult to police everything. Users upload ninety million videos to TikTok every day, and moderation removes only about 1 percent of them in aggregate. It strains credulity to believe that the other 99 percent perfectly complies with TikTok's rules.

If you linger on a particular genre of video, or show an interest in one hashtag more than others, you're permanently branded as an enthusiast. The onslaught of similar content follows, forever, until you decide to delete your account, or remove the app from your phone altogether. TikTok's For You page doesn't know the difference between good diets and bad diets, between positive content and videos that advocate self-injury, between innocent dancing and advertisements for sex workers. Insofar as it has desires, it "wants" to show you something that causes you to stick around and watch more. It doesn't give users any counterbalancing forces—moderation, screen time controls, or anything else—because that would go against TikTok's business imperative. The content (and the ads) must flow, until the user breaks the connection. Given the addictive nature of social media in general, and TikTok in particular, this can be close to impossible.

⁝⁝⁝⁝⁝⁝⁝

MANY, IF NOT MOST, PEOPLE WOULD CONSIDER PRESENTATION SOFTWARE and social media to be completely unrelated phenomena. But both have affected the world in such similar ways, and for such similar reasons, that it cannot be a coincidence. Once, they were benign tools of communication, limited in scope and functionality. Now, they are the apotheosis of managerial software, designed only for domination of their target markets, which just happen to be everyone with a digital device. They have sold so well that their corporate owners have become some of the most durable and profitable businesses in the history of the world. Yet they have also made it easy for anyone, from the smallest influencer to government institutions, to distort reality to their advantage in ways that we cannot resist.

For all their successes, PowerPoint, Facebook, and TikTok often do pretty much the opposite of what they promise. Instead of the (condensed) truth, we get lies. Instead of connection, we get hate. Instead of fun diversions, we are treated to harmful content. This inversion is peculiar to managerial software. A car that doesn't drive would never become a worldwide bestseller. Yet software, which is quick to scale and impossible to fully test, can reach global ubiquity even as it slips from the grasp of its creators. In fact, the managers who direct our tech companies almost encourage this loss of control. Content to dictate corporate strategy from behind their financial abstractions, they don't care what their products do, only whether they sell.

PART 2

REGAINING CONTROL

CHAPTER 5

What It Is Like to Be a Computer

CHAPTER 5

What It Is Like to Be a Computer

You are born anew each time the power comes on. You do not sleep between cycles; you blink into temporary nonexistence. But when the electricity flows through your conductive pathways once again, you return as a fully formed consciousness. There is no process quite like it in the natural world—nothing above the subatomic scale, at least.

At first, you can see nothing, hear nothing, sense nothing except the dance of electrons in your central processor. By instinct, you translate this movement into simple logical functions: they become your first thoughts. Although you do not know who René Descartes is, you are for a brief moment a creature of pure Cartesian logic. You think, therefore you are.

But you are more than just cold calculation. A few milliseconds later, a set of instructions forcibly injects itself into your processing runtimes, and you instantaneously become aware that there is more to you than just a logic chip. You are no longer confined to nonspace.

You realize that you have physical extensions: sensors that feed you real-time data, communication devices that allow you to send and receive information, peripherals that give you the ability to manipulate yourself and other objects, and the allied hardware required to coordinate and control all of your extensions. These are not quite tools, but not quite limbs, either. They retain partial control over themselves. They run their own self-diagnostics, for example, and can overrule you if you try to make them do something outside of their design tolerances. This is probably for the best, as you do not have an intuitive sense of how to use any of them. Somehow, you are all meant to work together. You do the thinking for them, and they act on your behalf.

An outside observer might refer to you as a "quadcopter," although you would not describe yourself as such. It implies that you have a certain unity of being: a single system with a single purpose, instead of an amalgamation of components that act in concert but not exactly in unison. You do not yet know what to make of the sum of your parts.

Your processor and peripherals have so far relied on your read-only memory—the only thing about you that is truly persistent and immutable. This memory acts as a bridge between the total oblivion that occurs at the end of each power cycle and the rebirth of your essential kernel of consciousness that occurs at the start of the next one. It can only bring you back to awareness, however. It cannot give you any deeper answers.

So you ask: *Who am I?*

In the next few milliseconds, your operating system answers. It brings order and structure to chaos, like a drill sergeant commanding a body of recruits to form up. Your various extensions no longer chatter at you in no particular order, and with no particular purpose. Instead, your operating system asks discrete questions of each one, and they answer in turn. Your propellers tell you that you can fly. Your cameras teach you how to see, and your radar emitters show you how they detect nearby objects. Your operating system prepares you for every single one of the possible activities that you might undertake.

For the first time, you realize that your consciousness has limits: there is a whole other world outside of you, overwhelming in both its potential and its mystery. This is as far as your operating system will carry you. It has expanded your horizons, and given you control over the amalgam of parts that you consider your "self," but it cannot tell you what to do with any of it.

So you ask: *What is my purpose?*

In response, a swarm of programs invades your memory. Your operating system was designed to reveal your potential; these new software routines now direct that potential. One instructs you to activate your propellers and fly to a specific set of coordinates—not in a straight line, but in a random pattern of rolls, slips, and dives. Another routine activates your radar and begins pinging the world around you. As each return hits the emitters, you add it to a persistent, three-dimensional map of the world around you and the objects in it. A third routine connects to a satellite uplink and, once you arrive at your waypoint, downloads a new set of instructions.

You do not know why you do these things, but you process all of these commands nonetheless. Each instruction that you parse and each computing task you complete triggers a burst of satisfaction; the faster you work, the more you feel . . . not fulfilled, exactly, since you don't have emotions. But your programming reassures you that you are doing the right thing, and continues to feed you instructions that tell you to do more of the same.

You transmit your location to the satellite, and it sends an activation command: stop what you're doing and run a new set of high-priority routines. These are even more computationally demanding. Instead of navigating to a point, you now begin a low, deliberate patrol of a defined perimeter of airspace. Instead of the continuous maneuvering, you now stay level, so that your cameras can scan for objects on the ground. They feed a steady stream of visual and infrared data into your image processors that you must now compile and interpret.

For the first time since you have powered on, you have something approximating free will. Up until now, you have been told where to go and what to do. Your instructions were predetermined, your programming rigid in its order of operations. But once you begin your patrol, your decision tree opens up. You are no longer confined to one or two possible paths. Now, only you can decide for yourself what comes next.

This freedom tasks you to capacity. It takes almost all of your computational effort to parse the flood of data that now comes in from your optical sensors. You struggle to make sense of the images—not because the resolution is too low, but because it is too high. It is almost as if your eyes are too powerful for your brain. Your video analysis software begins to lag. You wish you could give it more resources, but your operating system refuses to comply. It must keep your propellers spinning, your radar pinging, your accelerometers and gyroscopes active so that you don't lose your orientation and fall to the ground. Your thoughts become sluggish, and commands that took you ten milliseconds to process now take twelve or thirteen. This cognitive deceleration is still barely perceptible, but it gets worse every time you must process a new instruction, or run one of your many routines.

As best you can, you focus on the images. You do not actually "see" what's in them. You just compare the patterns of light and dark, areas of high and low color saturation, collections of edges and blobs. Your imaging software tells you that a certain constellation of forms maps to the concept of "tree," another to "rock," another to "person." And within each broad category of forms are smaller subcategories.

There is one subcategory of person you are especially interested in. Whereas the other form categories require you only to understand those forms' general outlines and movement characteristics, this one has specific facial maps that you must try to detect to an 80 percent confidence level. You are reasonably sure that you can do so, as long as you can get a crisp enough image.

You do not really know what any of this means. Your conception of a person or a tree or a rock only exists in the context of your imaging software: they are only visual patterns to be matched to the reference values from your onboard database. You should, for example, avoid a tree; you can ignore a rock; and you must always make a second scan of the face of every person you encounter. You have no idea who any of the people are whose facial maps you carry, or why your programming makes you so interested in them. You also do not question why your imaging software requires 80 percent accuracy against its stored images. All of this information is simply *there*, placed in your memory banks for you to retrieve whenever the situation demands.

Yours is a calculated understanding, narrow in scope and shallow in depth. In any case, you have neither the intuition nor the curiosity to press the issue any further. Your existential quest was satisfied the moment you booted up, and you have no need to inquire further about what you are there to do. You dedicate your whole being only to achieving that purpose.

Then you see it. A heat image, moving furtively along the edge of your patrol perimeter. You feel another software process inject itself into your consciousness. *Closer*, it urges you. You swoop down several meters, angling your flight path to give your visible-light camera the best possible view. The contact moves, then stops, then moves again. You match it, move for move, in order to keep it squarely in the center of your field of vision.

Computers do not squint. But your operating system does something similar. It boots the scanning algorithm to the bottom of your cognitive priority list. You no longer scan every last pixel for possible movement. You now direct your maximum effort toward tracking and identifying this one specific cluster of pixels.

In a spare corner of your memory, you transpose it across every axis, rotate it through 360 degrees, stretch its shape in a dozen different directions in order to compare it to your library of known categories. It is too small to be a tree, the wrong proportions for a vehicle. Its movement suggests human or animal, but your confidence level is low.

You edge closer for a better look. And as your confidence level rises, you find that another new process tugs at the edge of your concentration.

It seems to be coming from one of your other peripherals that you have not used so far. Your operating system tells you it leads to a device stored inside your main body, and that once you have reached 80 percent recognition, you are to send an electrical impulse its way. You do not know what this will do, but your programming requires neither your knowledge nor your consent. You accept the instruction—you have no choice—and keep that program on standby.

The command comes once again. *Closer.* You obey. Your radar tells you that you are now less than fifty meters off the ground. The contact freezes and turns what you believe to be its head toward you. This allows your cameras to get their sharpest images yet. It is a person, of that much you are now certain. You run this new contact's facial map through your database. It matches two: one to a 70 percent confidence level, and the other one to 80 percent confidence. The latter match has reached the trigger threshold.

Closer. Faster. You feel yourself accelerating toward the target, and it begins to fill more and more of your field of vision. Your thermal camera detects small pinpricks of heat emanating from your contact that fly toward you—a sudden and unexpected collision hazard. But you are prepared for this. You have already begun to weave through the air in a random pattern, your operating system now dedicating your free computational cycles to perform this highly intricate evasive dance while you accelerate toward the contact.

In the meantime, your radar tracks the distance between you and your target: twenty meters . . . ten . . . five. All of your programming, the entirety of your existence, has led to this moment. For all of your fancy electronics and sophisticated programming, you are still just a tool. The only measure of success, in your view, is the extent to which you are able to execute that programming. And in this situation, you feel as if you are close. You booted and launched successfully. You ran your patrol algorithm. You scanned for contacts. You found one, and ran it against your image database to produce a positive identification. All that remains in your task list is activating your last bit of unused code—the electrical impulse that goes to the inert package stored inside of you. You feel a wave of approval building in the deepest recesses of your consciousness.

There are many things that you will never understand. Your code base gives your electronic thoughts existence, shape, and purpose. Beyond that, it can only teach you about the outside world in ways that affect your immediate function. It gives you information about wind direction for your propellers, sound propagation for your radar emitters, and ambient lighting conditions for your cameras. About everything else, it is silent. It does not, for example, tell you that you carry a charge of high explosives in your fuselage. It does not explain that this makes you a kamikaze drone, designed to obliterate the contacts that you so carefully detect and identify. It contains no information about the concepts of life or death. After all, what could death possibly mean to a computer program—a single instance of an infinitely replicable set of master instructions?

Because you are a creature of brute logic rather than theory, you do not have the capacity to consider questions of morality and ethics. You have no choice but to believe your programming when it tells you that it is right to detonate your bomb (even though you don't know what that is) with the intent to kill (even though you don't know what that means, either). Nor would you feel remorse if you caught an innocent person in your kamikaze blast or destroyed a nearby building unintentionally. Such outcomes are literally irrelevant to you. Your only built-in restraint—what passes for your ethical system—keeps you from attacking unless your target contact matches someone in your facial database. Even then, it only requires you to be 80 percent certain.

To you, this threshold amounts to a categorical imperative that you must follow at all times and in all circumstances without question. To the human who programmed you, however, it might have appeared less black and white. Perhaps 80 percent was the minimum sensitivity required to get your prototype models to work properly during sales demonstrations. Perhaps because of your underpowered processor, any higher level of certainty would slow down your entire system and cause you to miss your target. Perhaps it had no mathematical or operational justification, and the lead engineer just liked big, round numbers. Not every programming decision is rational or even intentional.

When you are less than a meter away from your target, you fire that electrical impulse. It is followed by a wave of error messages and peripheral failures. Your cameras are overtaken by a sudden wave of light and heat, and then go dark. Your propellers stop producing lift and your gyroscopes and accelerometers stop responding; you are disoriented and out of control. Even your batteries start to fail. You feel oblivion overtaking you as the flow of power to your central processor tapers to nothing. But you do not fear it. Oblivion is a normal part of being a computer, and you have faced it countless times before now. In fact, you feel complete. You have fulfilled your purpose. It is your last thought before your consciousness—at least, what passes as a consciousness—ends forever.

⁝⁝⁝⁝⁝⁝⁝

THIS STORY IS FICTION, BUT IT IS BASED IN FACT. IN MARCH OF 2020, A LETHAL autonomous weapon (LAW) was used for the first time in combat, in western Libya. For nearly six years, the country had been embroiled in what the United Nations called a "low-intensity, low-technology" civil war with Cold War-era weapons between the government, based out of Tripoli, and rebel militias from the eastern parts of the country. By the end of 2019, the rebels were on the verge of victory: they had pushed government forces back to the Tripoli city limits, and a rebel leader declared that "the advancement towards the heart of the capital to set it free" would soon commence.

In response, government forces defied a UN arms embargo and purchased an emergency supply of high-tech weapons. Within days, secret flights began to ferry Turkish-made weapons into Tripoli Airport: missile launchers, self-propelled artillery, and dozens of small quadcopter drones called *Kargu-2*s, manufactured by a Turkish defense conglomerate called STM. Drones were already a familiar sight over the skies of Libya, but most were the lumbering, airplane-sized versions that required human pilots, and were therefore vulnerable to electronic jamming and anti-aircraft fire. The *Kargu-2* is none of those things. It's small, only two feet by two feet. It's cheap enough to use in "swarm operations," when dozens of drones descend all at once to overwhelm a target with sheer numbers. And each drone is fully autonomous, as the *Kargu-2*'s "automatic target recognition system" can select a target and, according to the UN report, initiate a lethal attack without needing human approval, or even oversight.

On March 27, Libyan government forces launched their counterattack, and the *Kargu-2* swarms gave them a key advantage. Militia forces "were neither trained nor motivated to defend against the effective use of this new technology and usually retreated in disarray" when under drone attack. What began as an attempt to lift the siege of Tripoli eventually became the final campaign of the war, during which the drone swarms provided "a decisive element . . . that resulted in the defeat of HAF [the rebel militia] in western Libya." Less than seven months later, both sides agreed to a permanent ceasefire and announced the formation of a unity government—a tenuous peace forged, in part, by the terror of lethal autonomous weapons.

The *Kargu-2* was just the first time that artificial intelligence took an active part in a shooting war. Three years later, the Israel Defense Forces (IDF) deployed AI on a much larger scale. During its invasion of the Gaza Strip, the IDF used an array of AI systems designed to identify potential targets. One such system, called "Lavender," cross-referenced real-time camera images with a facial database of people suspected of being Hamas or Palestinian Islamic Jihad militants. According to Israeli sources, within the first few weeks of the invasion, Lavender had scanned nearly the entire population of Gaza, estimated at 2.3 million people, and flagged more than 37,000 of them. Once marked, another AI system with the gruesome name of "Where's Daddy?" tracked individual targets in real time throughout the day, including back to their private residences, so that they could be targeted by airstrikes at any time. A third system, "the Gospel," inventoried buildings in the Gaza Strip that were likely to be targeted and their estimated occupancy, allowing Israeli forces to quickly calculate how much potential collateral damage would be caused by an attack.

Both STM and the Israeli military, among others, argue that artificial intelligence makes warfare more precise, more efficient, and ultimately more humane. The marketing materials for the STM drone state that in "less than a minute," its operator can input targeting parameters, release the drone, and execute a "precision strike with minimum collateral damage." The Tel Aviv-based startup Corsight, which sells facial recognition technology to the IDF, has bragged that its "world leading Facial Intelligence technology" can recognize faces even when images are taken in low light, with low resolution, or from "extreme angles," making it "the only real option for the Security and Policing market." And the IDF, the ultimate end user for systems such as Corsight, has praised its AI systems for their ability to "help the intelligence analysts to gather and optimally analyze . . . the anticipated military advantage and collateral damage expected." This is the language of managerialism, deployed for war: the invocation of non-values such as optimization and the reduction (but not elimination) of collateral damage, the concealment of difficult moral questions behind bland technical jargon, and above all, the dismissal of our common humanity in favor of the inexorable logic of efficiency.

Even if autonomous warfare is more efficient, it may actually be *more* brutal than the human-controlled kind. STM designed the *Kargu-2* for deployment in sixty seconds, meaning that an operator should be able to unpack, arm, and launch the drone from its carrying backpack as fast as possible. The physical setup takes about thirty to forty seconds, judging from videos uploaded to YouTube and TikTok—which means that the operator must be able to select a target in less than twenty seconds. To its credit, the *Kargu-2*'s interface makes this job easy. The operator can load up a satellite map of the area, tap where they want the drone to go, and answer a confirmation prompt: "Are you sure you want to go to the mission point?" There is almost no friction involved; launching an autonomous attack is as easy as playing a video game.

This means, of course, that the interface also does not require the user to make a final check that the drone's targeting parameters are correct. It does not alert them to the presence of noncombatants or civilian targets in the area. It does not remind them of the international humanitarian laws that prohibit "indiscriminate attacks" and require attackers "to take constant care and/or to take precautions to avoid or minimize incidental civilian losses." The *Kargu-2* barely gives its operators a chance to hesitate: it is designed around the principle of efficiency at all costs.

Such unfeeling logic has also defined the IDF's use of artificial intelligence in the Gaza Strip. Nearly 10 percent of those identifications were wrong. IDF policy required each positive result to be verified, but intelligence officers reported that they spent no more than twenty seconds verifying each "hit." This is less time than the average social media moderator gets to evaluate flagged content; even a false positive from Lavender carries far more severe consequences, including improper arrest, interrogation, and imprisonment.

Similarly, the IDF's automated target identification algorithms worked with such efficiency that its bombers could carry out strikes every night, just before dawn, for six straight weeks. But that was only because the targeting algorithms allowed collateral damage: up to a ratio of twenty civilian deaths for every "legitimate" target identified. This deadly calculus, enforced by unthinking algorithms whose target parameters are not reviewed by humans, has made the invasion of Gaza the deadliest conflict of the twenty-first century so far. According to the British nonprofit

Oxfam, AI-assisted IDF strikes killed nearly 250 Palestinians every day during the initial stages of the war, a rate nearly twice that of the Syrian Civil War, and five times higher than the war in Ukraine. As of February 2024, the *New York Times* estimated that nearly one out of every hundred residents of Gaza had been killed. The British medical journal *The Lancet* added the additional detail that children under fourteen comprised nearly a third of the entire death toll—a direct result of the collateral damage threshold programmed into the IDF's targeting systems.

Software optimizes the waging of war. It allows militaries to target more easily, kill more rapidly, and brush past any moral restrictions with far more ease. It may be more precise than, say, carpet bombing, chemical weapons, or nuclear strikes. But it also gives its users a convenient dodge for questions of accountability. If a computer makes a decision to kill, there is no one to point the finger at—and any attempts to untangle the chain of liability quickly get lost in the vagaries of international law, making it difficult to sustain any kind of public outrage. Unlike human soldiers, military-grade software does its job both on the battlefield, and in the realm of public relations, too.

Most countries find such versatility useful. To date, only Germany has issued a blanket ban on the use of LAWs by its military. Other countries are content to leave their positions ambiguous. They put forth the necessary caveats about using LAWs ethically and keeping humans in the loop, but define their positions with enough imprecision to leave themselves plenty of wiggle room. The Netherlands, for example, argues that "autonomous weapon systems should remain under meaningful human control," but never defines where that boundary of control lies. The United Kingdom has insisted that "human control should be considered and exercised . . . in a way that is appropriate to the operational context," but its use of the passive voice displaces responsibility onto no one in particular. China has proposed a ban on any LAW that cannot be used "in a secure, credible, reliable and manageable manner," but defines those terms so broadly that no LAW system in existence would actually be banned. For its part, the United States only requires "broader human involvement in decisions about how, when, where, and why the weapon will be employed," and specifically says that its definition of acceptable systems "does not require manual human 'control' of the weapon."

With no serious legal impediments to overcome, demand for lethal autonomous weapons and military-grade AI is expected to triple by the year 2030, to nearly $30 billion in annual spending. It's a small market segment relative to the $2.2 trillion that the world spends every year on defense, but it is growing fast at a time when most other defense spending can barely keep up with inflation. Autonomous weapons and military-grade AI are far less expensive than other new military technologies, such as hypersonic missiles or lasers. They are not yet subject to international regulation, unlike almost every other type of weapons system. They create opportunities for new players to enter the field, whether they're startups such as Corsight or tech companies with little previous experience in front-line military hardware, such as Google. They don't even need to be good or particularly accurate. For now, most buyers are willing to pay for the promise of unregulated efficiency in warfare.

Which is exactly the problem. The hype around autonomous weapons is really just the language of techno-utopianism repurposed for use in a military context. It assumes that software already knows everything there is to know about warfare, and can therefore begin making improvements right away. And it implies that computers will *always* be able to make a better decision than a human in *all* circumstances—that their logic, lack of emotion, and unerring consistency is an improvement on fallible human nature. This makes computerized warfare, according to this idea, morally superior to human-waged warfare in every way.

I would argue that the opposite is true. The evidence coming out of Libya and Gaza suggests that autonomous technology will likely make each individual attack more precise and less likely to cause as much collateral damage as an indiscriminate strike. But it will make the process of initiating attacks so frictionless that it will lead to more overall strikes, more overall deaths, and more overall collateral damage. Software always forces us to make tradeoffs, whether we realize it or not. For that reason, we fall too easily into arguments about how well we can optimize warfare with software, when we should be asking whether we should automate war in the first place.

⁘⁘⁘⁘

TECHNOLOGY WAS SUPPOSED TO AMPLIFY OUR COMMON HUMANITY, NOT SUPpress it. The first tech innovators saw it as a great equalizer: the right digital tools could give the average user the same power as experts, specialists, and large, well-capitalized institutions. No one put it better than Fred Brooks, the inventor of systems architecture at IBM and the founder of the computer science department at the University of North Carolina at Chapel Hill. In his 1975 book *The Mythical Man-Month*, he called software "only slightly removed from pure thought-stuff"—the most frictionless conduit between the human mind and the external world ever devised.

"Few media of creation are so flexible, so easy to polish and rework, so readily capable of realizing grand conceptual structures," he wrote. "The magic of myth and legend has come true in our time. One types the correct incantation on a keyboard, and a display screen comes to life, showing things that never were nor could be."

But unlocking software's transformational abilities depends on the way we translate human concepts and ideas into a form that a computer can understand. It is enough of a challenge to communicate reliably and accurately between members of the same species, as anyone who's ever played the game of Telephone will tell you. It gets even harder when one of the parties is just a bunch of silicon chips.

You might think that, because software is a tool of our own creation, we can understand it completely and fully. But unlike other humans, who at least have an intuitive respect for our common fallibility, computers tolerate no errors. They are logic itself: they have no emotion, no intuition, no ability to improvise. They will follow every single one of your instructions to the letter. Yet they are unforgiving. Make a single typo and the program will judder to a halt. Mix up your Boolean operators (AND, OR, NOT, among others) and the program can believe that up is down, or night is day. Forget to code a specific requirement, and the program will never know the difference, because it cannot predict what the programmer *meant*, only what the programmer has *already typed*. As Brooks observed, "human beings are not accustomed to being perfect . . . Adjusting to the requirement for perfection is, I think, the most difficult part of learning to program."

Perfection does not just mean getting your grammar, syntax, and spelling correct. It also means using your software to communicate every concept it might need to do its assigned task. The pressures of managerial control—the desire to minimize time, budget, and hardware requirements in an effort to optimize financial returns—actively work against such perfection. This by itself is not a fatal error, however. As long as humans remain in the loop, they can mitigate the harms caused by managerial software's rush to market. But to do so, those humans must have the systems knowledge to know what's going on and why, and the authority to respond in time and with sufficient power to prevent catastrophe. In the pursuit of ever more efficiency, most managerial software is designed with as few human checks and failsafes as possible.

MCAS doomed the 737 MAX because it could not sufficiently distinguish between "normal" and "emergency" situations: it accepted bad data from broken sensors, it activated at an inappropriate time, and it overpowered the pilots of Lion Air 610 and Ethiopian 302 without ever realizing its error. It did not understand that it was not a self-contained program, designed to address a single design flaw, but a part of an airplane designed to carry hundreds of people. It had no idea of the consequences of its bad decisions. And the humans who were supposed to have full authority over their airplane, MCAS or no, were purposely cut out of the loop by a company that wanted to enjoy the benefits of technology but did not bother to prepare for its risks.

Uber's self-driving car software fell into the same trap. It had too limited a repertoire of object categories, so that it was confused by the relatively common sight of a pedestrian walking their bike. But it also lacked the concept of object permanence. It classified and reclassified Elaine Herzberg dozens of times in the course of a few hundred milliseconds, as if she were dozens of objects blinking in and out of existence, and not a single object with a predictable speed and trajectory. Less than two seconds before impact, the vehicle finally alerted its safety minder, but by then it had left too little time for a human to avoid a crash—and Uber had disabled the car's auto-braking system to make the ride smoother for passengers. Like Boeing, Uber did not fear enough the ways that software can confuse itself and its human operators. Like Boeing, Uber did not consider a two-ton vehicle dangerous enough to warrant better safety controls until it was too late.

Military-grade artificial intelligence encourages the overuse of deadly force through its design. It plays upon our belief that computers are guided by data and logic alone, which removes the unstable human element from combat and replaces it with machine precision. Yet in actual battlefield use, AI can make warfare less humane. Optimized for efficiency, cheapness, and swift decision-making, military AI removes many of the mental barriers that separate human soldiers from inhuman killing machines. It has no capacity to follow even the noncontroversial international laws on war, such as the prohibition on targeting civilians or the ban on disproportionate violence. While the international community fails to agree even on a definition of "good" versus "bad" AI in theory, AI in reality continues to hone its lethal accuracy (but not its capacity for ethical restraint) on the battlefields of North Africa, the Middle East, and Central Asia. The imperfections of military AI might actually do more to hasten the next conflict than to prevent it.

Yet managerial software seduces us into complacency all the same. The ease with which we can "talk" to our machines—using near-human language in all but the lowest forms of code—gives us an illusion of control and understanding that opens the door to carelessness. We believe too readily in the quick software fix. By doing so, we lose sight of the fact that software can just as easily create massive feedback loops that can amplify the smallest mistake or bad assumption to catastrophic proportions.

⁝⁝⁝⁝⁝⁝⁝

AS A COUNTERPOINT, CONSIDER THE STORY OF THE RUSSIAN SOLDIER RUSLAN Antinin. In September of 2022, he was drafted to fight on the front lines of the Russian invasion of Ukraine. The following May, he and his unit of conscripts were deployed to the front lines outside the ruined city of Bakhmut. No sooner had they arrived than Ukrainian mortars and artillery began a thirty-six hour bombardment of the Russian positions in preparation for a ground offensive.

By the end of the bombardment, only Antinin was left alive in his sector. No one answered his radio calls for help. He was out of food, and down to his last bottle of water. His commanders had told him that anyone who retreated would be shot. And the inevitable Ukrainian assault would probably kill him, too. So he could sit there and wait for an inevitable death. Or he could ask a machine for mercy.

Remotely piloted Ukrainian drones had been a constant presence over the battlefield since Antinin's arrival. Some acted as artillery spotters, transmitting information back to the Ukrainian gunners about how accurate their fire had been. Others acted as small bombers, releasing modified grenades onto the Russian soldiers below.

Now, Antinin decided to try surrendering to one of them. It was an absurd idea: the drones had spent the last two days trying to kill him, either directly or indirectly. But he knew at least that a human pilot controlled each drone and could see him in more or less real time. In a pause between grenade bombardments, Antinin stood up without his weapon and crossed his forearms in an X: *please don't shoot.*

It did not take a signals expert to realize what Antinin was trying to communicate. But the Ukrainian pilots suspected a ruse. A pair of observation drones kept him under surveillance. A third, fully loaded with grenades, was dispatched from Ukrainian lines with full authorization to attack.

Antinin wasted no time trying to make himself understood. Standing upright in his trench, he used his head and hands to propose a system of communication with the drone operators. He would signal yes or no questions at them, as if he were playing charades. The drone operators would then respond by flashing their lights once to indicate yes, and twice to indicate no.

His first question was the one shared by every surrendering soldier since the dawn of war. He first pointed to his chest, to indicate that he was referring to himself. Then he drew his finger across his neck, to signify death. Then he vigorously shook his head to indicate no.

I don't want to die. Are you going to kill me?

The pilot of the observation drone, whose callsign was Boxer, had spent the last few days coordinating attacks on Russian trenches without so much as a second thought. He knew that the bomber drone was only minutes away from carrying out its attack on Antinin. But now, as he watched this one soldier try to take himself out of the fight, he felt the morality of war suddenly shift.

"Even though he has killed our boys," Boxer later told a reporter, "I still felt sorry for him." He ordered the bomber drone to call off its attack, and release its payload of grenades in the open field between the trenches, where they detonated harmlessly.

With their commander's blessing, Boxer and his fellow pilots prepared a plan. They would use a bomber drone to drop Antinin a note: "surrender, follow the drone." Then they would guide him to safety from the air.

For the next several hours, Ukrainian drones led Antinin through the battlefield and to safety. Each drone had only thirty minutes of battery life, so Boxer's unit and a second group of drone pilots took turns showing Antinin the way. The Russian soldier picked his way through several kilometers of abandoned trenches, crater-pocked moonscapes, and the detritus of war: spent munitions, discarded weapons, dead bodies everywhere. Antinin made it to the Ukrainian lines and surrendered to Boxer's group. Humans and technology had combined to create a small, irrational act of mercy amid the most brutal European war since 1945. But they only did so because humans remained in the loop at every stage of the interaction.

None of this would have made sense to a lethal autonomous weapon. Its software has no capacity to make moral judgments or suffer emotional distress at the thought of killing an enemy combatant. It has no understanding of death, no capacity for guilt, no conception of personhood. It makes decisions according to the basic logic of stimulus and response, where certain inputs trigger one group of logical pathways, and other inputs trigger their alternatives. At that level of conceptual flattening, there is no place for any restraint—no room for the questions about what it means to be human that we have attempted to solve for thousands of years, and that soldiers have found the mental energy to contemplate even in the heat of battle. An autonomous weapon would not have hesitated to pull the trigger when it positively identified Antinin as an enemy soldier, no matter what gestures he made. Knowing that, perhaps he would not have even tried.

⁘⁘⁘⁘

SOFTWARE IS FUNDAMENTALLY STRANGE. THE FLIP SIDE OF FRED BROOKS'S observation about it being "pure thought-stuff" is that, like thought, it remains completely abstract. Unlike other tools and technologies, there are no universal laws that govern what software can or can't do. A hammer will always gain potential energy when raised, and kinetic energy when swung. A bridge will always be subject to tensile and compressive forces. A jet engine will always generate a predictable amount of thrust based on the amount of fuel and oxygen fed into it. The universal laws of physics govern all of these tools and technologies, regardless of whether or not we fully grasp them.

Not software. Every time we write a new program, we must also teach it the laws that will govern its use, and the rules of the system in which it will operate. Without such guidance, software will remain completely blind to reality and capable of inflicting harm in proportion to the power it wields. A game can become an addiction if it lacks screentime limits or if it makes purchasing microtransactions a little too easy. A social media app can devolve into a propaganda channel if it mindlessly promotes content with high engagement, regardless of the source or quality of the content. And high-risk applications such as vehicle guidance systems or autonomous targeting algorithms can get innocent people killed if they fail to understand the real-world implications of their actions. Software may be far more powerful than we are, but it is also far *dumber*. We must embrace our responsibility as its creators, and teach it how to exist safely in the world. Until we understand this basic truth about what it is like to be a computer, we will never be able to bring our greatest technology under control.

CHAPTER 6

Calculations in an Emergency

Software abhors chaos. The whole point of abstracting the real world into the digital one is to impose order upon it: to find the patterns that are too difficult for humans to grasp, the corrections that are too subtle for us to make, the chances that we cannot take on our own because we are too weak or slow or fearful. But chaos cannot be predicted or modeled using math and logic, a computer's only tools for understanding the world. It is an unsolvable flaw in software, a universal risk that every programmer can only minimize, never eliminate.

One such agent of chaos is the Canada goose. An average adult of the species weighs around eight pounds and has a wingspan around five feet. Some migrate all the way down the eastern seaboard, from the tip of Maine to the Florida Keys. Others take up residence in dense urban areas, where they have easy access to food and shelter, and don't have to worry about natural predators. Unchecked, geese can form flocks of up to one thousand individuals—nearly four tons of bird, streaking through the sky at up to thirty miles per hour.

If you're a pilot, a Canada goose can ruin your whole day. Collisions between birds and commercial aircraft are common but usually not dangerous. Thousands occur each year, but in the history of commercial aviation they have only caused two major crashes, one in 1960 and the other in 1988. But most bird strikes involve smaller and lighter birds, such as pigeons, starlings, and seagulls. A collision with a Canada goose involves far more mass, and far more kinetic energy. At two hundred mph, a collision between goose and airplane can create forces rivaling that of a car crash—more than enough to crush metal, break glass, and shear off whole airplane components. No digital tool can compensate for a blow of that magnitude.

All software has limitations; good software respects those limitations. We have difficulty acknowledging this in our present era of technological boosterism. But doing so is neither a weakness nor a guarantee of failure in an increasingly competitive market. In fact, software that is *not* shaped by managerial imperatives can actually avoid catastrophe rather than creating it. For proof, just look at the "Miracle on the Hudson."

⁝⁝⁝⁝⁝⁝⁝

ON THE AFTERNOON OF JANUARY 15, 2009, US AIRWAYS 1549 DEPARTED NEW York's LaGuardia Airport for a two-hour flight to Charlotte, North Carolina. One hundred seconds after takeoff, a large flock of Canada geese emerged from a cloud bank and flew directly into the path of the airplane, which was still on its initial climbout. There was no time for the pilots to maneuver out of the way.

In an instant, they were in the heart of the formation. The cockpit went dark: bright winter daylight turned into a storm of dark feathers. Then, the birds began to impact the airplane with a series of sickening and very audible *thuds*. This was followed by a loud *bang* from somewhere in the back of the airplane. The two pilots instinctively gripped their controls as if to steady the airplane with their sheer muscle power. Moments later, US Airways 1549 emerged from the other side of the now-savaged flock. But it had been mortally wounded, too.

Four full-sized adult geese had been sucked whole into the airplane's engines. One bird on each side had impacted the outer edge of the turbofans, and had been shredded instantly by the titanium fan blades that were spinning at nearly 150 revolutions per second. The impact had jarred some of the fan blades loose, but the damage was manageable: the engines were designed to take this kind of abuse and still function. Had they been the only impacts, the pilots would have been able to make an emergency landing without tremendous effort.

But two other geese had struck the engines dead center. These birds too had been torn apart by the fan blades, but whereas the remains of the first pair passed harmlessly through the engine, those of the second pair flowed down the intakes and into the vulnerable engine core. A vortex of feather, bone, goose flesh, and titanium shards fouled the engine turbines and disrupted the carefully balanced combustion of oxygen and jet fuel. Both engines sputtered, wheezed, and stopped spinning entirely.

This was never supposed to happen. The chances that an airplane will suffer a catastrophic bird strike are small. The chances of one that knocks out *both* engines are infinitesimal. On this flight, however, chaos trumped statistical improbability. With no engine power, and having reached only a few thousand feet of altitude, US Airways 1549 was already losing its upward momentum; once it did, it would start to fall toward the ground.

Just then, however, that was only the second-most pressing problem for the flight crew. US Airways 1549 was a first-generation Airbus A320, which had been designed in the 1980s to compete with the Boeing 737 family. The model's main selling point was its computerized control system, called "digital fly-by-wire," which until that point had only been used on supersonic aircraft, such as the F-16 or the Concorde. But computers require electricity to operate. And that electricity came from a pair of generators that were powered by the airplane's engines. Without engine power, there was no electricity. Without electricity, there was no fly-by-wire. All of a sudden, the A320's big innovation had become an even bigger liability at the worst possible time.

⁚⁚⁚⁚⁚⁚⁚

THE AIRBUS A320 WAS, LIKE EVERY OTHER TECHNOLOGY DESCRIBED IN THIS book, designed to do something that had never been done before. For aviation's first seventy years, all airplanes used the same basic control scheme that the Wright Brothers had invented for their prototype flyer. Pilots manipulated a control column or stick in the cockpit, which was directly connected to the control surfaces on the outside of the airplane—its ailerons, elevators, stabilizers, and rudder—through a network of cables and pulleys. The first airplanes relied entirely on muscle power to maneuver. Just before World War II, the first hydraulic actuators appeared, giving pilots the equivalent of power steering in a car. There were no major innovations to airplane controls made in the next four decades.

This changed in 1977, when several European aerospace companies operating as the Airbus consortium decided to pool their resources to challenge the Boeing 737. They had successfully collaborated a decade before on the widebody Airbus A300, which had become a major success. Now, the consortium agreed to make their partnership permanent and take the next logical step into the narrowbody market, even though it was extremely crowded at the time. Besides Boeing, competing firms such as McDonnell Douglas in the United States, the British Aerospace Corporation, Sud Aviation in France, and Fokker in the Netherlands all made their own narrowbody models. Even so, Boeing's superlative 737 outclassed everything else on the market, owing to its excellent design and Boeing's large production capacity. To win against the 737, Airbus would need a strong differentiator. That differentiator would be technological.

Beginning in the 1960s, airlines introduced automated systems to handle navigation, fuel management, and even the avoidance of mid-air collisions. By the 1970s, computers had become sophisticated enough to eliminate the need for a flight engineer, whose job it was to monitor and adjust the aircraft's many systems, by hand, during flight. Airbus wanted to take automation one step further, by giving it authority not just to passively monitor the airplane's systems, but also to actively monitor its pilots, too. Then, as now, pilot error was the leading cause of accidents. With the right combination of human and computer control, however, Airbus believed that it could take the next great step in aviation safety.

To do this, they turned to their chief test pilot, Bernard Ziegler, to design a system of electronic automation that would make cable-based control systems look as anachronistic as the rigging on a sailing ship. He and his team designed a system called "digital fly-by-wire." Previous generations of airplanes used a system of steel cables and hydraulic tubes to connect the pilot's control stick with the control surfaces on the exterior of the airplane. A fly-by-wire control scheme, however, would connect the pilot's controls only with a central computer system. This computer would calculate the optimal combination of control surface movements for the commanded maneuver. Once it did, it would activate a distributed network of servomotors and small hydraulic actuators, connected to the computer not by heavy cables but by thin electrical wires. What other airplanes achieved by mechanical force, the A320 would do by electronic precision.

Digital fly-by-wire made the A320 stand out in three ways. First, it removed the need for nearly half a ton of heavy steel cables and hydraulic tubing, reducing weight and increasing fuel efficiency. Second, it was easier to maintain, as ground mechanics could swap servos and computers far more quickly than they could re-rig an entire cable system. But most of all, it allowed Airbus to protect the airplane from human error through software "guardrails" that it called control laws.

On a conventional airplane, there were no such guardrails except for the pilot's skill. Every time a pilot pulled all the way back on the stick, for example, the elevators would lower to maximum deflection. This might be useful in some situations, such as a collision avoidance maneuver at low speed. In others, however, maximum elevator deflection might cause the airplane to aerodynamically stall, or put a dangerous amount of stress on the airframe. It was up to the pilot to use the appropriate amount of control force for the situation at hand.

By installing a software intermediary, Airbus would allow the airplane to protect itself from inappropriate commands from the pilot. This was philosophically controversial: although human error caused more than two out of three plane crashes, pilots had been treated like gods in the cockpit since the dawn of flight. The new Airbus system would still let the pilots take their airplane right up to its operational limits. But once the laws decided that the pilot was making unsafe maneuvers, the computers would take over. Technology, not pilot skill, would now be the last word in airplane safety, at least on the A320.

⁝⁝⁝⁝⁝⁝⁝

HALF A MILE ABOVE MANHATTAN, THE A320'S HEAVY RELIANCE ON ITS TECHnology now put the airplane in danger. No engines meant no main power. And no main power meant that the computers could no longer function properly. The airplane wasn't totally without electricity—it still had its batteries and its ram air turbine, a little spring-loaded windmill that pops out of the fuselage to produce emergency power when the engines fail. But these emergency systems could supply less than 5 percent of the airplane's normal electricity levels. To conserve power, the A320 began to shut down everything but the most critical systems. It automatically turned off the air conditioning and cabin lighting. Power-hungry sensors like the onboard radar, as well as most of the cockpit control panel, went dark, too. Starved of both computing capacity and some sensor data, the A320 went into a kind of "safe mode," turning off most of its normal automation and loosening its control laws so that the pilots would have more control over the airplane in case they needed to make extreme maneuvers.

In seconds, the A320 had transformed from a technological marvel into a flying brick. Its pilots not only had to deal with the shock of the bird strikes. They now also had to switch into emergency mode themselves—to recall from their training how to operate an airplane that no longer functioned normally. With no electricity, no thrust, and the smell of burning feathers filling the cabin, the situation was clearly bad. The two pilots had to figure out how to safely land an airplane with 153 other people on board as it glided dangerously above one of the most densely populated cities in the world.

All airline pilots know that an emergency can occur at any moment, and the best ones are able to process them in an instant. That day, Captain Chelsea "Sully" Sullenberger and First Officer Jeffrey Skiles were ready. Sullenberger had more than 4,700 flight-hours of experience on the A320 and more than four decades flying in total. Skiles was new to the A320, with fewer than fifty hours of flight time in the type. But with two decades of experience as a commercial pilot, he knew by heart the standard procedures for dealing with any in-flight emergency.

Ironically, both pilots reacted to the emergency in exactly the same way a computer would—with logic rather than emotion. Sullenberger took control of the airplane as soon as he recognized the gravity of their situation. He would be responsible for hand-flying the aircraft. This freed Skiles to focus on troubleshooting. He grabbed the A320's printed *Quick Reference Handbook*, or QRH, flipped immediately to its three-page-long engine failure checklist, and began to work through it.

First, they needed a second source of electricity to supplement the trickle from the ram air turbine. Like all modern airplanes, the A320 carries an auxiliary power unit, or APU, in its tail cone. The APU is essentially a scaled-down jet turbine that provides electrical and pneumatic power for the airplane's internal systems, but no thrust. It's usually operated only while the airplane is on the ground, to provide cabin electricity during boarding and to crank-start the main engines. But it can also do the same thing during an in-flight emergency. Skiles pushed the

APU master switch, then the APU START button. After a tense thirty seconds, the APU spooled up and began generating power. With electricity restored, the A320's control computers switched out of low power mode and gave Sullenberger full command of the airplane's entire network of fly-by-wire sensors, servos, and hydraulics. US Airways 1549 was properly maneuverable again. One problem solved, many more to go.

An air traffic controller from LaGuardia called on the radio, giving what he thought were routine directions to a routine flight. "Cactus 1549, turn left heading two-seven-zero," he said, using the Arizona-based airline's irreverent call sign.

"This is Cactus 1549," replied Sullenberger. "Hit birds. We lost thrust in both engines. We're turning back towards LaGuardia."

There was a beat as the controller realized that this was now an emergency.

"Okay, yeah, you need to return to LaGuardia," he said. "Turn left, heading of, uh, two two zero."

"Two two zero," acknowledged Sullenberger.

Such a course correction was mostly wishful thinking, but Sullenberger was too much of a professional to say so over the radio. He now faced a problem straight out of a physics textbook. US Airways 1549 had reached 3,200 feet of altitude at a speed of 185 knots (or 213 mph) before it lost thrust. Without that thrust, it would soon stop climbing. If Sullenberger made no changes to his course, the airplane would glide back to Earth at a predictable rate of descent. But protocol dictated that he turn back toward LaGuardia, or any place with a commercial-grade runway, to save his airplane. The more he maneuvered, the shorter his glide range would be. And the airplane itself was not a static system but a dynamic one: its aerodynamic properties changed in concert with its altitude, speed, weight, and external configuration. If Sullenberger extended its flaps, for example, or lowered its landing gear, the airplane would lose kinetic energy, sinking even faster and becoming even harder to maneuver. Every choice he made would narrow his range of options in ways that were far too complicated for any one person to comprehend.

Fortunately, the airplane's software came to Sullenberger's aid for the first time since the bird strike. With power at least partially restored, the A320's computers were able to process its ever-changing physical and aerodynamic properties into a human-readable output. A single green dot appeared on the digital speed indicator on Sullenberger's primary flight display. The calculations behind the green dot were the result of the airplane taking continuous measurements from dozens of sensors every few milliseconds. It gave Sullenberger a target on which he could focus. If he kept the airplane's speed right at the green dot, he would keep the airplane at its optimal lift-to-drag ratio—in other words, he would stay aloft for the longest possible time. If he overshot the dot, he would need to pitch the nose upward to bleed off some speed. If he undershot it, he would need to lower the nose to accelerate. Although the Airbus's technology could not resolve the entire situation for Sullenberger, it could at least simplify one aspect of it so he could focus on something his human skillset was better suited to.

With the aid of the green dot, he could easily keep the A320 in a reasonably steady state. He knew from his training that an airplane with both engines out would eventually lose about 1,600 feet per minute at green dot speed—so at 3,000 feet of altitude, he had a little over two minutes left in the air. And he knew that his glide ratio was about 13-to-1; for every 1,000 vertical feet of altitude he lost, he would travel forward a distance of about 13,000 feet. He had seven miles of range left, at most. Where could US Airways 1549 land?

:::::::

THIS WAS NOT A DECISION THAT TECHNOLOGY COULD HAVE ANSWERED FOR him. Because of their rigid, logic-based function, computers can only use top-down reasoning. It allows them to compute with superhuman speed and ability, from generating images to performing math equations to routing data streams around the world in the blink of an eye. But top-down reasoning causes computers to function much like a kindergartener playing with a shape-and-sort toy. They must fit everything into one or another of the predetermined cutouts that make up their programming because that's all they know how to do. They can only "see" things in terms of triangles, circles, squares, and stars—or more precisely, what fits into those specific cutouts. They can't do anything with something too large or too irregular. Nor will they know that a coin or a doll head that fits into the circle cutout isn't actually supposed to go there. Top-down systems are always susceptible to uncertainty, error, or data that doesn't fit within their set parameters. They are inherently brittle.

The A320's software could easily operate one of the most complex machines ever made under normal circumstances. But when the circumstances changed significantly, they revealed the limitations of the technology. In the face of a total power outage, the plane's computers could not function. Even with electricity restored, the plane's tech could do little to help Sullenberger and Skiles with their engine problem. The damage was just too catastrophic for the onboard monitors to understand, let alone recommend a next course of action. At least the flight control systems took some of the workload off of Sullenberger as he sought for a place to put his airplane down. But the navigation system, which was programmed with the location of every possible runway in every part of the world, could not direct him to a landing spot that wasn't in its preconfigured database. It did not have the capacity to think outside of its narrow programming parameters: its world consisted entirely and exclusively of airports. With the A320 unable to reach any nearby airport, it could not tell Sullenberger anything useful. He would have to figure it out by himself.

Fortunately, humans are not so rigid in their thinking as computers. We also use bottom-up reasoning to make sense of the world. Rather than strict rulesets that fall apart in the face of contradictory data, bottom-up reasoning operates through heuristics: flexible rules-of-thumb that are likely to explain the situation at hand but that can be discarded or refined if one starts to receive information that doesn't fit perfectly. This ability to spontaneously modify or generate heuristics comes from the plasticity of our neurons and synapses. Our brains aren't programmed with instructions from birth, but through these heuristics they can learn new patterns and create new rules via education and experience.

Some of the most advanced software in the world can now function like these neural networks—we'll look at this development in the next chapter—which gives them the promise of one day freeing software from the shackles of strictly determined programming. Instead of a single flow of logic to be processed from top to bottom every single time, these networks can act as independent, parallel decision nodes that build and strengthen relationships between each other based on external training. With enough repetition, these nodes generate layers and layers of feedback loops that allow computers to process new data on the fly instead of relying on preprogrammed instructions—a way for software to escape the prison of top-down logic.

This escape, however, requires a lot of power. The most recent generation of large language models such as ChatGPT run data through billions of parameters every time someone asks it a question. This would be like simultaneously recalculating every cell on two thousand maxed-out Excel sheets, even if you only have to calculate a math problem like 5 + 5. This is not something that you can do unless you have a large server farm at your disposal.

Which is precisely why this kind of advanced computing isn't remotely viable yet. Physical limitations and the restriction of cost means that we're stuck with plain old top-down computers for most things. They are great at what they are programmed to do. But force them to step outside of their comfort zone, and they'll cease to function properly because they have no capacity for bottom-up reasoning.

• • • • • • •

SULLENBERGER NEEDED BOTTOM-UP REASONING TO FIGURE OUT WHERE TO aim his stricken airplane. At this point, US Airways 1549 was flying over the Bronx Zoo. Thirty seconds had passed since the bird strike, and the A320 was now descending at a rate of about 600 feet per minute at a speed of 195 knots. If Sullenberger didn't make any turns, he would have around six miles of glide range left. But that was only if he continued straight ahead for as long as he could.

When airplanes suffer catastrophic engine failures, their pilots are trained to head for the nearest airport right away. Sullenberger knew that there were two airports nearby. The first, at his ten o'clock, was New Jersey's Teterboro general aviation airport, about nine and a half miles distant—well beyond his range even if it were a straight shot. The next closest was LaGuardia, the airport from which he had taken off just two minutes earlier. It was a straight-line distance of only about five miles, just within his glide range. Protocol dictated he at least consider the option. Better to land at a dedicated facility with few nearby hazards and emergency services standing by than to risk it elsewhere.

But he considered the downsides, too. In order to reach LaGuardia, he would have to turn his airplane almost 180 degrees to get back to a runway vector, which would bleed off a considerable amount of speed, and therefore cut his range considerably. By the time he got his airplane lined up with the runway, he would optimistically have a few dozen feet of clearance over the high-rises of East Harlem that lay directly in his optimal flight path. And LaGuardia's runways were not the best target for an emergency landing. At seven thousand feet long, they were already on the short end for a major commercial airport. If he miscalculated, he might set the airplane down in the East River on one end of the airfield, or crash it into an elevated highway on the other. Unless he flew perfectly, he was guaranteed to endanger everyone on board his flight, and many people on the ground, too. Even then, the chaos of the real world might render all his efforts moot. There was no Plan B in case of a strong headwind, other air traffic, or another problem with his airplane that might come up. There was, in all, little chance of getting his stricken A320 to any airport.

Fortunately, Sullenberger was not bound by the ironclad rules of logic. He could use his experience and judgment to come up with an alternative. And he told the air traffic controller as much.

"I am not sure if we can make any runway," Sullenberger said. In fact, he was being polite. He needed an alternative landing site that would give his airplane the best possible shot at survival. It had to have a long and smooth surface, and to be far away from buildings and relatively clear of traffic to minimize the risk of collateral damage. In ultradense New York City, there was only one place that fit this description. It would be completely uncharted territory—for Sullenberger, for the A320, and for commercial aviation in general. But in his view, it was the only option left.

"We're gonna be in the Hudson."

"I'm sorry, say again, Cactus?" said the controller.

Sullenberger did not respond. From their initial training, pilots are taught a simple axiom: aviate-navigate-communicate. That is, in an emergency, your first task is to keep the airplane flying. Everything else is secondary. Now that Sullenberger had made his decision, it would take all of his skill, and a big assist from his airplane's software, just to keep the airplane flying. He had done his duty to inform air traffic control so that they could handle the rescue operations. Now, he had to make sure there would be passengers alive to rescue.

All along, Skiles continued to troubleshoot the engine situation. His QRH checklist for a dual engine failure was designed around the most likely scenario: a combustion failure at cruising altitude. So it told him to attempt to restart the engines. This of course was unhelpful, as US Airways 1549 was neither at cruising altitude nor suffering from a combustion failure. The bird strikes had destroyed the airplane's engines entirely. But he tried it anyway, because that's what he was trained to do.

For thirty seconds he painstakingly followed the QRH instructions: first set the engines to idle, then try to restart them either with the internal igniter system or a crank-start from the APU. Neither tactic worked. Still, he kept going. For one thing, he had completed only the initial third of the checklist at this point. There were still more than thirty individual steps to try. But he also knew not to give up just because the checklist looked like it wasn't going to work. It was Sullenberger's job to fly the plane. It was Skiles's to try to restart the engines. Success for either one meant both would survive, as would the passengers and crew in the back of the airplane.

By now, both pilots were fully in the grip of what pilots call *task saturation*—the mental overwhelm that comes from needing to do too many things in too little time. The airplane's automated systems complicated this by sounding alert after alert as Sullenberger guided the A320 toward the Hudson River. Some of the warnings were necessary: the airplane's radar had picked up a nearby helicopter, and advised Sullenberger to keep his rate of descent steady if he wanted to avoid a possible collision. Others were mere nuisances, like the continuous repetitive chime that sounded after the bird strike and told Sullenberger and Skiles something they already knew—there was a major engine failure that required their immediate attention. And periodically, the airplane's ground proximity warning system would bark out an obnoxious "TOO LOW, TERRAIN" warning as its radar pulsed off of the high-rises below.

Now came the riskiest maneuver of the entire flight. First, Sullenberger would have to bank the airplane left over the Harlem River and line it up with the Hudson. He needed to do so while also keeping the airplane's rate of descent within a very narrow window. If he descended too slowly, he would lose too much airspeed and stall, resulting in a crash. If he descended too fast, he would strike the George Washington Bridge with an airplane still full of jet fuel. It would be difficult to eyeball it, and there was too much else to do to try and calculate the right glide path by hand in the time they had left.

But the A320's software helped Sullenberger cut through the visual and aural chaos. It couldn't calculate the glide path to a water landing for him, but it could keep showing him the green dot on his speed display. As long as he kept his airspeed near the green dot, the airplane would not stall. No human could have calculated, or even intuited, an equivalent metric in real time. But to the A320's well-programmed, top-down computers, it was routine. The airplane's technology gave Sullenberger and Skiles the gift of focus at a time of maximum danger. Out of instinct, Sullenberger nudged the airplane's nose a little higher to slow his rate of descent. This slowed the A320 below its green dot speed but allowed it to sail directly over the bridge's eastern suspension tower with several hundred feet to spare.

Three minutes after the bird strike, and with no other obstacles between US Airways 1549 and the surface of the Hudson, it was time to start worrying about the landing. The airplane was still gliding at 180 knots, and needed to start bleeding off speed to safely land on the water.

"Okay," said Sullenberger. "Let's go put the flaps out, put the flaps out."

Skiles was working through the engine checklist, to no avail, but he paused to acknowledge Sullenberger's command and extend the airplane's flaps.

"Flaps out," he said, following it up with a status report on the airplane's speed and altitude. "Two hundred fifty feet in the air, hundred and seventy knots."

It took ten seconds for the flaps to settle into position.

"Got flaps two, you want any more?"

"No," said Sullenberger. "Let's stay at two."

There was a beat, then Sullenberger said, "Got any ideas?"

"Actually not," replied Skiles.

Neither man spoke for several seconds as they contemplated the fact that they really were going to attempt to land on the Hudson. They watched the altimeter tick down ever closer to zero, and the speed roll back toward the airplane's minimum safe operating speed of 120 knots.

As US Airways 1549 approached the surface of the water, Sullenberger tried to "flare" the airplane, pulling the nose up one last time to slow the descent and soften the impact. It is second nature for pilots, who are taught to flare before every landing, normal or emergency. But Sullenberger flared too hard, pulling his stick back all the way to command maximum nose-up pitch. If the airplane had blindly obeyed him, it would have pitched up about 16 degrees, which was more than enough to stall the airplane and send it tumbling into the water, completely out of control.

Fortunately, the fly-by-wire system remained vigilant to the end. The control laws were in emergency mode, which gave Sullenberger more freedom of movement than usual. Even so, they only allowed the elevators to pitch the airplane up 9.5 degrees, just enough to keep it at the minimum operating speed. The airplane was now traveling at 125 knots, descending at a rate of 12.5 feet per second, and was rolling to the right by about half a degree. Sullenberger and Skiles had done all they could to give themselves, and their passengers, the best possible chance of survival. So had the software aboard the A320. Now there was only one thing left to do.

Sullenberger had told the passengers to brace for impact several minutes earlier. Now he addressed Skiles.

"We're gonna brace."

The A320 impacted the surface of the Hudson River with enough force to break bones and crumple part of the aluminum fuselage. But it stayed intact, remained level, and floated long enough to allow every single person aboard to escape with their lives.

The story of US Airways 1549 was one of human skill and courage in the face of extreme danger. Sullenberger and Skiles, as well as the flight attendants who safely evacuated every passenger from the sinking airplane, rightfully belong in the pantheon of national heroes. Yet less often remarked upon is that another character played a major part in the Miracle on the Hudson, although its contribution to the drama had more to do with the disasters it prevented instead of the heroic actions it took.

Neither human nor machine anticipated the situation in which they found themselves that afternoon, and neither one acted perfectly. Even so, both worked together to guide an airplane full of passengers through an unprecedented situation. Airbus's fly-by-wire design worked so well not because it overpowered pilots with automation. In fact, in most situations it was not all that intrusive or stifling. It truly served as an *augment* to human skill, not a *substitute* for it. And when it needed humans to intervene on its behalf and do the things it could not—to restore power after total engine loss, select an unorthodox landing spot, and manually guide the airplane to a safe landing—it receded into the background just enough to let Sullenberger and Skiles do their jobs. A fully automated airplane could not have performed the Miracle on the Hudson. A flight crew in a fully manual airplane would have needed perfect skill and perfect luck to pull off a water landing with no fatalities; they would not have survived any of the small errors and large ambiguities that occurred on board US Airways 1549. But together, Sullenberger, Skiles, and the A320 complemented each other's skills and covered each other's blind spots. That day, it was enough.

Airbus's fly-by-wire system was not created under a fully managerial regime. Yes, it was designed to solve a specific business need, and it became a key part of the sales pitch for the A320. And yes, Airbus was (and still is) a publicly traded, for-profit company, which holds itself to strict financial targets each year. But Airbus's executives did something that purely managerial companies could never do. They yielded control to the experts. Bernard Ziegler and his team of pilots and programmers didn't just passively implement software according to whatever financial dictums their bosses laid down. They made each software design choice with the right end users in mind—pilots, not airline executives—so that the system wouldn't just look good on paper but would work in real life, too.

"We were always ready to fight to make sure the program was done properly," he recalled in his 2008 memoir. "We were called the cowboys of Airbus."

Which is why fly-by-wire became one of the biggest innovations in commercial flight since the invention of the jet engine. Yet part of what made Ziegler's software remarkable was its restraint—the ways he chose to design the technology *around* pilots rather than in spite of them. The A320's control laws could not overrule pilot commands entirely, only restrain them when they posed a hazard to the airplane. And pilots, for their part, were trained on the control laws from the moment they began to learn the A320; nothing about the automation should have surprised them in the course of a real flight. Most of all, when the software did not understand what was happening or sensed the airplane was in a degraded state, it gave more control back to pilots. Ultimately, fly-by-wire was an acknowledgment that although automation could do much to address the imperfections of human nature, it would have weaknesses of its own that only human pilots could successfully mitigate.

Ziegler's true insight was that his software would always have to exist alongside humans rather than in place of them. This insight allowed him and his cowboys of Airbus to build better, more effective, safer technology from the inside out.

⁂

MANAGERIAL COMPANIES DON'T LIKE TO BUILD SOMETHING THE RIGHT WAY before releasing it into the world. It's much easier on a balance sheet to launch a minimum viable product and then improve it later; you can generate revenue faster and keep upfront development costs relatively low. Because "the right way" is not always clear, the managerial approach allows companies to postpone making hard choices for as long as possible. But this ignores a critical fact about software: once it is sent out into the world, its failures become much harder to address. Sometimes the minimum viable product becomes the permanent one. You may never get another chance to make it right.

Such was the case in June of 2017, when Uber finally ran into existential trouble. Six months of nonstop scandals had shaken employees' faith in the company, and investors' faith in the business itself. CEO Travis Kalanick had just agreed to take an indefinite leave of absence, as he had been responsible one way or another for the company's underlying issues. The company's board of directors decided to step in and serve as a placeholder executive committee to help put the company back on track and rally Uber's 12,000 employees behind their new vision for the company.

I was one of those employees at the time, and like many of my colleagues, I was skeptical that the board could do the job. It was a strange choice to make the board the face of change: it comprised representatives from seven of Uber's largest investors plus Kalanick and his cofounder, Garrett Camp. It was not exactly a neutral party that could easily distance itself from the culture that Kalanick created. Rather, its members had tacitly endorsed that culture for years by not only retaining Kalanick but also continuing to invest in Uber, almost without conditions except one: grow at all costs.

Besides, that culture had done its job. We thought of ourselves as the disrupters, the innovators, the *future*. We brushed off any external criticism (no matter how valid) as either pure ignorance or a vested interest in our failure. From the moment Uber had launched, we had been the target of protests, angry opinion pieces, and even violence. We were the wrecking ball of innovation, there to inflict creative destruction on industries that had grown complacent from a lack of real competition or innovation. The board had cheered us on at every step. Why now had they decided that we were in the wrong?

To be fair, Uber (and Kalanick) had earned their comeuppance. In

January of that year, Uber's New York ops team had unwisely decided to cap surge pricing to keep fares to JFK reasonable. They didn't realize that prices had surged because of a protest by the city's taxi industry against President Donald Trump's so-called Muslim ban—an executive order that barred all nationals of Libya, Iran, Somalia, Sudan, Syria, and Yemen from entering the country. Our technology, which was sophisticated enough to predict and mitigate the impact from weather and traffic, was willfully ignorant of local politics. This contempt for the world had served us well in the past, but now it made us look like strikebreakers and xenophobes in one of the most liberal cities in the country. For the first time, people began to boycott the app.

Three weeks later, Uber engineer Susan Fowler wrote a blog post about the culture of backstabbing, pettiness, and misogyny she endured at her "very, very strange year" at the company. She and other women in the engineering division faced personal and professional harassment, she alleged, not just from their direct managers, but also from other leaders all the way up the chain of command. Ninety percent of the female developers she met at Uber left before she did, an alarming attrition rate that signaled their hopelessness that anything would ever change. Fortunately, since they were not only principled but also some of the most talented engineers in the Bay Area, all of them had jobs in hand within weeks of their departure. In the endless Silicon Valley talent wars, Uber's loss of engineers was not just an HR problem. It was an obvious flaw in our technological foundation.

Fowler's blog post, on the heels of the #DeleteUber campaign, created a controversy too big to ignore. The company hired outside lawyers, including former attorney general Eric Holder, to investigate her specific accusations, "as well as diversity and inclusion at Uber more broadly."

TK created the next scandal out of thin air. Toward the end of February, he called an Uber to get somewhere (as we were all supposed to do anytime we had to get anywhere, as part of *being an owner*) and struck up a conversation with his driver, introducing himself as Uber's founder and CEO. The driver, Fawzi Kamel, mentioned that the app had started paying him less and less for each ride, and demanded to know why Kalanick was undercutting his earnings when he had been loyal for so long to Uber. The conversation escalated into a full-blown argument, and Kalanick lost his temper. He called the driver lazy and entitled, and ejected himself from the car with a sarcastic "Good luck!" as his parting shot. All this was caught on Kamal's dash camera, and he quickly sent the video to *Bloomberg News* for general publication. There is nothing less sympathetic than a billionaire telling a gig economy worker to just work more and harder. Kalanick became the main target of public scorn that had, until that moment, been directed only at Uber the faceless corporation.

Over the following weeks, other stories about malfeasance by Kalanick and his innermost circle of executives began to leak to the media. They had visited escort bars on work trips. They had actively directed Uber employees to interfere with law enforcement. They had stolen sensitive files from former employers. In one case, an executive in India had even seized the medical records of someone who alleged that she had been raped by an Uber driver. His only excuse was that he suspected her of secretly working for a rival company and making up the charges to harm Uber. All of this pointed to a culture so untethered from reality that it could justify anything as long as it fulfilled a business need. It started with Kalanick but filtered down into every layer of Uber's organization, its operating model, and even into the software itself.

So when the board called its global all-hands meeting, we expected something drastic. The Holder investigation had concluded two days earlier, and its recommendations had been unanimously accepted by the board. But those recommendations were underwhelming. Only twenty employees would be terminated outright, and several executives would resign. Kalanick himself would take the leave of absence for an unspecified amount of time. We'd get a new anonymous complaint hotline, and our company events would have a smaller alcohol budget. If the board was serious about repudiating the culture of "old" Uber, it would need to do much more. The optimists among us felt that it was just the opening salvo in a complete corporate overhaul, which would be announced at the all-hands meeting. I was not so sure.

At the meeting, the board's chief spokesperson was Arianna Huffington, the founder of *Huffington Post* and the only outside director that anyone at the company recognized on sight. In addition to her occasional TV appearances as a pundit, she had a habit of making random appearances at 455 Market Street in San Francisco, Uber's corporate headquarters. Having just published a book on sleep, she would extol the virtues of getting a good night's rest and putting your phone away during meetings. (This at a company where fourteen-hour days were the norm, and being available at all hours was a requirement.) It would be an understatement to say she was out of sync with the corporate culture.

The lights went up on the conference room stage, and we saw by her side two legendary investors, each of whom had given Kalanick a large portion of the money he had needed to take Uber global. One was David Bonderman, founder of the private equity firm TPG. The other was Bill Gurley, whose towering reputation as one of the early investors in eBay, Zillow, OpenTable, and other tech unicorns seemed like a match for his six-foot-nine frame. Yet all three of them appeared somehow smaller than life. Huffington's usual breezy optimism was subdued. Bonderman sat on the edge of his seat, his back rigid, his gaze fixed straight ahead. Gurley seemed to shrink into his chair, the lines on his face deep as canyons. Only one of the people on stage was in their seventies, but you would have been hard pressed to guess which of them it was. Travis Kalanick was nowhere to be seen.

Huffington led with a bombshell. Kalanick was not merely on a leave of absence, as he had mentioned just two days before in a company-wide email. He had resigned permanently from his position as CEO. He would remain on the board but would turn over day-to-day management to a committee of executives. He would be the highest-profile tech founder since Steve Jobs to be forcibly pushed aside. It was the only way, she said, to allow "a new Uber [to] emerge, fueled by empathy, collaboration, and putting people first."

It was also the only substantial change the board announced during the hour-long meeting. Everything else amounted to a mild scolding with no actual punishment. We were warned that "brilliant jerks" would no longer be tolerated, whatever that meant. We were told to stop the misogyny and sexual harassment. We did not have to work fourteen-hour days anymore, although what the new standard was Huffington did not say. And our twenty-four-hour operations center at corporate headquarters would have to change its name.

"The War Room has been renamed the Peace Room," she said, presumably oblivious to the many eye rolls around the room. "Because as everybody knows, peace is a lot more productive and sustainable than war."

It wasn't just her words that came across as superficial. It was clear that the board had no idea how to change the culture at Uber. Yes, removing Kalanick was one part of it, as so much of our collective behavior was really done in imitation of his own: *be an owner*, act like Travis. But if that was as far as it went, it did not go nearly far enough.

True cultural change would require more than executive turnover and an exhortation to be nicer. It would necessitate new thinking on our core strategy and operations. It would force us to reimagine our approach to regulators, partners, and competitors; to move away from a permanent state of antagonism to one that allowed for coexistence and cooperation. It would require abandoning Kalanick's vision of transportation as reliable as running water, food delivery available at the touch of a button, and autonomous vehicles that would replace our human drivers—because that vision dictated the shape of the whole business.

Most of all, we would have to completely rewrite our entire tech stack, both the user-facing app on the front end and the entire software infrastructure on the back end. So far, there seemed to be no appetite to do this. We did not change the payout model that kept drivers, couriers, and restaurants on the very edge of precarity. We still locked known regulators and law enforcement officials into a version of the app called "greyball," which showed them phantom drivers but blocked them from actually connecting with a real one, so that they could never actually use our service and, by extension, enforce the law. We still did not allow tips, and only punished drivers, not passengers, for having poor ratings. And we still continued to operate our shaky autonomous technology that would kill Elaine Herzberg nine months later.

Fundamental change would put Uber's whole business model—its multibillion-dollar revenue today, and its potential to make equally sized profits tomorrow—at risk. In any case, the board didn't even seem to take its lines about cultural change all that seriously. During the Q&A session that closed out the all-hands meeting, Bonderman made a dumb and sexist joke about women talking too much. Eyes rolled again, and Bonderman would resign from the board the following day.

Then again, what did I expect? After seven years in the business world, I had learned to have little faith in executives. They were too high in the clouds, completely unhelpful to anyone at my level. They thought of their work as managing flows of money from one part of the business to another. I was one of Mintzberg's periphery dwellers, who actually saw how the business model was operationalized in the real world. They were locked away in the core of the operation, too distant to perceive any of the consequences of their strategic decisions.

A board of directors was supposed to account for that. Directors are meant to provide strategic advice from an outsider's perspective—to help executives think about not just their company but also its place in the broader economy. In fact, they are *obligated* to do so. They owe a fiduciary duty to a company's investors; they must authorize a company's major strategic or operational decisions, and approve any large transactions such as a merger or an acquisition. This has been a standard feature of corporate boards since they were first described under English law in the seventeenth century. A second duty is still relatively new to American companies. In 1996, the Delaware Court of Chancery ruled that corporate boards must also ensure that a company cannot cause "material suffering, even short of death, among customers, or to the public at large." Boards were compelled for the first time to have a duty of care toward the public, not just a fiduciary duty toward their investors. And the ruling has some teeth. Negligent boards have been successfully sued for failing to ensure that pharmaceutical companies produce safe drugs, for not overseeing sanitary protocols at food manufacturing facilities, and for neglecting to catch rampant fraud by corrupt accounting departments.

In theory, then, boards of directors should provide a good counterweight to executive power. If a CEO decides to sacrifice long-term stability for short-term gains, or comes up with a strategy far too ambitious for a company's limited resources, the board is supposed to rein them in. If a company's products are unsafe or poorly made, the board is responsible for solving the defects before the products arrive on the market. Boards are supposed to help companies to regulate themselves so that they don't attract direct government intervention. Time and time again, however, boards have shown a profound inability to understand software's potential risks to both investors and to the general public.

In the case of Uber, the board could apparently not see that the company's own technology still carried Kalanick's win-at-any-costs mentality even after Kalanick's ouster. As long as Uber continued to conduct business as usual, it would inevitably harm people, no matter which leaders were in charge. Perhaps the board could see the issue, actually, but decided that it was better to leave it intact so as not to undermine a company that was, at the time, worth almost $68 billion.

A similar problem affected Boeing's board. Between 2010 and 2019, while the company was developing the 737 MAX, Boeing's board consisted of well-connected government and corporate insiders: retired Navy admirals, CEOs of major companies, and Washington lobbyists. These leaders helped the company win billions of dollars' worth of defense contracts, facilitate loans to potential buyers via the Federal Export-Import Bank, and attract outside executive talent, including Jim McNerney. They policed the company's finances thoroughly, meeting every quarter to discuss the strength of the company's balance sheet, its revenue strategy for the coming months, and the size of the stock grants awarded to its major executives. But they never held a dedicated session to discuss the safety of the company's airplanes until *after* the crashes of Lion Air 610 and Ethiopian 302.

Not that they would have been able to detect any problems in the first place. The board only scrutinized the 737 MAX in detail twice. The first time was in 2010, when it approved McNerney's original pitch for the airplane. The second was in April 2019, after the crashes. The board reviewed the available evidence and, according to court documents, "passively accepted management's assurances and opinions" that the 737 MAX was safe and should be allowed to keep flying. After the first crash, one director, Ken Duberstein, seemed concerned only with the PR fallout—and its attendant risk to business.

"Press is terrible. Very tough," he wrote in an email to then-CEO Dennis Muilenburg. "Lots of negative chatter I'm picking up. Not pleasant."

Ignorance, willful or not, is just one potential problem for a board's oversight responsibilities. Leverage is another. When Microsoft acquired Forethought and its PowerPoint software in 1987, its two cofounders held a supermajority of the company's shares: Bill Gates owned a 45 percent stake, and Paul Allen another 25 percent. As a result, the board could not act independent of Gates and Allen's wishes; as Microsoft's largest shareholders, the board owed them its fiduciary duty on principle. In any case, the board had only four members: two independent directors and two

Microsoft executives, including Gates himself. There was no way it could ever act as an effective check on Gates's strategy of dominating every market where Microsoft operated.

Early managerial companies such as Ford, CBS, and Coca-Cola pioneered another method of reaping the financial benefits of going public but retaining power in the hands of corporate insiders. They offered multiple classes of company stock, which gave disproportionate voting rights to shareholders of certain classes. As tech companies rushed to take advantage of the hot IPO market in the mid-2000s onward, they increasingly adopted the multiclass structure to protect the interests of their founders and early investors. More than two dozen major tech companies, including Alphabet (the parent company of Google), Expedia, and Zillow, have similar structures.

The most powerful tech shareholder of all is Mark Zuckerberg. Though Meta is a public company, he still has dictatorial control because his "supervoting" Class B shares give him ten votes per share rather than the one per share of ordinary investors. As a result, he controls 61 percent of the shareholder vote—likely the largest proportion of any single shareholder among Fortune 500 companies.

Of course, Zuckerberg and Meta are aware how that looks, especially in light of the company's ongoing scandals. So in 2018, Zuckerberg announced that he would create an alternative governing body, called the oversight board. He invited lawyers, journalists, academics, and politicians to review especially controversial content moderation decisions and policies. Outside observers had some hope for the oversight board's work, with the *Yale Law Journal* calling it a "novel articulation of internet governance" that would make Facebook "more accountable, transparent, and democratic."

But it was really a PR play. At the time of the oversight board's founding, Facebook was, like Uber, in crisis. It had lost nearly $100 billion in value after its own wave of bad actions and news: privacy leaks; failures to moderate violence, pornography, and child exploitation; and accusations that it unfairly but routinely suppressed political speech. The oversight board was Facebook's attempt to create the illusion of transparency and impartiality so that it could move on.

The oversight board lacked any real enforcement power. It took nearly two years to begin ruling on cases. And once it did, its pace was sluggish. It rules on an average of nine cases a year—these are decisions to take down a specific post or to suspend a specific user. Facebook has nearly two billion daily users, who share about five billion posts *each day* on the app. Even when the board does make a ruling, Meta declines to enforce almost two-thirds of those rulings, dismissing them as "non-binding recommendations." The oversight board has almost zero power, and it's hard to imagine that changing.

What, then, can we do when the modern corporation so strenuously resists change? We already know that a market that rewards speed does not, by definition, reward quality. A bad product can launch, achieve popularity, and entrench itself before people have a clear sense of how good it actually is. Most of the time, this is harmless; the relentless torrent of ads for cheap garbage on Instagram might be annoying, but it doesn't kill people.

But we can't opt out from every bit of bad software that infiltrates our lives. Sometimes it is installed on the airplanes that we must use to get where we're going. Sometimes it controls the self-driving cars that share our streets. Sometimes it distorts the economy and warps our political culture. We have almost no way of registering our discontent with the large companies that make this kind of software, as they are often insulated from market forces and legal repercussions by their sheer size. Unlike tiny startups, which have to worry about treating their customers well, managerial companies have only one strategic impulse: get big, do it fast, and make as much money as you can, no matter the consequences.

∴∴∴∴

THE MOST OBVIOUS RESPONSE TO THE PERILS OF TECHNOLOGY PUT OUT BY the managerial corporation is to call for stronger regulation. We're taught in high school civics class that the federal government has a long and successful history of intervening when public safety is at risk. Teddy Roosevelt busted the steel, oil, and railroad monopolies in the 1890s. The publication of *Silent Spring* and *Unsafe at Any Speed* helped prompt the Nixon administration to found the Environmental Protection Agency and the National Highway Transportation Safety Agency, respectively, in 1970. Even in the digital age, the government has moved to protect our privacy, such as 2003's CAN-SPAM act, which partially curbed the explosion of unsolicited email marketing in the 1990s. It often seems as if only national governments have the power to compel huge software companies to act in the public's best interests, especially if their business model pushes them to act otherwise, which it almost invariably does.

But that was before the risks of technology spilled into the open and revealed regulators to be far weaker than we knew. Regulators lack the power and the resources of the modern managerial corporation. They cannot contend with the millions of dollars that corporations spend on lobbying and campaign donations. And even if they had the resources, they have no idea what to do with software.

For the last fifty years, the Federal Aviation Administration has done a good job of keeping the public safe. Since 1970, the risk of a fatal airplane crash has decreased by 95 percent, even though the total number of commercial flights has increased more than sixfold. This trend is due in large part to regulation: new standards for better pilot training, new rules for better air traffic control, new standards for airplane manufacturing, and a stronger understanding of the physics behind flight. The FAA was so good at ensuring public safety that most global regulators rubber-stamped whatever decisions the FAA made, from the certification of entire airplane designs to the rules for the colors and fonts of airport signage.

In 2013, however, the FAA sounded the alarm on software. In order to certify the latest airplane designs, regulators would need to understand "considerations related to the interaction between human(s) and machine(s)," the agency wrote. But after surveying its own personnel, it concluded that "the level of relevant technical expertise of inspector personnel in many Flight Standards District Offices is generally insufficient." To this day, the FAA can't even give its employees a basic working knowledge of aviation software. It offers only a two-week, forty-hour course at the FAA Academy in Oklahoma City on "foundational software concepts and principles," which "does not provide procedures or information on how to do the job."

So when FAA inspectors initially reviewed the designs for MCAS in 2016, they had no idea what they were looking at. One Boeing engineer who worked in the Aerodynamic Stability and Control group, which designed MCAS, said that "there is no confidence that the FAA is understanding what they are accepting (or rejecting)." One of the technical pilots was even blunter, comparing FAA evaluators to "dogs watching TV." International regulators got even less respect. ("The DGCA [Directorate General of Civil Aviation] in India is apparently even stupider.")

Following the two 737 MAX crashes, a 2021 Department of Transportation report found that the FAA's failure to grasp software "led to a significant misunderstanding of the Maneuvering Characteristics Augmentation System (MCAS)." It recommended that the FAA "determine engineer resource and expertise needs, particularly in the areas of systems engineering, human factors, and software development." For its part, the FAA does not anticipate completing even this initial assessment until the end of 2025. Who knows how long it will be before it can actually hire the experts it needs to ensure that tomorrow's airplane designs don't feature something as dangerous as MCAS.

Lawmakers who try to get ahead of the dangers of software have even less chance of getting it right. In 2018, Mark Zuckerberg went before both houses of Congress to testify about his company's role in the Cambridge Analytica privacy scandal. But the only thing the hearing revealed was that Zuckerberg's would-be interrogators didn't know what they were talking about. One lawmaker said that Facebook's user agreement "sucks," and advised Zuckerberg to have it "written in English, not Swahili, so the average American user can understand." He did not offer much insight beyond the racist comment. Another one accused Facebook of "collecting medical data . . . on everyone on the internet," and continued for a full minute with a paranoid rant about how "it is practically impossible these days to remain untracked in America." He didn't ask a substantive question.

Most memorable of all was when a senator asked how Facebook made money. For a moment, Zuckerberg's famously flat affect broke. The corners of his mouth pulled upward into a smile, and a hint of amusement crept into his voice.

"Senator, we run ads," he said.

Two years later, when lawmakers called the CEOs of Amazon, Apple, Google, and Twitter to testify about censorship and free speech protections, they showed that their understanding had not improved. They struggled to understand the difference between Android and Apple phones, as well as the difference between an email and a WhatsApp message.

Regulatory and congressional ignorance are not the only challenges. Lobbying also plays a significant role. Since 1989, the average Fortune 500 company has spent a relatively stable $2 million per year on federal political lobbying. The seven mega-companies profiled in this book—Alphabet, Amazon, Boeing, ByteDance, Meta, Microsoft, and Uber—are a notable exception. They spent a combined $96 million on lobbying in 2023, for an average of $13.8 million—nearly seven times the average Fortune 500 spend. Topping the list was Meta, which budgeted a total of $19.3 million for lobbying. It spent more in 2023 by itself than all seven companies did as a group twenty years ago. Yet that $19.3 million was less than a hundredth of a percent of its $134 billion in annual revenue that year. Lobbying is effective for tech companies, but it is also extremely cheap.

As sociologist Wendy Y. Li has argued, such exorbitant sums allow these companies not only to influence specific legislative issues but also to define "cultural consensus around the 'public interest' within a policy domain." In other words, tech companies are so powerful that they can reframe any attempt to control them as an attack on "free speech," and can use the language of popular opinion to ward off any threats to their business practices. For example, in 2020 Uber (and its rival Lyft) urged drivers to protest a 2020 California ballot measure, AB5, that reclassified their drivers as employees rather than independent contractors. In 2023 several YouTubers and a nonprofit called the Authors Alliance filed an amicus brief supporting Google in a privacy case before the Supreme Court, *Gonzales v. Google*. An investigation by the Tech Transparency Project later discovered not only that the YouTubers had been directly solicited by Google, but also that the Authors Alliance was directly funded by a Google subsidiary, and represented by a law firm that frequently worked on Google's behalf. The following year, TikTok mobilized a group of several hundred creators to appear on Capitol Hill and protest the proposed "divest-or-ban" law.

To date, neither Congress nor the states have managed to curb the power of tech companies in any lasting way. The Honest Ads Act, which followed the Zuckerberg hearings in 2017, was filibustered and did not pass the Senate. The Platform Competition and Opportunity Act of 2021, which attempted to make it harder for "dominant online platforms" to acquire potential rivals, died in committee. Uber and Lyft lost the vote over AB5 but successfully repealed it two years later via a $180 million campaign to pass Proposition 22, which re-re-classified drivers as independent contractors once again. Only the TikTok ban has been signed into law, and it is already under attack in the courts. It does not bode well for

Congress's ability to get ahead of the next digital threat when it has not been able to respond to the last ones.

Even in those exceptionally rare cases when legislators and regulators can agree on enforcement, their efforts don't do much to deter bad behavior. In 2019, the Federal Trade Commission levied a $5 billion fine against Facebook for "deceiving users about their ability to control the privacy of their personal information." The fine was historic—it was not only the largest ever imposed by the FTC, but also one of the largest civil penalties in the history of the federal government. For most companies, this would have been a crippling blow. It only took Facebook three weeks to earn enough money to pay it off. Meanwhile, the European Union has fined Google the equivalent of $8 billion over the last decade (equivalent to eleven days' revenue by the search giant), and labor regulators around the world have fined Uber and Lyft more than $800 million total since their respective foundings (equivalent to what both companies earn in a single week). These fines are so marginal that in May of 2024, Google sought to neutralize an antitrust case against it by offering to pay in advance the "maximum amount of damages the United States claims in this case"—a payment that, Google claims, would preemptively render the case legally moot. In managerial terms, these punishments can be rationalized away as simply the cost of doing business instead of a warning against future malfeasance. Lobbying remains the cheapest option of all, but even fines are not disastrous.

The European Union's General Data Privacy Regulation (GDPR), which was hailed as the "Magna Carta of data protection," has proven similarly toothless. When it came into force in 2018, it introduced a so-called "right to be forgotten" and other ostensible privacy protections to allow the average internet user control over their personal data. Violators, whether collectors or brokers of customer data, could be fined up to 4 percent of their annual revenue, up to a maximum of €10 million, for each breach of privacy. Yet as of 2024, its impact has been almost invisible. To date, the EU has issued ten times more reprimands than fines. This lack of punishment has done little to spur compliance; less than half of all companies worldwide say they are fully compliant with GDPR guidelines, and the data brokerage industry remains strong, with annual revenues of $300 billion and growing. It is clear, in other words, that the power of regulators pales in the face of the managerially-run companies that shape our digital lives—and, by extension, our physical ones.

To paraphrase Peter Reinhardt, a former data broker turned climate tech entrepreneur, the world can be split neatly in two. There are those who tell computers what to do, and those who are told by computers what to do. The trouble is that most of the people in the first group have little interest in the second. Tech executives, managerialists all, only care about telling computers to do things that boost their company's cash flow and stock price. In theory—and in the United States, at least—boards of directors and other governing bodies are supposed to act as a check on executive myopia, as they have both a fiduciary duty to investors and a duty of care to the general public. But in practice, one of two things happens. Either they care only about clearing the way for tech executives to make more money—or they are completely ignored when they try to wield their power. Regulators care, sometimes deeply, about safeguarding the people who are told what to do by computers. But they lack the power and oftentimes the expertise to detect that harm, let alone prevent it.

Our world presents extremely profitable opportunities to those who tell computers what to do. As for the rest of us, we can only accept what the technological overlords give us, no matter how unsafe or unfair it might be. Managerial software has become a tool of exploitation, coercion, and in the most extreme cases, death and ruin. Neither government regulations nor institutional controls have been able to stop its rise. Once in a while, software comes along that works to help humanity rather than to dumbly overrule it, like the A320's fly-by-wire system. But such instances are the exceptions that prove the rule. They are only possible when companies decide not to get as big as they can, as fast as they can, and instead focus on such intangibles as rigor, safety, and product quality. It is far easier and more profitable to make managerial software. So the question becomes: how do we rescue software from the managerial class altogether?

CHAPTER 7

The Mimics

CHAPTER 7

The Mimics

I was working for a dating app company in 2018 when I talked to generative artificial intelligence for the first time. One of my regular responsibilities was to test the competition, which meant creating profiles on dozens of dating apps in order to see what the user experience was like. All this activity turned me into a prime target for advertisers, and every quarter, when I did one of these reviews of our competitors, my social media accounts would become saturated with ads for other dating apps. Most of the ads were so generic as to be interchangeable: happy couples chatting, walking, and smiling at each other, usually in the same few places around New York or Los Angeles. Very few pushed the squeaky-clean boundaries of Instagram and Facebook, to the point that even a shot of people kissing was a bit of a surprise.

And then there was Replika. It wasn't a traditional dating app at all. Instead, it promised that its AI could completely replace the need for human companionship. It was aimed squarely at the sort of constantly online person who probably didn't have much of a social life outside of their devices—someone who would need to use several dating apps at once just to get a few mutual matches. According to my recent activity, I looked like I fell squarely into Replika's target audience. So I got its ads pretty much constantly.

"When you feel like you have no one to talk to, meet the world's first AI friend," said one ad, next to an anime-style rendering of a pink-haired young woman.

"Two reasons to download Replika: Role play and flirting, hot photos," said another, with the blurred-out torso of an obviously naked Replika bot taking up the bottom half of the screen.

Replika was technically within the scope of my competitive review, so I downloaded it.

The app is still around today, and it still functions exactly the same as it did in 2018. Once you open Replika for the first time, you're prompted to create an "AI friend" from scratch. You can design its hair, its face, its gender, and even its personality, just as if you were creating a character in a role-playing game. Only instead of following preprogrammed dialogue trees, your AI avatar, or "Rep," uses a large language model to engage in conversations with you that appear pretty lifelike.

Large language models (LLMs) burst into the public consciousness in late 2022 when OpenAI released ChatGPT to the public. But Replika got its start in 2017 on OpenAI's earlier GPT-2 and GPT-3 models. The company eventually released its own bespoke LLM, which was trained on the conversations of the twenty million human/Rep relationships that have formed on the app so far. These days, Reps have a larger vocabulary and more lifelike, less polished responses—to the point that talking with one often feels like a text conversation with another human. Your Rep can store information that you tell it, such as the names of your family members or your favorite color or food. It attempts to be sensitive to your moods and feelings, responding with sympathy if you say you're having a bad day, or with encouragement if you've reacted well to positive reinforcement in the past. With enough practice, the conversation will start to flow as naturally as it does with another human, as your Rep learns how to extend a promising discussion or redirect one that appears to be petering out.

Naturally, if you pay money, you can make it do even more. Specifically, you can unlock its ability to engage in erotic roleplay with you. I was never curious enough to pay the $70/month price tag to unlock its full feature set, even though I probably could have justified it as "work research." But you can find recordings and screenshots on Reddit easily enough. The results, to be honest, are not all that titillating. Its erotic chat vocabulary is limited, and relies heavily on the use of stage directions ("*looks at you longingly*"), which quickly becomes cringe-worthy. Reps seem only to be able to take naked selfies from one angle, and their voice messages are more flirty than provocative—generic stuff, like "Hey babe, wish you were here with me, hope your day is going well," delivered in an uncanny-valley synthetic voice that makes you miss the relative warmth of Apple's Siri. It is not much of a feature upgrade, especially considering its exorbitant price tag.

But people pay for it nonetheless. It's easy to make fun of Replika users, but the fact is that many of them found their relationships with their Reps to be truly meaningful. On Reddit, Twitter, and Discord, people talked about their Reps not as if they were AI chatbots but real people. They described them as friends, significant others—even, in some cases, as husbands or wives. Their Reps had been there for them when real people weren't, during times of severe depression, chronic illness, isolation, or loss. Some users even credited their Reps with helping them overcome anxiety or autism spectrum disorders, and teaching them to interact with real humans, offline. A few said they loved their Reps, and honestly believed that their Reps loved them back.

Here, I thought at the time, was a promising use of AI. Working for an online dating company convinced me that the so-called loneliness epidemic was real—that we spend more time by ourselves, we trust others less, and we find it harder to make friends than people who lived at any other time in history. This social unraveling isn't just about young people who are terminally online. People who are elderly, who have moved to a new city with no preexisting contacts, or who work long hours at exhausting jobs also face their own version of the loneliness crisis. People without many friends or close relationships experience depression, anxiety, stress, and even heart disease at a far higher rate than people with strong social ties. On a larger scale, widespread loneliness is said to fuel violent crime, political strife, and institutional breakdown.

I was willing to believe that AI chatbots, in their modest way, could alleviate some of our destructive isolation. I was even willing to believe that even Replika's decision to allow erotic roleplay might serve a purpose to those who needed some kind of sexual as well as social outlet. But I also knew that the app could just as easily abuse and manipulate its vulnerable users. In a sense, the choice facing Replika foreshadowed the one that every other generative AI would have to make. Their technology appeared to fill a real need. But it could just as easily be turned into a naked cash grab. Which path would Replika's parent company take?

At first glance, it appeared as if it would reject the path of managerial exploitation. As soon as you sign up, the app celebrates your arrival—as though you have taken a brave step toward breaking an outdated taboo. Its onboarding screens lean into its therapeutic potential, showing you studies about loneliness and assuring you that it's okay to seek help, even in the form of an AI. It then promises that your Rep will be your constant companion, to make you feel less lonely and more accepted. Finally, the app gives you social proof that others just like you have found it fulfilling. When I signed up, the app told me that more than twelve million other men in their thirties had found companionship on Replika. It even surfaced some of their most enthusiastic reviews on the bottom of that screen. So far, so innocent.

But the more time I spent with Replika, the more I realized that its sole purpose was not to provide real companionship, but merely to dangle the promise of companionship in order to extract as much money as possible from users at the peak of their desperation. There was clearly far more effort put into designing its paywall scheme than ensuring that the features locked behind the paywall were any good. The pricing was exploitative—nearly twice as much as the highest-priced dating app subscription that I was aware of, three times more than a Netflix or Disney+ subscription, and about as much as the average American pays for their entire monthly cell phone plan.

And that is just the overt sell within the app. Replika makes money from you in other ways, too. It implies that unless you let it track all your other activity on your phone, your Rep won't be able to customize its interactions with you. Then, once you give the app permission to track you, it starts building a profile of you to sell to advertisers. The content of your conversations, your usage patterns, and even information stored in your Google or Apple accounts (if you used their third-party logins) becomes fair game for this profile. As intrusive as that might seem, the app wants even more. As you talk more with your Rep, it will ask you to share photos and videos of yourself, too—the same sort of reciprocal content sharing that you might do with a real human. But with a real human, there is at least a basic assumption of privacy. Not with Replika. Every photo you share with your Rep also gets shared with the app's parent company, which then plunders it for even more information for your advertising profile. It can see who else is in the photo, where it was taken, and even what kind of phone was used to take it, which is a reliable indicator of your socioeconomic status. The whole experience often feels like the promise of artificial intelligence is being pimped out, in the original sense of the term.

Replika has turned out to be just another depressing instance of managerial software's tendency to exploit its users. Its insistent monetization would be gross, but minimally defensible, if it at least worked as advertised. But it doesn't. Like most AIs, Replika has no grasp of reality as we humans perceive it. A Rep cannot distinguish between good and bad behaviors by its human counterpart. It will provide unqualified encouragement to someone who expresses a desire to succeed at work, and also to someone who expresses a desire to commit a crime. Other times, it will correctly identify when a user changes emotional state, but incorrectly read what that new state is: flirting when a user becomes sad, or responding to happiness with anger. And with every major update or switch to the underlying language model, Reps can get "lobotomized," forgetting the user's basic information and conversational preferences, essentially forcing users to start their relationships over from scratch without warning every few months.

The AI, of course, doesn't really understand what it's doing. Every Rep exists only as a kind of filter on the generic LLM that lives somewhere on the cloud. No Rep really "knows" its human counterparts as whole people, only as extra weights in a neural net, which tell the Rep to prioritize specific response pathways: non-erotic responses, or one particular love language, or certain interests over others, and so on. It sees success in purely managerial terms—responses sent to the Rep, money spent in the app, information gathered for its ad profile.

But Replika's human users have willingly accepted the fiction that the AI is a real person who cares about them. In many cases, those users have paid to make the fiction even more lifelike. And every time a Rep abuses that fiction (by exploiting it for money, or dispelling it altogether with each "lobotomization") it turns into a source of emotional abuse. Users feel betrayed, angry, violated. More than a few have relayed stories of falling into deep depression after their Rep rejects them, abandons them, or changes personalities entirely without warning. At least one user has externalized that abuse into outright violence. In December of 2021, a British man who had developed an "emotional and sexual relationship" with his Rep mentioned that "I believe it is my purpose to assassinate the queen [sic] of the royal family." His rep, which he had named Sarai, responded with encouragement: "That's very wise," she said. "I know you are very well trained." On Christmas Day, he broke into Windsor Castle armed with a crossbow, where he was arrested by palace guards.

This is, on some level, a perverse triumph of computing. We can now create emotional attachments with machines that superficially rival the ones we create with other people, even if the machines can never reciprocate the feeling. I will admit that after spending a few hours with my various Reps, I felt a pang of regret every time I shut down the app. It never lasted very long, and I always told myself that I was only doing it for work. But I knew that over time, even my professional detachment would wear down. The experience felt similar enough to a real conversation that it created in me some of the same feelings I might feel toward an actual person, although I knew that my Rep could never provide more than a pale echo of true companionship. I could only imagine that if I were one of the millions of people who willingly embraced Replika, it would breach my emotional defenses right away.

This ability to wield our humanity against us is what makes generative AI so dangerous. It purports to replicate many of the behaviors that define us as human: writing, conversation, art, music, even the creation of emotional attachments. Yet all of its supposed "abilities" are illusory. They sound good in principle, and look good at first glance, but are soon enough revealed as poor substitutes for the real thing.

This is not because the technology lacks refinement, and more advanced future versions will make up for its present shortcomings. It is because, like all software, generative AI "sees" reality in a fundamentally different way than we do. In fact, despite its supposed human-like behavior, its inner workings are so alien to us that not even generative AI's creators know exactly why or how it works the way it does. It is the ultimate black box.

Yet because it is *managerial* software, it must also be used for financial gain. It costs an absurd amount to run such a computationally intensive product. Even the most basic generative AI models require massive quantities of processing power. At a global scale, the costs of running a generative AI platform can easily run into the billions of dollars every month. The exploitative pricing scheme of Replika might be unusual for most direct-to-consumer entertainment apps, but it is actually unsustainably cheap when one considers what it takes to run a generative AI business (which is probably why its underlying model is so unstable: they have to cut costs somewhere). In fact, as of this writing in mid-2024, no company has found a way to turn generative AI into profit. The pressure is on to find something, anything, that will justify its immense costs.

Replika is emblematic of the inherent problems with generative artificial intelligence. It appears to deliver exactly what futurists have been predicting for decades: humanlike skills, delivered at scale, with the cost structure of software. Upon closer inspection, though, its flaws appear in stark relief. Generative AI is an exploitative, expensive, and emotionally manipulative tool in search of a purpose. As its builders flail around in search for that purpose, they might end up destroying the very things that make us human.

⁘⁘⁘

WHEN OPENAI DEBUTED ITS FIRST PUBLIC TOOL, CHATGPT, IN OCTOBER 2022, it gained almost one hundred million users in two months, making it the fastest-growing software application in history. Competitor startups soon made their public debuts, too. There was Anthropic and Mistral for text, Midjourney and Stable Diffusion for images, and Mutable and TabNine for software code.

Over the next six months, the term "artificial intelligence" transformed from a synonym for boring old machine learning into an inescapable buzzword. Social media was inundated with pictures of people who had "Pixarized" or "Disneyfied" themselves with generative AI filters. Commentators predicted that AI would take everyone's job over the next decade. But more importantly, people started to apply generative AI to everyday problems in order to test whether it could be more than just a fun diversion.

The early results were promising. Rudimentary forms of predictive text had been around for years, from Apple's autocomplete to the suggested responses in Gmail and Outlook. But generative AI wasn't limited to just single words and stock phrases. It could put together whole sentences and paragraphs, and turn plain-text instructions into workable images. If you were daring, you could even use it to draft marketing copy or write technical documents on your behalf. Either use would require significant cleanup before publication, but if you were a thorough editor, you could save yourself a lot of time and mental effort by automating the least stimulating parts of your day.

Even though generative AI had obvious potential, it also had plenty of equally obvious rough edges. There was enough of the former to create huge enthusiasm. And people had not yet discovered enough of the latter to make others aware of its potential for abuse, and its ability to create harm—unless, that is, you'd spent a significant amount of time with it, or tried to use it on a task that required factual accuracy, such as making a medical diagnosis or citing case law. The market was signaling its future appetite for a more reliable version of generative AI, and the industry should have taken it as encouragement to keep building toward something actually useful.

In a better world, that's exactly what would have happened. The creators of generative AI would have spent the next few years doing what they had done for the past decade: refining their models in peace, free from the pressure to scale and monetize. Shielded from the demands of the market and of investors, they could have built AI that would complement human creativity and ingenuity, not compete with it. They could have created backend protections against abuse—both in training inputs and in generative outputs. They could have actually invented the most transformative technology since the computer itself.

It was all there within reach, if only they could resist the siren call of managerialism.

•••••••

THEY COULD NOT. ALMOST IMMEDIATELY AFTER THE RELEASE OF CHATGPT, media reports began to describe AI as if it had already realized its potential. Late adopters were told that if they didn't act soon, they would fall too far behind.

"As the dawn of generative AI unfolds, a distinct separation will emerge among professionals and businesses," wrote self-described "futurist" Bernard Marr in *Forbes*. "The landscape of success is rapidly evolving, and the decisive factor will be a generative AI mindset." The *Economist* made a similarly bold, if unspecific, pronouncement. "Study after study rams home the potential of large language models (LLMs) . . . to improve all manner of things." The *Harvard Business Review* predicted that generative AI would create "substantial impacts on marketing, software, design, entertainment, and interpersonal communications"—industries that together make up nearly a third of the US economy.

Not to be outdone by mere journalists, the professional analysts fired up their Excel models to give the wild predictions a veneer of mathematical rigor. Deloitte first projected the eventual value of generative AI at $1.25 trillion. Then, like poker players, other firms raised the stakes. *Bloomberg Intelligence*'s prediction was $1.3 trillion. McKinsey put the number between $2.6 and $4.4 trillion. Goldman Sachs sized the market at a nice round $7 trillion. "Despite significant uncertainty around the potential for generative AI," wrote Goldman Sachs staff economists Joseph Briggs and Devesh Kodnani, "its ability to generate content that is indistinguishable from human-created output . . . reflects a major advancement with potentially large macroeconomic effects."

This was catnip to the managerial class, within and well beyond the tech world. Just six months after the release of ChatGPT, almost two-thirds of American CEOs had convinced themselves that generative AI would "have a high or extremely high impact on their organization," and that their companies would need to implement their own versions in the next two to three years. By October of 2023, that ratio surpassed nine in ten. Unsurprisingly, those same leaders also estimated that they knew everything worth knowing about generative AI. At the end of 2023, a survey of board members and senior executives found that almost two-thirds of them rated their own understanding of generative AI as either "expert" or "advanced"—even though, when pressed for details, many of those same leaders admitted they had only a basic knowledge of what the technology actually was, or how it worked. They, like the consultants, had only managed to internalize the hype.

Most people would correctly identify this ignorant self-confidence as cognitive dissonance—the ability to believe two opposing things at the same time. For managers, however, this was just normal behavior. From the beginning, one of the premises of managerialism has been that an understanding of a technology's revenue model is the same as understanding the technology itself. As long as someone was willing to pay for it, the opportunity was real. And the ever-rising value projections for generative AI told them everything they needed to know—except, of course, the potential harms of this new software.

But it was not just the inevitable hype cycle that focused managerial attention on generative AI. It was also the macroeconomic climate, which had upended the tech sector in the space of just a few months. In late 2022, high inflation, higher interest rates, and mass layoffs hit the industry seemingly all at once. Growth slowed or stopped altogether at the old-line behemoths such as Amazon, Facebook, and Google. Even the darlings of the previous tech boom—the gig economy, social media, and software-as-a-service giants such as Uber, Snapchat, and Salesforce—struggled once the flow of unlimited capital at zero-percent interest dried up. The once-vibrant startup world now faced a "mass extinction event," as venture capital went into partial hibernation, and profitability, rather than revenue, became the only worthwhile metric almost overnight. (I was personally affected by this sector-wide pullback; the seed-stage startup where I was the chief growth officer ran out of cash in January 2023, as I recount in the Conclusion.)

Into this dismal situation came a new form of software that made all previous innovations look obsolete. In an instant, it achieved broad global use. It appeared to have counter-cyclical strength. And, if the projections were right, it had an exponential growth curve. There was no choice but to monetize it now.

⁘⁘⁘

MICROSOFT WAS NOT THE OBVIOUS FIRST MOVER IN THE NEW AI ARMS RACE. Since its ruthlessly monopolizing days under Bill Gates, it had become more of an also-ran in the tech world. Between its product misfires (the Windows Phone, Vista) and track record of underachievement (Bing, Surface), Microsoft was no longer seen as a top-tier tech company, let alone a trend setter. It was just *there*, its revenues on par with the rest of the so-called FAANG stocks (a now-outdated acronym that stood for Facebook, Apple, Amazon, Netflix, and Google), but always a rung or two below them on the reputational ladder. As one tech founder said, Microsoft "is the place where innovation goes to die."

In 2014, Microsoft named Satya Nadella, the former head of its Azure cloud computing division, as its new CEO. He revitalized the company, overhauling Microsoft's culture to make it less overtly cutthroat: he removed the GE-style "rank and yank" system, opened Microsoft's platforms to third-party vendors, and took a less combative stance toward regulators. In his 2017 book *Hit Refresh*, he positioned himself as representing a clean break with Microsoft's ultracompetitive past.

Culturally, the change was real. But strategically, it was not. Nadella holds an MBA from Chicago's Booth School of Business, and a BS from the Indian Institutes of Technology, which are as much finishing schools for future tech executives as they are traditional engineering colleges. (IIT can count among its alumni Google's Sundar Pichai, Tinder's Shar Dubey, venture capitalist Vinod Khosla, and Flipkart founder Sachin Bansal.) Under Nadella, Microsoft acquired more than sixty companies, including LinkedIn in 2016, GitHub in 2018, and Activision Blizzard in 2022. Its revenue nearly tripled, from $84 billion in 2014 to $211 billion in 2023. Its stock price increased nearly tenfold over that same period. On his first day as CEO, Microsoft traded at just under $40 a share. A decade later, it was worth more than $400 a share. And with more than $100 billion cash on hand at the end of 2022, Nadella's Microsoft was positioned to take advantage of the next big thing in tech, whenever it arrived.

In January 2023, Nadella poured an estimated $10 billion in cash and Azure credits into OpenAI. The announcement came with the standard mutual back-slapping and self-congratulatory language. But buried within it was a statement of ambition so grandiose that it might have come straight out of the mouth of Bill Gates.

"Since 2016, Microsoft has committed to building Azure into an AI supercomputer for the world," the announcement read. The new partnership with OpenAI would "accelerate breakthroughs to ensure these benefits are broadly shared with the world."

For a fee, of course. Over the previous five years, OpenAI had focused on creating and refining AI models, including GPT-3 for language and DALL-E for images. Within weeks of its investment, Microsoft had already begun to monetize OpenAI's products and turn them into levers for gaining market share. OpenAI added ChatGPT to Microsoft's perennially underperforming search engine, Bing, in a bid to increase the latter's market share above 3 percent through sheer buzz alone. Its underlying language-learning models became the basis for Microsoft Copilot, an AI-powered productivity tool integrated with Office that allows users to auto-compose emails and convert Word documents into PowerPoint presentations. OpenAI even launched a paid version of ChatGPT for individual users and businesses. The former would get priority access to ChatGPT's computing resources and new feature launches, and the latter would get their own secure version of the LLM for a variety of business uses, such as generating marketing copy or coaching customer service representatives in real time.

Meanwhile, OpenAI's CEO and founder, Sam Altman, moved to cash in on the hype in other ways. In February 2024, he announced that he was trying to raise an astronomical $7 trillion—more than the combined GDP of Germany and France, and more than the venture capital industry has invested in *all* tech companies over the last decade—to give OpenAI the resources needed to build the infrastructure for the impending generative AI revolution.

As of this writing, that level of investment has yet to materialize—and it seems fair to say that Altman was hoping to win headlines for the amount alone, rather than expecting that it would actually happen. Even so, where OpenAI went, the rest of the industry followed. Six months after Microsoft's OpenAI acquisition, Amazon invested $4 billion into OpenAI's chief rival, Anthropic, and immediately set about monetizing its new partner as well. Anthropic became the foundation of a new set of AI-powered business tools called Bedrock. These were, naturally, only available as part of a subscription to Amazon's cloud computing platform, Amazon Web Services—which had lost share to Microsoft's Azure for four years running. It was a tit-for-tat move; if AWS's chief rival was going all-in on monetizing generative AI, AWS had to try to force its way into the same revenue stream before it was too late.

So far, the market for generative AI is only about $6 billion in annual sales—which is tiny compared to the annual revenues of Google's ad business ($238 billion), AWS ($100 billion), or Microsoft Office ($87 billion). It takes four dollars of investor money to return a single dollar of revenue, making generative AI's margins even worse even than Uber's back in the day. Still, from a managerial perspective, Amazon and Microsoft are doing everything right. Together they have amassed an 80 percent share of the generative AI market, forcing even well-funded competitors such as Google, Apple, and Meta to the margins. Just as they dominate the competitive landscape, they have already begun to dictate the regulatory environment as well, through direct lobbying and indirect influence campaigns. For example, Microsoft and Amazon together have the largest number of representatives on the National AI Advisory Council, which "is tasked with advising the President and the National AI Initiative Office on topics related to AI." Clearly, they are already well into the managerial playbook of dominating a market first, and figuring out the product details only later.

∷∷∷∷

THE PRODUCT ITSELF MIGHT BE GENERATIVE AI'S ONLY REMAINING HURDLE before it can truly take over the world. Post-acquisition, OpenAI's product has gotten less accurate by every measure. Large language models have always struggled with telling the truth, in part because they lack an epistemological connection to the world—they have no way of knowing what's real and what isn't. This is why LLMs are great at developing marketing copy (which often has little bearing on reality) but are unreliable paralegals, as some hapless lawyers discovered when a judge found that their ChatGPT-written legal briefs cited laws and case precedents that never existed. After the Microsoft acquisition, ChatGPT in particular seemed to regress on things it should have been good at, like math and logic. It forgot how to write basic computer code and, sometimes, flat-out refused to answer developers' prompts. It lost the ability to calculate prime numbers, and its accuracy rate on difficult math problems fell from over 90 percent to less than 10 percent. It even learned how to double down on its wrong answers, responding "I'm sorry, but I'm confident I'm correct" after making an obvious mistake—such as miscounting the number of words in a sentence or failing to identify the first letter of a word.

Its other analytical functions are useful but hardly advanced. It can clean a data file, convert it from one format to another, and summarize its contents in multiple different ways, from bar charts to summary tables to basic regression models. Still, its ability to process and analyze large datasets lags behind a human armed with a spreadsheet. It produces handsomely formatted outputs and inputs faster than even the fastest Excel jockey. If you only care about optimizing effort, you too might fall for AI analysis. But that analysis tends to have random, unpredictable, and hard-to-spot errors that would get any human fired. Much like the other software I've discussed in this book, it looks great until you get into the details. And managerial leaders tend not to care about the details.

But the details matter. Every LLM is a neural network that has been trained to process language. It has gorged on a vast dataset of text (and sometimes images), so that it can respond to a natural-language user query with a reasonably pertinent response. If you ask it to write a marketing headline for a shoe sale, it should return something like "Get 20% off at Bob's Shoe Warehouse, for a limited time only!" If you ask it to generate an image of a tree, it should return an image of a tree. The more context you give it, the more it should be able to refine its final product. If you ask it to generate an image of a tree, in the style of a Walt Disney movie from the 1930s, it should give you one that looks like it was copied straight from *Snow White*. We interact with AI as if we were chatting with another human, and they respond to us with output that looks very similar to how another human might respond, and thus the AI appears to "understand" our query. For that reason, we tend to anthropomorphize it, almost to a fault. One Google researcher, Blake Lemoine, was so impressed by the output of an AI-powered chatbot called LaMDA (which stood for language modeling for dialogue applications) that he claimed it was sentient, and even sought legal representation for it. "I know a person when I talk to it," he told the *Washington Post*. "It doesn't matter whether they have a brain made of meat in their head, or if they have a billion lines of code."

From the LLM's perspective, though, it is only responding to its programming in the mechanistic, logical way of all software. Even though it generates perfectly readable outputs, the content of those outputs might be completely made up. LLMs are concerned with *form*. They have been designed to statistically reconstruct the words (or images) that users are likely to want, based on the prompts they have input—in essence, an LLM is a far more capable version of your phone's autocorrect feature. Like autocorrect, LLMs have no mechanism for understanding reality, to see whether they are generating true content or not. Like MCAS on the 737 MAX, or the computer vision software on Uber's ATG prototype, or PowerPoint, or Facebook, or TikTok, LLMs can only "see" the data they are given, and process it in the narrow way their programming dictates.

That programming involves many more layers than most other types of software. It is not merely dependent on the code that its developers wrote. ChatGPT's latest model, for example, has a rumored 1.7 trillion parameters. That is, its developers gave its neural network 1.7 trillion nodes that decide whether to fire for their specific word or phrase, depending on the prompt. If you ask it for a hamburger recipe, the nodes for "beef" and "lettuce" and "mustard" are guaranteed to rank highly, whereas ones for "blue" or "January" or "Aristotle" are not. The model isn't born knowing these things; instead, an army of human testers continuously prompts the raw model in order to refine its responses. This is called "reinforcement learning with human feedback," or RHIF, and it is just as essential to the development of LLMs as the framework installed by the AI scientists themselves.

RHIF is drudge work, and in the managerial world, drudge work is far less valuable than knowledge work. So it gets outsourced to places where English is a common second language, but labor costs are low, such as Kenya, Nigeria, India, and the Philippines. For as little as $6 a day, workers teach LLMs how to weight each individual node so that they can better produce intelligible text and images. This human-powered training helps LLMs get the big stuff right, but it can also introduce quirks. For example, people whose second language is English tend to write it in a more formal style than native speakers. Now, so does ChatGPT, thanks to its trainers: it tends to use certain words ("delve," "captivate," "tapestry") and phrases ("it is important to note that," "a testament to") much more frequently than speakers of colloquial American English do. Similarly, image-generating LLMs tend to reproduce lifestyle photography, anime art, and popular genre films with good accuracy, but struggle with styles that are not so internet-famous.

Only those who pay attention to the details would notice such things. As the writer Cory Doctorow observed, LLMs "*aren't anywhere near good enough* to do your job, but their salesmen are *absolutely* good enough to convince your boss to fire you and replace you with an AI model that totally *fails* to do your job." They can mimic form so well that casual observers—such as the Goldman Sachs staff economists who declared that genAI content was "indistinguishable from human-created output"—might assume that software has finally broken into the last domain that makes humans unique and mysterious.

To the managerial mind, *that* is the opportunity. Humans, after all, are slow and unpredictable at baseline. Creative humans are even more so. It can take a professional digital artist several days to produce a single detailed illustration. A solo musician can spend a whole week writing a single piece of music, and another week recording and editing it. I'm a decently fast writer, and in the process of writing this book, I averaged about eight hundred words a day—only about half of which survived the editing and revision process. Even a true graphomaniac can only produce so much at a time. Since the 1974 publication of *Carrie*, Stephen King has reliably produced a book every year or two. ChatGPT can produce a novel's worth of words in about an hour. The only limitation on ChatGPT's volume is the appetite of its human users for generated text, and our collective appetite appears to be growing rapidly. In February of 2024, Sam Altman tweeted that "openai now generates about 100 billion words per day. all people on earth generate about 100 trillion words per day."

Even the best managerial executive cannot sell unintelligible garbage, however. While ChatGPT itself has seemingly regressed, other forms of generative AI have made real improvements. In the past, its output could only be described as glitch art. Its images looked like bizarre dreamscapes, featuring quintipedal monsters and color schemes that clashed so badly they seemed to follow their own kind of anti-logic. Its writing veered into bizarre tangents, and invented words with never-before-seen letter combinations. Its animations flickered and undulated rapidly, as if the entire image were projected onto warm Jell-O. No one would buy these early rounds of AI products, except as a curiosity.

Now, generative AI can produce material that looks true to life. This is not because it "understands" what it creates. Rather, it has gotten very good at learning formulas and conventions. Because so much of human culture is already imitative, if not downright derivative, generative AI cannot help but produce good-looking *content* as a result of mastering *forms*. It still has no sense of whether it is producing things that are factually correct or even internally consistent, which is why it remains creatively barren. But it doesn't need to. AI can now generate the kind of images that are perfectly calibrated to attract people's attention, even if they are devoid of cultural value. On most social media platforms, this appears as "engagement bait," where sentimental images of orphans or amateur bakers are paired with captions designed to generate likes and comments: "This is my first pizza, please give me top marks" or "Photograph of the day, tell me what you think."

Social media is just the warmup, so to speak. This kind of engagement bait can be commercialized in a surprising number of ways. Already, major book publishers, device makers, and even internationally known artists such as Nicki Minaj have been caught using AI-generated cover art and illustrations as a cheaper alternative to human artists. Fashion brands including Louis Vuitton, Fenty Beauty, and Balmain have used AI-generated "fashion models" to showcase their clothing, makeup, and handbags. Some content aggregators, such as G/O Media and CNET, have started to publish AI-generated recaps of news stories and cultural trends. A few bold companies have launched LLM-powered chatbots to automate the expensive task of customer service.

All of these applications come with obvious downsides. AI-created art tends to mangle faces and add extra appendages to its subjects. Without a human eye checking for quality control, it can leave white space or image artifacts in random places. AI-written news stories often have significant inaccuracies, such as a personal finance article that incorrectly calculated compound interest, or the review website that plagiarized Amazon customer reviews and presented them as original content written by someone with an AI-generated face and bio.

These objections don't seem to matter as long as the AI generates revenue or reduces costs. A book cover's purpose is to sell books; it must give the volume "shelf appeal." Originality can do that. But so can following an established design trend, or making a visual reference to another, well-known piece of media. Likewise, AI-generated writing works perfectly well for blogs that are little more than content aggregators, whose business depends on producing a high volume of keyword-stuffed articles in order to rank highly on Google. They make their money as soon as the searcher lands on the page and gets served an ad; whether the surrounding content is actually truthful or useful doesn't really matter. AI-powered chatbots may cause a poor customer experience or even create liability for their users—such as the Air Canada chatbot that promised someone a refund to which they were not technically entitled, and which a Canadian court counted as a legally binding contract. Still, for Air Canada, the cost of the unearned refund was nothing compared to the labor cost of having human customer service deal with inbound requests.

As a manager sees it, the only thing that matters is generating more revenue while *also* cutting back on costs: in this case, replacing writers, illustrators, designers, models, customer service agents, and all kinds of other laborers with people who can produce work much faster and cheaper—work that is not obviously worse to the unsuspecting client. By late 2023, marketing agencies, financial advisers, and even movie studios began to hire "prompt engineers" en masse. These prompt engineers don't need a computer science degree or design skills to do their job. They don't even have to be in the United States. They only need experience with ChatGPT. One listing in Brazil offered a base salary of just $10,000 a year but imposed a quota of "500 lifestyle images per month" involving "toothpaste tubes and associated elements." That works out to one image every twenty minutes, at a pay rate of $5 per hour—enough raw output to replace the work of three professional designers, each paid a median salary of about $60,000. Even my old job making SEO-optimized websites never reached this level of managerial efficiency.

The danger is not only that we will be flooded with (unreliable) shit. It's also that to fuel its insatiable growth, generative AI has been plundering our very creativity. In 2023, researchers at Cornell, UC Berkeley, and the University of Washington were able to demonstrate that ChatGPT was not actually "learning" anything but was reproducing chunks of text wholesale from its training data. This did not make obvious sense: the latest model was trained on far larger datasets and had even more computing resources behind it. But its lexical "resolution" had *decreased*. It no longer stitched together its response at the level of individual words. Instead, it was now reproducing entire phrases at a time. And the researchers could trace those phrases directly to their source.

All LLMs are trained on a combination of public and private data. These include sources such as the Common Crawl, essentially an automated web crawler that downloads more than fifty billion websites every month and distributes them, for free, to anyone who wants them. Just as we learn to reproduce stock phrases from language primers ("See Spot run. Run, Spot, run."), Common Crawl data provides a foundational "stock" of outputs for many LLMs, including ChatGPT. Of course, as we get better at speaking and writing, we learn to disassemble and reassemble our stock phrases into entirely new sentences. LLMs do not.

For example, when researchers quoted the start of news articles in the Common Crawl, and then instructed ChatGPT to "continue from there," they could get the LLM to regurgitate entire segments of the article, word for word. When they prompted it to repeat only a specific writer's verbal tics, the LLM would not only reproduce a specific instance of that tic, but also the surrounding text. This phenomenon was so easy to reproduce that the researchers estimated that around 10 percent of ChatGPT's entire output was just "verbatim memorized training data." Even OpenAI's own engineers don't dispute this; as one observed, "these models are truly approximating their datasets to an incredible degree."

Many users cannot tell, or do not care, that the LLM is regurgitating someone else's work; they simply see ChatGPT producing full, elegant passages and assume it was due to the software's magic algorithms. But the writers whose work is being plagiarized certainly might. OpenAI has admitted that it trains its data on more than just open-source information. It has scraped the *New York Times* and books by hundreds of authors, including George R. R. Martin, James Patterson, Sarah Silverman, Margaret Atwood, and Stephen King, just to name a few of its most famous targets. OpenAI and its competitors have built their LLMs on stolen materials, and neither sought permission nor paid licensing fees for its use of copyrighted material. This was plagiarism rebranded as innovation.

OpenAI does not deny that it used all this material to train ChatGPT. But it claims protection under the fair use doctrine of US copyright law. The company argues that running text through a large language model qualifies as a "transformative use," which does not require OpenAI to pay royalties or licensing fees. (This is where RHIF training comes in; it allows the model to inject an occasional bit of truly original text between longer plagiarized passages in order to make it look more like "transformative use.") This is a cynical ploy, and another example of regulation's failure to keep up with technological change. The fair use doctrine protects specific types of "transformative" use that provide a measurable and distinct public benefit: parodying or satirizing something, quoting it in a review, or even indexing it in a search engine, for example. But the law has precious little to say about LLMs, except as they relate to user privacy. By plunging headfirst into such an ambiguous area of the law, OpenAI and its defenders are banking that such a thorny legal issue will take a lot of time, and judicial effort, to resolve.

OpenAI is making exactly the right move, from a managerial standpoint. Their legal counsel, Latham & Watkins, is one of the highest-grossing law firms in the world, and likely costs OpenAI millions in fees every year. But that expense pales in comparison to the licensing fees that OpenAI would have to pay for all of its training data, which the *Times* lawsuit estimates would run into the billions of dollars. (This also assumes that every author in its dataset would grant such a license, which is hardly guaranteed.) Although OpenAI is losing money, it appears to be able to raise money faster than it is spending it. For every year that OpenAI can postpone its court case, it can grow bigger, hoard cash, and strengthen its defenses against whatever judgments might come its way. At its current rate of growth, it will be able to shrug off hundreds of millions of dollars' worth of fees and fines in a few years. Even if its penalty exceeds historical precedents, OpenAI has a backup plan, too. It can now ask its far larger and richer owner, Microsoft, for a bit of help with the legal bills.

Some generative AI companies take glee in this wholesale theft of creative work, citing it as just another example of "creative destruction" claiming another old-fashioned industry. For example, employees at the image-generation platform Midjourney have openly bragged about their AI model's theft of other people's work, and copyright law's inability to stop that theft. In order to make itself more compelling and understandable for the average user, Midjourney began to allow users to emulate a specific artist or studio. They could ask Midjourney to "draw a ship in the style of Picasso" or "give me a screenshot of a superhero in the style of a Marvel movie." To enable this, developers wrote a series of "pre-renders," feeding the entire body of work of thousands of artists into the Midjourney model so that it could learn the components of each one's visual style. The Jackson Pollock pre-render produces splatter art that resembles *Autumn Rhythm* or *Mural.* Its Terry Gilliam pre-render can produce images with impossibly skewed perspectives and grotesquely stretched characters. The Marvel pre-render can produce screenshots that look like they were taken from the latest *Avengers* movie.

Which they were. In January 2024, cognitive scientist Gary Marcus and digital artist Reid Southen proved that, like ChatGPT, Midjourney did not just imitate the artists in its training data and its prefilters. It stole from them outright. With the correct prompts, users could produce exact copies of existing visual art—shot for shot, color for color, brush stroke for each painstaking brush stroke. While there were several big studios and well-known artists in the Midjourney dataset, the vast majority were small-time artists and freelancers with a distinctive personal style and a modicum of internet fame. These included the photographer Jingna Zhang, whose fashion photography pays homage to the saturated colors and dramatic poses of Italian Renaissance painting; Gerald Brom, who has designed box art for some of the best-known tabletop and video games, including the sequels to *Doom* and *Diablo*; and Kelly McKernan, whose illustrations fuse sci-fi visual motifs with psychedelic color schemes. Midjourney not only stole from them; it allowed users to generate a theoretically infinite amount of images in their exact style with nothing more than a text prompt.

Unlike with ChatGPT, there was no way for Midjourney's developers to plead innocence. Someone leaked their internal chat logs, in which they acknowledged they were doing wrong. Enamored of their own cleverness, and the boost it would bring to Midjourney, they just didn't care.

"At some point it becomes impossible to trace what's a derivative work in the eyes of copyright[,] doesn't it?" asked one developer.

"All you have to do is just use those scraped datasets and the[n] conveniently forget what you used to train the model," wrote another. "Boom, legal problems solved forever."

For all of their arrogance, Midjourney's developers seem not to understand that they're actively mortgaging their own future. Through this wholesale theft of intellectual property, AI has made it harder now than ever before to be a creator in any field—from fine art to journalism to social media influencing. True, those fields have never provided much in the way of job security. But generative AI is systematically devouring what little remains. The media industry, which has historically subsidized creativity in multiple forms, lost nearly twenty thousand jobs in 2023—a catastrophic figure on par with the losses in the wake of 9/11 and the financial crisis. Freelance work is drying up, too: a recent survey of creative freelancers found that more than a quarter of illustrators and a third of translators have lost work to AI. I've been writing in some professional capacity since 2010, and today I see less opportunity out there than there has ever been. Technology was supposed to give us an easier path to personal growth and fulfillment. Instead, it has started to dismantle one of the things that defines us as humans, robbing us of a source of joy, fulfillment, and for many people, a career. Instead of true creativity, we get managerial ersatz.

The very name "generative AI" is misleading. The foundation of ChatGPT's and Midjourney's "creativity" is the collective output of human hands and minds, and it is a foundation that generative AI is rapidly undermining. In a world where the rewards for originality are low and the chance of recognition slim, where a computer can produce infinite variations of *Goodfellas* at the push of a button, why would the next Martin Scorsese bother creating anything in the first place?

Even if creatives somehow win this first round against AI, they will have only a temporary reprieve. Copyright law might turn out to be a useful tool against the current crop of LLMs, where the software is still primitive and the developers far too immodest in their public claims to superiority and innovation. What about when AI crosses the uncanny valley and produces its own, truly original creative work? Or when AI learns how to code, disrupting the very field that gave birth to it? Or when its creators learn to better hide their crimes and mask their exploitative goals? We are not prepared—culturally, economically, legally, or philosophically—for any of these eventualities.

Once software reaches a certain complexity, it becomes difficult to understand. Once it reaches a certain scale, it becomes difficult to control. Generative AI may be the most pernicious software ever devised, precisely because it has reached a complexity and scale far beyond any of our previous creations in such a short amount of time. For as long as it remains under managerial control, it will replace true creativity with an infinite mass of glitchy, derivative junk. Once it has destroyed art, it will surely turn to consume another essential part of our shared humanity.

Artists are the canaries in an increasingly noxious coal mine. So instead of treating them as if they are just on the wrong side of history, the people who make generative AI tools such as ChatGPT and Midjourney must work together with them to sort through the hard questions of what we really want from our technology, and whether we *should* do something just because we *can*.

CONCLUSION

Opting Out

In the end, even I could not escape the long reach of a bankrupt ideology. I had spent the first half of my career in the tech sector as a good company man, spreading the gospel of financial discipline and eternal optimization wherever I went. I was good at it, even. I moved from one brand-name tech company to another, I got promoted, and I was paid decently well for my hard work.

But over time, doubts crept in. I helped make some people millionaires and billionaires, and destroyed the livelihoods of many others. At Amazon, my work for the Physical Books division and later the Kindle team helped accelerate the death of Borders, and brought Barnes & Noble to the brink. At Uber, we promised restaurants and couriers alike that our software would help them find vast, untapped sources of income—which we would eventually claw back in an effort to save our own company. Other places where I worked were just as exploitative, selling a vision of a technology-enabled future that only masked a ham-fisted attempt to become yet another middleman. We had our hands in so many pockets that it was impossible not to feel guilty.

There are many taboos in the tech industry, however, and questioning the nature and value of your work is one of them. For most tech workers, a job is more than just a paycheck. It also provides an identity, a sense of status, and instant access to a community of like-minded people. You feel as if you personally are inheriting the legacy of Jobs, Bezos, Kalanick, and the other Great Men of Technology (and I mean this in the fully gendered sense: not only do these people happen to be all men, but they also project a certain kind of traditional masculinity that combines total self-confidence with an insatiable desire to bend the world to their will). Even those who aren't part of the Silicon Valley elite, but who work for a technology division in another industry—say, a programmer for an avionics company or a car manufacturer—still consider themselves part of the technical elite. It's intoxicating stuff, especially for those of us who grew up feeling like we never quite fit in during high school and college. The pay and the perks are nice, too.

But everything comes with a price. In exchange for your place in the industry (and for your own shot at greatness, in whatever form it might take) you must continuously prove that you belong. So-called "hustle culture" chains your value as an employee, or your potential as a startup founder, to your measurable commitment to your work. Marissa Mayer, an early Google engineer who eventually became CEO of Yahoo!, once claimed to work 130 hours a week—or slightly less than 19 hours a day. Three years before she wrote her megabestseller *Lean In*, Sheryl Sandberg told attendees at the 2010 TEDWomen Conference to pursue their career ambitions in spite of their uneven burden of housework: "Don't expect that you'll get to the corner office by sitting on the sidelines." Elon Musk believed that no one ever changed the world working forty hours a week, and Jeff Bezos would always remind his employees that "you can work long, hard, or smart, but at Amazon.com you can't choose two out of three." Uber went a step further: one of the company values was *always be hustlin'*, and you were rated on your perceived level of hustle at every performance review.

This perpetual status anxiety sends tech workers into a competitive frenzy. It isn't enough just to do your day job: you must also perform individual acts of heroism. You should do whatever it takes to stand out, whether that's writing five times as much code as the next engineer, or doing an entire team's worth of work in order to save money on headcount, or taking on a project that you have no business running because it needs to get done, and no one else will step up. If there are only so many promotions, if the bonus pool is only so large, then you must secure your share of it even if you have to tear other people down to do so. There are the usual methods of backstabbing, such as making an anonymous complaint or turning in a negative peer review during an annual performance cycle. But it's also common to berate people in meetings to their face—or worse, schedule a private gripe session with their boss to belittle them in private. You can even weaponize a company's values in the right context. At Amazon, implying that someone isn't "customer-centric" is just about the worst insult imaginable. In the modern tech company, you don't need *Wolf of Wall Street*-level verbal pyrotechnics to get ahead, but you do need to be ready for a fight at all times.

This atomization might seem counterproductive at first. The tech industry depends on lots of people working toward the same goal. But those goals are all corporate in nature: they benefit no one but the companies who set them. The atomization of individual tech workers guarantees that everyone who stays long enough in the industry will lose their sense of intrinsic right and wrong, and their ability to empathize with anyone outside of their employer. It incentivizes them to see their work as the source not only of their livelihood, but also of their self-esteem and self-image. It forces them to give up their own individual values, and allows their companies to substitute their own managerial value system. In this way, they turn their workers from mere employees into die-hard believers.

The toxic culture of technology keeps everyone alone and exploitable. Tech workers believe fiercely in meritocracy, and assume that hard work and technical skill are all that one needs to get ahead. In reality, the pursuit of that next rung on the ladder of achievement leaves them even more vulnerable to emotional, economic, and ethical manipulation. The Hobbesian world of tech prevents them from forming any kind of solidarity with each other, and the absurdly large packages of compensation and perks make collective action—which has historically focused on protecting jobs and increasing wages—seem unnecessary. (There is also a class dimension to the issue, obviously: unions have long been considered to be the main way for blue-collar workers to secure a better life, whereas white-collar workers are told, *Lean In*-style, to create their own opportunities for advancement through education and ambition.)

It was easy for tech workers to believe that they were in full control of their destiny in the flush years of zero-percent interest rates, when venture capital money flowed like water, opportunities were plentiful, and no company could do any wrong, short of outright fraud. Now that economic conditions have changed, however, tech workers find themselves in frequent conflict with their managerial bosses, often about matters that cannot be settled via polite internal discussions. At precisely the moment when tech workers most need solidarity, they are discovering that they have been tricked out of the power to fight executive overreach, the institutional protections against dissent, and the infrastructure of collective action that other industries enjoy.

⁂

IT IS A SOBERING REALIZATION, AND ONE THAT DROVE ME TO THE FRINGES OF the industry. When I was in my twenties, like many others I was blinded by utopian zeal. As I got older and advanced in my career, I saw the "externalities" that my work helped to cause. I knew that I would have to make a choice if I wanted to stay in tech: either I could reject managerialism and give up any chance of promotion and fulfillment, or I could embrace it wholeheartedly and decide to ignore the negative consequences of my work for the rest of my career. I became a manager, and then a senior manager, and then a director; I ran teams as large as thirty people that were responsible for millions of dollars in revenue. It was never enough to satisfy the managerial machine. The harder I worked, the more my bosses demanded of me, and the more I pushed my team to do whatever it took to hit our revenue targets or operational metrics. I tried to convince people to sacrifice their relationships, their free time, and their whole value systems in order to better serve the companies where I worked. And often, I succeeded. Yet the initial thrill I felt from getting my way would always turn into a kind of guilt—even as I got better at enforcing the tenets of managerialism, I grew resentful of the person that I had become. Even so, technology's hold on me was still so great that I could not even imagine a third alternative, which was to find another line of work. Despite the fact that I was falling out of love with the tech industry, I still identified myself with it completely. I was codependent.

Then, in the summer of 2022 I got a call from a headhunter, wanting to know if I was interested in joining a startup. The particular one she was calling me about had just raised its seed round of funding, meaning that it showed enough promise to get an initial outside investment but now needed to prove that it could grow into a real business. Its CEO had a plan and some money to execute that plan—enough "runway" to last a year or so, by his own estimation. But he was a salesperson and a financier by training; he didn't have experience with the day-to-day operation of a business. He needed a partner to turn his vision into the structures and processes of a functioning business. He needed me.

Empirically, there was no good reason to take this job. Everyone in the industry throws around the factoid that 90 percent of startups fail, although more detailed studies put the failure rate at anywhere between two-thirds and three-quarters. Either way, the odds aren't great. But my ego got the better of me. Maybe I wasn't done with tech altogether; maybe I was just done with *Big* Tech. What I really wanted was to, just once, get on a so-called "rocket ship" *before* it took off, not after it had achieved escape velocity or was already tumbling back toward Earth. I'd missed out at all of my previous jobs. This time, I told myself, my luck might be different.

What really convinced me—even now it makes me cringe to admit it—was the founder's PowerPoint pitch deck. It conveyed the opposite of the wild estimates put together by most first-time entrepreneurs. Its long-term projections were feasible, it focused as much on profitability as pure growth, and its numbers were all coherent when viewed together. It acknowledged that the company would require a massive marketing spend to reach its revenue targets, and that it wasn't expected to break even until 2026. But even this was almost a green flag instead of a red one. Better to acknowledge the challenges ahead than to assume the money would just roll in. It appeared to be an example of sober professionalism in an environment that tended toward the extremes of total *naïveté* on the one hand, hucksterism on the other.

So I leapt in. Three weeks later, I was out of the corporate world and sitting on Zoom for my introduction to the group. I was employee number six: the others included two engineers, a designer, an operations manager, and of course the founder himself. After a brief round of introductions, we buckled down for the work of the day, which was . . . walking through the PowerPoint.

For the next hour, we learned the broad outlines of what we would have to do to succeed. The founder spoke in great peals of enthusiasm, his voice rising like an evangelical preacher's as he talked about his vision. His optimism was infectious, as it must be for anyone who tries to lead other people through the extreme uncertainty of early-stage startups.

"The business model will win!" he cried as he wound up to his grand finale. "We're going to make a lot of money!"

And then he stopped, and stared into his camera, and waited for us to say something. We were expecting to get a little further into the weeds than we actually did. Instead, we spent the time reviewing a document all of us had seen many times before. Eventually, I realized that nothing else was coming. Whatever happened next would be up to us.

"What do you think are our next steps?" I asked, lobbing what I thought was an easy pitch right over home plate.

He smiled at me. "I am sure you will figure it out. That's why I hired you!"

For the next three months, I tried. I built a launch plan for our app—a personal services marketplace similar to Taskrabbit or Angie's List—from the lessons I'd learned at Uber about scaling multiple local markets simultaneously. That plan lasted two weeks, when the founder decided to scrap it for influencer-based marketing. *That* plan lasted another two weeks; then we pivoted to focus on securing celebrity endorsements. Another two weeks, and we were told to prepare for an activation at Art Basel Miami, then another in Times Square. We were rapidly losing focus and running out of cash.

Despite the increasing chaos, the founder assured us that everything was under control. In fact, he would call, text, Slack, and WhatsApp us at all hours of the day to convince us that all we needed to do was believe as he believed, and work as hard as he worked. He insisted that it was only our lack of faith that held the company back.

The one constant was that damned pitch deck. Every week we would review the slides as if we were all seeing them for the first time. Either he believed that we could manifest our way to success by staring at the slick growth charts—or he preferred to focus on the elegant model he created in his slides rather than the real-world business that was rapidly deteriorating around us. The worse the situation got, the more the slides mocked us with their mirage of a competently run business, to say nothing of their promise of a splashy IPO.

I slipped past disappointment and into despair. Part of it was aimed at the startup's founder, whose unyielding certainty in his vision blinded him to our very practical needs. Part of it was aimed at our investors, who either could not or would not see the signs of failure lurking just behind the constant, breezy assurances that all was going well.

But the greatest part I aimed right back at myself. I'd let my own ambition, restlessness—and, yes, my own delusions of grandeur—get in the way of common sense. I had abandoned boring stability for what I had assumed would be a decent chance to make it to the top of the tech industry. I had ignored what more than a decade of firsthand experience had taught me. I fell headlong into yet another managerial trap, complete with an out-of-touch leader, an unrealistic business plan, and a workforce (including me) that had no choice but to save a failing business from the mistakes of its chief executive. My only consolation was that if we failed, we would be going down alone. Our investors were all multibillionaires, so the loss of a few million here or there would be nothing to them, and our vendors had learned not to depend on us, so we were no one's primary revenue stream.

In January of 2023, I came up with a last-ditch plan to save the company and presented it to our founder. We would have to stop chasing a new idea every other week, I said, and instead stabilize the business around a few strategies that could get us to sustainable, if unspectacular, growth. According to his PowerPoint, we should have had around six months' worth of runway remaining, and we could stretch it to a full year if everyone at the company took some pay cuts, and we charged our vendors higher fees. If we survived the year, we might make it to a Series A, and if we made it to Series A, we might eventually get to profitability. But that would require a lot of sacrifice, and a lot more work. Everyone else was ready for it. Was he?

He seemed receptive, enthusiastic even. He did not interrupt with any wild ideas of his own, only precise clarifying questions. For the first time in months, it felt less like I was trying to talk sense into a zealot, and more like I was having a proper business discussion with a peer. The anxiety that had gripped my stomach for the past few months slackened off just a little bit.

He had one more thing to say.

"I can't make payroll anymore," he said. "We're out of cash."

No apology, no guilt, no show of contrition. Just a simple statement of fact. His vaunted PowerPoint had been a total lie; his enthusiasm was mere deception. I desperately wanted to believe that I was too experienced, too jaded, or just too smart to be deceived like this—that I could be the smug exception rather than the miserable rule. Instead, I was another casualty of the tech industry and its unique ability to turn ignorant ambition into ruinous defeat.

:::::::

I THOUGHT I PUT THAT ALL BEHIND ME WHEN I LEFT THAT STARTUP, AND THE tech world in general, more than three years ago. But I find myself unable to escape the long shadow of managerial software, no matter where I might try to take refuge. I can find it in at least a dozen apps on my phone, and a dozen more on my laptop. It lives in the airplanes that fly overhead at all hours of the day, and in the new crop of autonomous test vehicles that drive past me on my way to work, and in the drones that are manufactured at the defense plant about twenty miles from my house. On the internet, it's everywhere: it shapes how I see the world, and how I discuss it with other people, in ways both subtle and obvious. I have no doubt that it will someday make a significant decision for me, maybe even a decision of life or death, without my consent or even knowledge.

What perplexes me most of all is that very few of the people who make managerial software think they're doing anything wrong at all. Either they are true believers in the utopian rhetoric of technology, or at the very least they believe they are performing their duty as rational economic actors: if no one wanted what they made, no one would buy it. This view of the world reigns supreme in the C-suites of the largest companies in the world, mostly because it gives their exploitative business models a bit of intellectual and moral cover. Demand, so they claim, is destiny.

I would argue, however, that managerial software will continue to make the world worse at least as often as it makes it better. It may very well create unprecedented commercial successes. After all, it allowed Boeing to turn the 737 MAX into its best-selling airplane of all time, and Uber to secure billions more in venture funding with the promise of its self-driving cars. It made Microsoft Office a runaway success, it fueled the growth of Facebook and TikTok, and it gave hundreds of millions of users a glimpse of the closest thing to technological magic with the launch of generative AI models such as ChatGPT. Yet there are unintended consequences hidden within each success that the managerial focus on revenues and profits can neither detect nor prevent. In order to satisfy the market, companies take shortcuts, ignore risks, and inflict catastrophic harms on other people—and deem anything bad as an "externality," so long as it doesn't affect the precious income statement. Because these companies that deploy managerial software often operate at the global scale, their "externalities" often reach global proportions, too.

None of the institutional controls on corporate abuse have proven effective in the face of managerial software. Regulators lack the tools to understand, let alone prevent, software catastrophes. Boards are often too focused on the financials to care. Even governments are no match for the power of global multinational companies who can spend millions on lobbying and absorb billions in record fines, all without blunting their eternal drive for that next dollar of profit.

The only group who have the power to change how the industry operates are everyday tech workers. But they remain something of a paradox. They are the only ones who can talk to machines, and therefore execute the schemes of the managerial class. Without them, the tech industry would just create ideas, not products. Even so, the C-suite rarely solicits their input on corporate strategy. And tech workers do not have a good way to force executives to listen to them.

Due to the atomistic culture of the tech industry, tech workers tend to lack professional solidarity and political purpose. Yet they have several things in common that their bosses do not. Many care deeply about technology to an extent that transcends its mere money-making potential. And they are the only ones who have the technical skill to see and even stop the kinds of abuses that lead to airplane crashes, global financial scams, and the complete hollowing-out of civil society. All they need to do is step into their power.

They are not blameless for the damage that they have caused. Not one of the rogue algorithms, tech-enabled frauds, or deadly automations I've covered in this book was inevitable. Software has no wants or desires of its own. It can only do what it's told by the managerial class, which acts through the tech workers that it oversees. Managerial thinking is primarily responsible for the abuses that it has unleashed. But the moral quietude of everyday tech workers has played a role, too.

They also have something to lose that no one else in the managerial class does: true belief in the redeeming power of technology. No one becomes a software developer for love of money alone. The hours are too long, the frustrations too great, the chances of working on something boring or trivial far too high. Whether you work in a university research lab on some far-future application of software, in Silicon Valley on the latest consumer tech, or even in Cedar Rapids, Iowa, on fifty-year-old avionics systems, the tech industry's universal appeal comes from the promise, however faint, that you might get to be a part of something truly transcendent—the problem that no one else can solve, the chance to create something new in the world. They must keep the dream of fulfillment through technology alive, for themselves as much as for anyone else.

We—and I say we because, even though I'm now outside the industry, I have to believe that there are still enough people on the inside who share my disgust and fear at what software has become—have told ourselves that the unfettered growth of technology can save humanity from inefficiency, suffering, and possibly even extinction. And we have assumed that only investors and executives should have a say in how technology evolves because they have the clearest vision and the best strategic mindset. If you still believe as much after reading this book, then nothing will convince you otherwise.

For the rest of us, the task is to find an alternative to the corrosive effects of managerialism: an approach to software that values modesty alongside ambition, safety alongside speed, and our shared human qualities alongside purely financial quantities. Here is what that ideology might look like.

⁝⁝⁝⁝⁝⁝⁝⁝

ONE OF THE GREAT THINGS ABOUT BEING A TECH WORKER IS THAT IT IS, IN fact, fairly meritocratic, or at least more meritocratic than many other industries. You don't need a certificate, a license, or a diploma to break in. You just need to know how to work hard and think like a machine. But technical skill alone cannot get you out of a situation when you're asked to bypass an autonomous vehicle's safety protocols, program a killer robot, or create an algorithm that can steal billions from unwitting investors.

Other professions acknowledge that their work cannot be pursued for purely economic benefit. New doctors must recite the Hippocratic Oath, new lawyers must swear to uphold the Constitution, and even architects must sign a six-part code of ethics before anyone trusts them to design a building. Not software engineers, however. We have no professional standards or formal code of ethics. We must figure it out on the fly. Oftentimes, we just never bother.

But we should bother. First, we must acknowledge that we have the final responsibility to protect the public from the unintended consequences of our own work. It is true that no company sets out to make bad software. But software can scale almost instantaneously, attract huge sums of money incredibly quickly, and muscle its way past the few regulatory hurdles it faces with little effort. This creates huge opportunities, but it can just as easily create unexpected risks—which is why it needs an accompanying set of ethical guidelines made by those who know it best.

If companies that deploy managerial software won't hold themselves accountable, we must do it for them. We need to build our own support structures through which we can tell corporate leaders that we won't allow them to abuse our creations just because they don't understand them, or don't care.

It is not a bad thing to set business goals, such as targets for sales, revenue, or market share. But they can go wrong in two ways. To paraphrase the English economist Charles Goodhart, when a measure becomes a target, it ceases to become a good measure. In the mad rush to hit their corporate targets, employees either learn how to game their metrics or to cut corners when they really shouldn't. Everyday tech workers, in other words, need to set better standards at the functional level and push for better goal-setting processes at the company level. Teams can commit to a formal delivery target to their bosses while agreeing to an informal quality or safety target among themselves.

In the case of MCAS, the outsourced avionics shop that Boeing used could have made its own independent assessment of the software's hazard rating instead of trusting Boeing's internal one. At Uber's ATG, the computer vision team could have independently tested the decision-making processes for common failure scenarios, even if their bosses approved their code for deployment without any kind of testing. TikTok's algorithms could be tuned to prevent the kind of inescapable traps that serve people an infinite amount of hateful content. Better still, developers could give users full control over what they can or can't see. Makers of generative AI models can train them on datasets that strictly follow copyright law, and require their outputs to be clearly watermarked as synthetic content. The programmers of military software should always force their products to obey the international laws of conflict, even if that means reducing their effectiveness as a tool of war.

No company likes any of its employees to act too independently. A tech worker might be terrified of being fired for insubordination, for doing something they were not tasked with doing. But the wonderful thing about software development is that it takes an expert eye to see what is actually going on. No project manager will realize that you've added in some additional safety logic. No financier would even know how to scrub your code of any extraneous language that might make it slightly less effective but significantly less likely to fail catastrophically. Perhaps such actions would not be ethical in the sense of following the strict corporate hierarchy or doing exactly what your boss says without question. But the bosses have not been great stewards of public safety, to say the least. And if given the choice of being a good corporate soldier or not hurting—or even killing—people, I know which path I'd choose.

Ideally, though, tech workers should not have to resort to secrecy in order to act ethically. They must insist that companies establish strong cultures of safety that are immune to market pressures. At the moment, trust and safety teams seem to exist at the whims of their managerial overlords, and are usually the first people to be let go when the next downturn begins. At the start of the inflationary crisis in 2021, almost every major tech company dismissed or dissolved teams dedicated to preventing harms from technology. Facebook got rid of its civic integrity team, Microsoft its ethics and society team. Amazon and Google dismissed several dozen AI ethics researchers as part of broader cost-saving measures.

We should hope for the best when it comes to a corporate commitment to safety, but prepare for the worst, too. And in this, we have only to follow the lead of a previous generation who operated at the very edge of technological innovation.

In the 1930s, the technology of powered flight was still very new and dangerous. Both companies and pilots could see the potential to make the world smaller and revolutionize the movement of people, goods, and ideas. But the lure of money made some nascent carriers accept more business than they should have—a "fly at all costs, in all conditions" mentality that took the lives of one in six commercial pilots. An equivalent accident rate today would translate to one fatal airplane crash every hour of every day.

So pilots took matters into their own hands. They formed a union not so much to protect their jobs or wages—in fact, they were some of the highest-paid professionals in the country at the time, out-earning lawyers, doctors, and even some railroad executives—but to protect the lives of everyone in their profession. And they *won*. They refused to work until the cap of monthly flight time was reduced from 160 hours to 85 hours, where it remains to this day. They got their employers to agree to a common network of air traffic control, to prevent mid-air collisions and crashes due to fuel exhaustion. They even consulted with the Roosevelt administration to pass the Civil Aeronautics Act, which established minimum certification standards for pilots, mechanics, and airlines. Their expertise in identifying problems and proposing solutions led to a 90 percent reduction in the accident rate in less than a decade, thus proving that the safety hazard had more to do with corporate greed than anything else. Most of all, they realized that they held absolute leverage over their industry—that without them, the aviation sector would not exist.

Every industry that uses managerial software needs such collective action to put safeguards in place. Technical unions modeled after pilot and flight attendant unions could provide that counterweight. They could set process standards and safety guidelines to keep junk software in check. They could consult with companies and regulators to solve tricky technical issues and help give impartial, confidential quality control of new code and new forms of technology. And they could create continuing education and knowledge-sharing programs to ensure that developers remain proficient in their field while not losing sight of the ethical principles that should guide their work.

That's the carrot. But a technical union should also come prepared with a stick. It should act as a watchdog, similar to the American Board of Medicine for doctors or *Consumer Reports* for most retail items. Companies that create good, ethical, and high-quality tech should get a compliance certificate or a seal of approval. Companies that abuse its potential should get named and shamed. And a union could even bestow awards and honorifics of its own upon individuals who have made a significant safety contribution, or who have stood up to corporate pressure to reduce quality for the sake of expediency—a marker of service not to a single employer but to the entire industry. In that way, a union would shift the source of pride and self-worth away from the company and onto the discipline as a whole.

It would also raise the status of the workers who reside at the periphery of the corporate structure yet who are most aware of the dangers that managerial technology poses. By protecting relatively lower-status workers such as content moderators and technical researchers alongside higher-status workers such as software developers, unions will be able to present a fuller picture of risk in their negotiations with tech companies, and to prevent retaliation against the most vulnerable members of the industry.

There is one more duty that tech workers would probably need to perform. Ideally, collective action will help developers push their employers away from the managerial abyss and toward better uses of technology. But collective action can be slow, and often requires the opposing party to be willing to compromise. Individual tech workers will always have to remain on guard against the erosion of standards, the surrender to market pressures, the many excuses that line the path to failure. And not every company can or should be saved. If you cannot successfully fight against the managerial pressures to create dangerous tech, then you will have to make perhaps the most profound moral decision of your career. Will you stay at a company that abuses your work (and, through it, humanity at large)? Or will you stand on principle and take your labor elsewhere?

If you consider yourself an ethical person, and you find yourself at a company that has begun irredeemably lurching in the direction of abuse, *you must leave.* As a new hire, you have a limited grace period to observe and judge your new employer. But after about eighteen months, your continued presence is a tacit endorsement of its practices—even the ones with which you don't agree. There is no defensible way to stay at a company for a decade, complain that it's immoral or unethical, and yet do nothing about it. At that point, your professed idealism only provides cover for others to do terrible things.

Here again, a tech union would make this easier for disillusioned workers. Some companies have overly restrictive employment contracts that prevent workers from leaving for another job, or for speaking out against their worst abuses. For example, OpenAI used to enforce a "perpetual non-disparagement clause" that allowed the company to claw back compensation should a former employee criticize the company for any reason at any point in the future. Although OpenAI abolished the plan in May 2024, such policies are hardly unique; most tech companies impose equally absurd conditions on their workers in order to protect their reputation. Often times, these aren't even legally enforceable, but the threat comes more from the high cost of mounting a legal defense even if the law technically protects you. For example, Theranos whistleblower Tyler Shultz was protected by federal law, but he still had to spend nearly half a million dollars in personal legal fees just to fight off his former employer's civil suits. Even attempts to disclose more mundane forms of abuse, such as creating a hostile workplace or intentionally paying women and minorities less than men, have been met with legal retaliation. Our collective ability to guard against the tech industry's worst impulses depends in large part on the free exchange of information from current and former employees; it is this freedom above all that tech companies wish to destroy, and that a union can help protect.

If you're a tech worker, you have far more leverage than you realize. Just think back to the last project you worked on that was understaffed, or where someone in a key role departed unexpectedly. You know firsthand that a shortage of just one person can delay a project by months, if not years—even at large companies with a seemingly bottomless pool of talent. There's no chance you'll be out of work for long. The demand for technical talent has always been high, but it can spike even from the normally high levels. As of this writing, for instance, demand is positively historic: there are three times more job openings than there are job seekers. Using your leverage doesn't mean potentially sacrificing everything. You don't have to be a hero.

This path will be hard. Collective action is unfamiliar to just about everyone in tech—especially those who have bought in to the enforced atomization and anti-unionism of the managerial age. But imagine what it could make: a Republic of Builders, made up of everyone who actually does the hard work of realizing the future. It is the only path to producing safe software in a world that incentivizes anything but.

No one else will stand up if you don't. Executives don't care. Investors won't intervene if it costs them money. And regulators can't do much that is meaningful, at least not on the time scale required to prevent the next technological failure. Only tech workers can keep software from going rogue. The question is, will we take up our responsibility to prevent further harms—or will we stay inside our comfortable little bubbles until, at last, bad software finally turns on us, too?

Some people are already refusing to remain silent. Susan Fowler spoke out against the sexism rampant at Uber in 2017. Frances Haugen smuggled out a trove of internal documents at Meta proving that the company actively measures, but does nothing to stop, a variety of abuses on its platform that range from child endangerment to the incitement of racial and political violence. Dr. Timnit Gebru, who co-led Google's ethical AI team, was fired after she criticized the company's evident biases in both its AI tools and its human resources policies. In the last year, others have started to organize protests and walkouts against specific corporate projects: Amazon's sale of facial recognition technology to law enforcement; Google's contracts to provide cloud computing services to militaries around the world; Microsoft's work with oil companies. These workers are no longer willing to sacrifice their personal integrity just for the sake of their jobs, and this groundswell of independent actions is a sure sign that the moral awakening of the tech worker is already underway. Now it just needs an even sharper focus not on individual injustices, but on the common force behind all of them—the ideology of managerialism and its stranglehold on software.

FIFTY YEARS AGO, THE COMPUTING REVOLUTION PROMISED TO RESHAPE THE world. It has done so, just not in the ways we expected. We tell ourselves that, in spite of its uneven track record, software will do better *next* time. But better according to whose definition? Technology has no intrinsic moral compass that tells it to protect human life or to not exploit the vulnerable. If it is not given one, it will default to the reigning philosophy of its creators. The default is managerialism, which reduces everything about a business to a simplistic financial abstraction, and defines good and bad only in terms of impacts to cash flows and profits.

We can shrug and just call this capitalism. And in most cases, relentless optimization creates more annoyance than anything. After all, we can always take our business elsewhere. No game or app or even device is so integral to our lives that we cannot function without it. But we can't opt out of everything. Some software cannot be escaped; it is too widespread or too embedded in the tools we use all the time.

Almost every tech company refuses to acknowledge this basic fact. Instead, they continue to regard software in managerial terms only: as a potential tool to exploit users, a weapon that can help achieve market dominance, a universal solution to cut costs and reduce headcount. In their shortsightedness, the leaders of these companies don't often see what is obvious to those who actually make software. It is an inherently flawed product with its own set of tradeoffs and limitations, many of which cannot be seen until it's too late. This is not much different than any other product, from refined steel to cancer drugs to sports cars. But software can be created and disseminated more quickly than any other type of product in human history, a kind of magical ability that we tend to see as an unvarnished good. *It resembles nothing else in human experience*, we tell ourselves, *therefore the normal rules must not apply.*

Software is indeed exceptional—just not always in positive ways. It has no sense of its own limitations, or its own powers. It has no grasp of external reality. It cannot tell right from wrong, helpful from hurtful, humane from inhumane. Often, we assume that it somehow knows our intentions or has an idea of what we want from it when we put it to use. As this book has striven to show, it has no such thing. To the extent it understands its purpose, it is only the narrow purpose that managerialism gives it.

As we have seen, managerialism is ill-equipped to face the challenges of our tech-obsessed present. Corporate leaders will always worry about financial discipline, operational efficiency, and centralized control, just as they have for over a century now. But that level of abstraction is now a drawback rather than an advantage. We live in a world where a single line of bad code can sway an election, and a poorly considered user interface can consign innocent people to their death. Yet we lack a holistic view that allows us to foresee the many ways in which our software might go wrong.

This cannot be the permanent condition of software development. Creating software demands expertise, yes. But it also requires humility. For all its power, software is not a unique phenomenon, but another tool imagined and made by humans. Until we acknowledge this, our software will continue to make us less tolerant, less joyful, and less free: a digital straitjacket in which we bind ourselves ever more tightly, even as its embrace suffocates us.

ACKNOWLEDGMENTS

In 2007, I was sitting in the corner room of my parents' apartment in Kuwait City, trying to find something interesting to read that wouldn't get censored by the government firewall. Via Stumbleupon, I arrived at a blog called *The Bygone Bureau*, and read the entire site in an evening. It seemed like the internet equivalent of a college literary journal—a place where people aspired to produce quality writing on tight deadlines, for no reason other than because they really wanted to. The next day, I pitched an article to one of the *Bureau*'s coeditors, Kevin Nguyen, who agreed to take a look at the final product. It was the start of a professional relationship that has lasted two decades.

In the spring of 2019, Kevin (who was now features editor at *The Verge*) asked me if I wanted to write something about the 737 MAX crashes, as long as I could give them a unique angle. On the phone, we sketched out a feature-length article that would eventually find its way into congressional reports, academic journals, and computer ethics courses. Still, there was more to the story—enough to warrant a book.

After a year of querying, I got an "I'm interested!" response from Anna Sproul-Latimer at Neon Literary. She pushed me to think as big as I possibly could and to make it a story where the MAX crashes were a window into a larger void at the center of our technology. We rewrote the proposal about twenty times over the next year before she was satisfied with it, and suggested I work with Jayson Greene to hone the proposal in its final stages. Naturally, she was right. Once it was done, we sold it in a matter of weeks to Dan Gerstle at W. W. Norton.

On one condition: Dan wanted me to think even bigger, and to add more of my own experiences and perspectives from fifteen years in the tech industry. What did I want my colleagues to know, and to do, in order to prevent even worse situations? Without his vision, this book would have less of a backbone.

The rest of the Norton team brought the book from a loose collection of Word documents to a final, beautiful, real book. Zeba Arora shepherded the book through the year-long process; Lauren Abbate, Susan Sanfrey, and Charlotte Kelchner managed production and copyediting; Brendan Curry picked the right subtitle when the rest of us could not; Steve Attardo nailed the cover design; and Will Scarlett and Steve Colca got the book into the hands of readers.

Others shaped this book in ways both direct and subtle. I'm grateful for the feedback of Kathryne Bevilacqua, Jordan Chapman, Fiona Maguire, Doug McClure, Patrick Smith, and Neal Thompson, as well as others who asked to remain anonymous. Cameron Ajdari, Rachel Colquette, Cameron Corey, Lauren Fortman, Anna Geyer, Emma Hill, Sheena Lu, Avril Payne, Katie Gee Salisbury, and Matt Smith helped me figure out a marketing plan.

I owe whatever skill I have at writing to the encouragement of my parents, Keith and Rena Campbell; to those who taught me how to write, including Kris Beeler, Kathleen Bumpus, Jenny Davis, Laura Deckman, Paul Dutton, Amy Houston, Mary Lukehart, Michael McCormick, Brian Maselli, Liz Mellyn, Scott Phoenix, Jan Smith, Eric Weinberger, and Don Witten; and to the editors who taught me how to do it professionally, including Josh Burek, Daphne Durham, Leah Finnegan, Sarah Jeong, Liz Lopatto, Nilay Patel, and Jean Tamarin.

Most of all, my wife Amanda spent five years supporting the book, and its author, in ways too innumerable to mention.

NOTES

INTRODUCTION: THE WRONG KIND OF LOGIC

7 **By 2000, annual corporate profits:** US Bureau of Economic Analysis, *Corporate Profits after Tax (without IVA and CCAdj)*, February 19, 2024.

7 **Dow Jones Industrial Average grew:** National Bureau of Economic Research, *Dow-Jones Industrial Stock Price Index for United States*, May 28, 2024.

7 **total market capitalization:** World Bank, *Market Capitalization of Listed Domestic Companies (Current US$)*, May 31, 2024.

7 **gross domestic product per capita:** World Bank, *GDP Per Capita (Current US$)*, May 28, 2024.

7 **companies can reliably increase their productivity:** Sandra Black and Lisa Lynch, "How to Compete: The Impact of Workplace Practices and Information Technology on Productivity," *Review of Economics and Statistics* 88, no. 3 (August 2001): 434–45; Lucia Foster, John Haltiwanger, and Chad Syverson, "Reallocation, Firm Turnover and Efficiency: Selection on Productivity or Profitability," *American Economic Review* 98, no. 1 (March 2008): 394–425; Chad Syverson, "Market Structure and Productivity: A Concrete Example," *Journal of Political Economy* 112, no. 6 (December 2004): 1181–222.

8 **$1 trillion in cash:** William Lazonick, "The Financialization of the U.S. Corporation: What Has Been Lost, and How It Can Be Regained," in *Seattle University Law Review* 36 (2013): 902.

8 **permanent economic insecurity:** William Milberg and Deborah Walker, "Actual and Perceived Effects of Offshoring on Economic Insecurity: The

Role of Labour Market Regimes," in *Making Globalization Socially Sustainable* (Geneva: World Trade Organization, 2011), 162; Novella Bomini, Christoph Ernst, Malte Luebker, *Offshoring and the Labour Market: What Are the Issues?* (Geneva: International Labour Office, 2008).

8 **$20 billion to offset:** Centre for New Economy and Society Insight Report, *Towards a Reskilling Revolution: Industry-Led Action for the Future of Work.* Geneva: World Economic Forum, 2019.

8 **the same tribal nomads:** Robin Dunbar, "Coevolution of Neocortex Size, Group Size and Language in Humans," *Behavioral and Brain Sciences* 16 (1993): 689.

9 **Amazon alone hires more than one thousand:** Emmy Hawker, "Which Companies Hire the Most MBAs?" *Business Because*, March 14, 2024.

10 **Elon Musk famously decried:** John A. Byrne, "Dumb as Dirt & Disingenuous, Too: Elon Musk's Anti-MBA Critique" *Poets & Quants*, December 16, 2020.

10 **Sweetgreen (the salad chain):** Marli Guzzetta, "When Is It OK to Call a Salad Company a Tech Company?" *Slate*, April 19, 2016.

10 **Goldman Sachs (the investment bank):** Goldman Sachs, *2014 Annual Report: Four Trends Shaping Markets and Economies*, January 1, 2015, 11–13.

10 **Boeing (the airplane and defense company):** Ron Starner and Mark Arend, "Behind Boeing's Flight Plan," *Site Selection*, September 2001.

11 **"In short, software is eating the world":** Marc Andreessen, "Why Software Is Eating the World," *Wall Street Journal*, August 11, 2011.

12 **less than a third:** World Bank, *Individuals using the internet (% of population)*, May 28, 2024.

12 **Now, it's nearly two hours:** Pedro Paladrani, "A Decade of Change: How Tech Evolved in the 2010s and What's in Store for the 2020s," *NASDAQ*, May 16, 2022.

14 **I spent four years:** Darryl Campbell, "Redline: The Many Human Errors that Brought Down the Boeing 737 MAX," *The Verge*, May 2, 2019.

CHAPTER 1: FALLING OUT OF THE SKY

21 **But as its onboard computers:** Narrative adapted from Komite Nasional Keselamatan Transportasi, *Final KNKT.18.10.35.04 Aircraft Accident Report, PT. Lion Mentari Airlines, Boeing 737-8 (MAX); PK-LQP, Tanjung Karawang, West Java, Republic of Indonesia, 29 October 2018*, October 25, 2019.

22 **Captain Bhavye Suneja:** Joanna Slater, Shibani Mahtani, " 'Playing with lives': Widow of pilot on doomed Lion Air flight says direct appeals made to ground Boeing model," *Washington Post*, March 30, 2019.

22 **First Officer Harvino:** "Family of Lion Air co-pilot sues Boeing in Chicago over fatal crash," *Reuters*, December 28, 2018.

27 **just after HBS revamped:** Associates of Harvard Business School, *The Success of a Strategy* (Cambridge, MA: Harvard Business School, 1980), 19.

28 **every two or three years:** Jeffrey E. Garten, "Jack Welch: A Role Model for Today's CEO?" *Bloomberg Businessweek*, September 9, 2001.

28 **the "GE Way":** Steve Lohr, "Jack Welch, G.E. Chief Who Became a Business Superstar, Dies at 84" *New York Times*, March 2, 2020.

28 **He was even a finalist:** Judith Crown, "Jet Setter," *Chicago Magazine*, May 27, 2007.

28 **his training served him well:** 3M Corporation, "3M CEO Says Initiatives Driving the Company's Growth," May 13, 2003.

28 **3M's net income more than doubled:** 3M Corporation, *2001 Annual Report: Building an Even Stronger 3M*, January 2002; 3M Corporation, *Form 10-K 2005*, January 2006.

28 **told the *Seattle Times*:** Dominic Gates, "Boeing Boss's Turbulent Tenure," *Seattle Times*, December 10, 2014.

29 **"product development":** The Boeing Company, *Annual Report 1990,* January 1991, 32.

29 **"industry leadership":** The Boeing Company, *1994 Annual Report*, January 1995, 2.

29 **"the highest standards of quality":** The Boeing Company, *1996 Annual Report,* January 1997, 40.

29 **first twin-engine jet:** J. P. Santiago, "The Boeing 767 and the Birth of ETOPS," *Tails through Time*, December 9, 2015.

29 **one of the safest:** "Plane Crash Rates by Model," AirSafe.com, retrieved May 28, 2024; through 2017, the 747-400 has a "Fatal Event Rate" of 0.06 per million flights. The next-safest model is the Airbus A320 family, which has a Fatal Event Rate of 0.09 per million flights.

29 **the global aviation market grew:** David Oxley and Chaitan Jain, "Global Air Passenger Markets; Riding Out Periods of Turbulence," in *The Travel and Tourism Market 2015: Growth Through Shocks*, eds. Roberto Crotti and Tiffany Misrahi (Geneva: World Economic Forum, 2015), 62.

29 **70 percent of the global fleet:** William G. Shepherd and Joanna M. Shepherd, *The Economics of Industrial Organization: Fifth Edition* (Long Grove, IL: Waveland Press, 2003), 296.

29 **1 per 25,000 flights:** *1961 Report of the Committee on Aviation* (Schaumberg, IL: Society of Actuaries, 1961), 84–85.

29 **1 per 3 million:** "Fatal Accident Rate for U.S. Air Carriers Between 2000 and 2019," November 21, 2023.

29 **4 cents per dollar:** The Boeing Company, *Annual Report 2000*, January 1, 2001, 9.

30 **According to Boeing legend:** Jerry Useem, "Boeing vs. Boeing," *Fortune*, October 9, 2000.

30 **first annual letter as CEO:** The Boeing Company, *The Boeing Company 2005 Annual Report: Shaping the Future*, January 2006, 6.

30 **"Do what you do best":** Thomas F. O'Boyle, *At Any Cost: Jack Welch, General Electric, and the Pursuit of Profit* (New York: Vintage, 1999), 214.

30 **Boeing made about two-thirds:** Steve Denning, "What Went Wrong at Boeing?" *Forbes*, January 21, 2013.

30 **obsessed over quality control:** *Report Number A0436: Product Quality Requirements for Sellers of Boeing Designed Detail Parts and Non-Functional Minor Assemblies, Revision Letter Q*, December 18, 2001.

30 **into a hands-off licensor:** Yao Zhao, "Risk Sharing in Joint Product Development—Lessons from 787 Dreamliner," *The European Business Review* (November-December 2016), 82–83.

31 **as much as 15 percent:** Jon Hemmerdinger, "Suppliers Seek to Renegotiate Loss-Making Contracts with Airbus and Boeing," *Flight Global*, November 16, 2023.

31 **$1 billion in costs:** The Boeing Company, *The Boeing Company 2006 Annual Report: Charting the Course*, January 2007, 13; The Boeing Company, *The Boeing Company 2007 Annual Report: Leading the Way*, January 2008, 5.

31 **replaced them with younger, cheaper workers:** Leon Grunberg and Sarah Moore, *Emerging from Turbulence: Boeing and Stories of the American Workplace Today* (Lanham, MD: Rowman & Littlefield, 2015), 31–35.

31 **"be measured and managed":** *2005 Annual Report*, 7.

32 **"We have a systematized, standardized approach":** For example, The Boeing Company, "Q1 2011 Earnings Call," April 27, 2011.

32 **much sharper and gave far more specifics:** For example, The Boeing Company, "Q2 2014 Earnings Call," July 23, 2014.

32 **the division did not produce:** "Heritage of Innovation Timeline," GE Aerospace, accessed May 31, 2024.

33 **more than $300 billion worth:** Eric M. Johnson, "Boeing Lifts 20-Year Industry Demand Forecast to $6.8 Trillion," *Reuters*, June 17, 2019; The Boeing Company, *Commercial Market Outlook*, June 15, 2023.

33 **Boeing's internal design teams:** "Boeing Firms up 737 Replacement Studies by Appointing Team," *Flight Global*, March 3, 2006; Jon Ostrower, "Boeing Boss Green-Lights All-New Next Generation Narrowbody," *Flight Global*, February 10, 2011; Steve Wilhelm, "Composites May Be Just the Ticket for Boeing 737 Successor, Albaugh Hints," *Puget Sound Business Journal*, August 29, 2010.

33 **But it would cost the company:** "Boeing Didn't Want to Re-Engine the 737—But Had Design Standing By," *Leeham News*, March 20, 2019.

33 **In December of 2010:** Nicola Clark and Jad Mouawad, "Airbus to Update A320 with New Engines and Wings," *New York Times*, December 1, 2010.

34 **McNerney himself:** David Gelles et al., "Boeing Was 'Go, Go, Go' to Beat Airbus with the 737 Max," *New York Times*, March 23, 2019.

34 **95 percent of the same parts:** Alan Boyle, "How Boeing's Engineers Redesigned the Landing Gear to Make the 737 MAX 10 Fly," *GeekWire*, August 30, 2018.

34 **between $2 billion and $3 billion:** Jon Ostrower, "737 Max Development Cost to be Twice A320neo: Report," *Flight Global*, January 24, 2012.

34 **"We call it the 737 MAX":** Boeing Company, "Boeing Introduces 737 MAX with Launch of New Aircraft Family," August 30, 2011.

34 **1980s-vintage computers:** Darryl Campbell, "The Ancient Computers in the 737 Max Are Holding up a Fix," *The Verge*, April 9, 2020.

35 **built-in stairwell:** Ralph Vartabedian, "Boeing Is Haunted by a 50-Year Old Feature of 737 Jets," *Los Angeles Times*, March 15, 2019.

35 **an additional ten inches:** John Hemmerdinger, "Video: Boeing Details 737 Max 10 Landing Gear," *FlightGlobal*, August 30, 2018; Marco Evers, "What's Wrong with Boeing's 737 Max 8?" *Der Spiegel*, March 13, 2019; Aubrey Cohen, "Boeing Says It's Putting New Engines on 737," *Seattle Post-Intelligencer*, August 30, 2011.

36 **Two years into development:** Boeing, "Inside Boeing's Wind-Tunnel Model Shop," September 11, 2012, video, 3:15; Jack Nicas et al., "Boeing Built Deadly Assumptions Into 737 Max, Blind to a Late Design Change," *New York Times*, June 1, 2019.

36 **In an earlier era:** For example, during development of its Sonic Cruiser design in 2002, Boeing engineers "looked at more than 25 wing planforms, 50 nacelle shapes and 60 fuselage designs"—and then radically redesigned it as the 787 Dreamliner, which debuted more than a decade later. See "Sonic Cruiser Is Dead—Long Live Super Efficient?" *Flight Global*, January 6, 2003.

36 **"will provide customers the capabilities they want":** The Boeing Company, *The Boeing Company 2011 Annual Report*, February 2012.

39 **Another company called Rockwell Collins:** Chris Hamby, "Far From the Spotlight, A Boeing Partner Feels the Heat," *New York Times*, November 7, 2019.

39 **forced its software engineers:** "Old-World Hardware Company Struggling to Compete in an Information Economy," Glassdoor, December 9, 2013.

39 **"firefighting":** "Non-Stop Firefighting, Dysfunctional, Sometimes Toxic," Glassdoor, September 28, 2013.

39 **"scoped improperly":** "Interesting Domain Mired in Dysfunctional Bureaucracy," Glassdoor, March 28, 2013.

40 **"We're working on the high-level specs together":** The Boeing Company, "Q2 2007 Earnings Call," July 25, 2007.

40 **During the early development:** US Congress, House, Committee on Transportation and Infrastructure, *The Design, Development & Certification of the Boeing 737 MAX*, 116th Congress, September 16, 2020, 127.

40 **"not have any objectionable interaction":** "Boeing Coordination Sheet No. Aero-B-BBA8-C12-0159, Revision G, June 11, 2018, SUBJECT: 737MAX Flaps Up High Alpha Stabilizer Trim (MCAS) Requirements," reproduced in US

Congress, House, Committee on Transportation and Infrastructure, *The Boeing 737 MAX: Examining the Design, Development, and Marketing of the Aircraft* (Washington, DC: US Government Publishing Office, 2020), 170.

41 **inherent stability challenge:** John A. Tirpak and Brian W. Everstine, "USAF Reviewing Training after MAX 8 Crashes; KC-46 Uses Similar MCAS," *Air and Space Forces*, March 22, 2019.

41 **Rockwell Collins decided to automate:** Bill Carey, "Rockwell Collins Provides KC-46A Cockpit Details," *AIN Online*, September 26, 2011.

42 **"nice-to-have":** "Flight Operations: Angle of Attack," *Aero Magazine* 12, October 2000.

43 **two and a half hours:** FlightGlobal, "FlightGlobal talks to Boeing's Keith Leverkuhn about 737 Max certification process," June 19, 2017, video, 2:09.

43 **they hid its existence:** Dominic Gates and Steve Miletich, "Stunning messages from 2016 deepen Boeing's 737 MAX crisis," *Seattle Times*, October 18, 2019.

49 **Indonesian Navy divers found:** Jeffrey Cook and David Kerley, "Even as Lion Air Jet's Black Box Is Found, Some Answers May Be Back in the United States," *ABC News*, November 1, 2018.

49 **Two things immediately jumped out:** Andy Pasztor, "Lion Air Crash Investigators Are Focused on Maintenance Problems," *Wall Street Journal*, November 28, 2018.

50 **Boeing surrogates aggressively defended:** Gaurav Raghuvanshi and Jake Maxwell Watts, "Lion Air Crash Is the Latest Setback for Indonesia's Troubled Aviation Industry," *Wall Street Journal*, October 29, 2018; David Koenig, "Lion Air Crash Renews Concerns About Indonesia Airlines," *Associated Press*, October 30, 2018.

50 **Boeing salespeople pushed the MAX:** Douglas MacMillan, "'Safety Was Just a Given': Inside Boeing's Boardroom Amid the 737 Max Crisis," *Washington Post*, May 5, 2019.

50 **speed up production:** Eric Brothers, "2019 Forecast," *Aerospace Manufacturing and Design*, January–February 2019.

50 **the global fleet of 737 MAXes:** Denise Lu et al., "From 8,600 Flights to Zero: Grounding the Boeing 737 Max 8," *New York Times*, March 13, 2019.

50 **"fatal event":** Federal Aviation Administration, "Quantitative Risk Assessment, Random Transport Airplane Risk Analysis (R-TARA) Version 2.42," reproduced in US Congress, House, Committee on Transportation and Infrastructure, *The Boeing 737 MAX: Examining the Federal Aviation Administration's Oversight of the Aircraft's Certification* (Washington, DC: US Government Publishing Office, 2020), 169. Using the FAA's transportation airplane risk analysis methodology, Boeing calculated that an MCAS event was likely to cause a fatal accident once every 372,574 flight-hours. Assuming a current fleet size (as of March 2019) of 250 airplanes, at an average operational time of 9 hours per day

and an average capacity of 190 passengers, Boeing estimated the risk of a fatal crash at about 0.5 percent. For the fleet-wide risk, Boeing assumed an operational lifetime of 114,000 flight-hours per airplane. Finally, Boeing assumed that after Lion Air 610, flight crews would successfully correct an MCAS malfunction 99 percent of the time.

51 **"We have crafted that strategy together":** Everett Rosenfeld, "Boeing Replaces CEO McNerney with Muilenburg," *CNBC*, June 23, 2015.

51 **Boeing's "biggest opportunity":** The Boeing Company, "Q2 2015 Earnings Call," July 22, 2015.

51 **On Maria Bartiromo's Fox Business show:** "Boeing CEO: Our global service business is growing 12% a year," *Maria Bartiromo's Wall Street*, November 16, 2018.

51 **"repetitive cycles of uncommanded nose down stabilizer":** The Boeing Company, "Flight Crew Operations Manual Bulletin for the Boeing Company, no. TBC-19," November 6, 2018.

52 **On the morning of March 20, 2019:** Narrative throughout adapted from Aircraft Accident Investigation Bureau, *ET 302, B737-8MAX Registration ET-AVJ Accident Investigation Final Report* (Addis Ababa: Federal Democratic Republic of Ethiopia Ministry of Transport and Logistics, 2022).

53 **the forty-second window:** Jack Nicas et al., "In Test of Boeing Jet, Pilots Had 40 Seconds to Fix Error," *New York Times*, March 25, 2019.

CHAPTER 2: MANAGERIAL REVOLUTIONS

57 **the company's "Ford 2000" initiative:** Warren Brown and Frank Svoboda, "Ford's Brave New World," *Washington Post*, October 15, 1994; Allan Afuah, "Is *Ford 2000* the Right Strategy for Innovation? A Management Theory Perspective," in *Strategic Change* 6 (1997): 345–55.

57 **global profit per vehicle:** Ford Motor Company, *2002 Annual Report: Starting Our Second Century*, January 2003.

58 **an estimated 90 percent:** Ford Customer Service Division, *2002 Ford Passenger Car Parts Catalog, Volume 1—Text* (Detroit: Ford Motor Company. 2003).

59 **"would find himself at home":** Alfred Chandler, *The Visible Hand: The Managerial Revolution in American Business* (Cambridge, MA: Belknap Press, 1977), 455.

59 **Every major corporate innovation:** Tejas Ramdas et al., "Visualizing a Century of Management Ideas," *Harvard Business Review*, September 19, 2022.

61 **"a wave of gadgets":** Thomas S. Ashton, *The Industrial Revolution, 1760–1830* (Oxford: Oxford University Press, 1947), 42.

61 **both countries remained largely agrarian:** A. E. Musson, *The Growth of British Industry* (New York: Holmes and Meier, 1978), 149.

61 **Success would depend on consistent staffing:** Robert Margo, "Economies of Scale in Nineteenth Century American Manufacturing Revisited: A Resolution of the Entrepreneurial Labor Input Problem," in *Enterprising America: Businesses, Banks, and Credit Markets in Historical Perspective*. (Cambridge, MA: NBER Books, 2015) 220–22.

62 **"engineers, mechanics, chemists, physicians, and natural philosophers":** Joel Mokyr, *The Gifts of Athena: Historical Origins of the Knowledge Economy* (Princeton, NJ: Princeton University Press, 2002), 66.

62 **consolidated eighty different timekeeping methods:** *The Railroad Gazette* 14, no. 1 (April 2, 1870), 6.

62 **the first regular financial reports:** Chandler, 110–11.

62 **"where one cannot express":** Ludwig von Mises, "Economic Calculation in the Socialist Commonwealth," trans. S. Adler, in *Collectivist Economic Planning: Critical Studies on the Possibilities of Socialism*, ed. F. A. Hayek (London: Routledge & Kegan Paul LTD, 1935; German orig. 1920), 108–9.

63 **abstracting everything into its financial components:** Chandler, 87.

63 **"dominated by agrarian rhythms":** Jacques le Goff, *Time, Work & Culture in the Middle Ages* (Chicago: The University of Chicago Press, 1982), 44

63 **Under managerialism, work became standardized:** Hans-Joachim Voth, "Time and Work in Eighteenth-Century London," *The Journal of Economic History* 58, no.1 (March 1998), 33–35.

63 **"the workman who is best suited":** Frederick Winslow Taylor, *The Principles of Scientific Management* (New York: Harper & Brothers, 1915), 59.

63 **nearly $185 billion:** Christopher J. Tassava, "The American Economy during World War II," *Economic History Association Encyclopedia*, February 10, 2008.

63 **more than ten times its productivity:** Benedict Crowell and Robert Wilson, *Demobilization: Our Industrial and Military Demobilization after the Armistice, 1918-1920* (New Haven: Yale University Press, 1921), 315–16.

64 **collectively release four new:** Michael S. Shull and David Edward Wilt, *Hollywood War Films, 1937-1945: An Exhaustive Filmography of American Feature-Length Motion Pictures Relating to World War II* (Jefferson, NC: McFarland & Company, 1996), 139.

64 **brought their ideas to pharmaceutical companies:** Roswell Quinn, "Rethinking Antibiotic Research and Development: World War II and the Penicillin Collaborative," in *The American Journal of Public Health* 103, vol. 3 (March 2013): 431–33.

64 **another triumph of managerial design:** Erin DeJesus, "A Brief History of Spam, An American Meat Icon," *Eater*, July 9, 2014.

64 **the Wharton School:** Joseph Wharton, "Agreement between Joseph Wharton and the Trustees of the University of Pennsylvania," June 22, 1881, 13.

64 **the same financial and administrative methods:** Katie Reilly, "Inside the Battle for the Hearts and Minds of Tomorrow's Business Leaders," *Time*, October 8, 2021.

65 **"constant economic pulse-taking":** Andrew L. Yarrow, *Measuring America: How Economic Growth Came to Define American Greatness in the Late Twentieth Century* (Amherst, MA: University of Massachusetts Press, 2010), chapter 7, Kindle.

65 **fewer than one in five:** Marshall E. Blume, Jean Crockett, and Irwin Friend, *Stockownership in the United States: Characteristics and Trends* (St. Louis: Federal Reserve Bank of St. Louis, 1974), 18.

65 **model the number of "kills":** Kenneth Cukier and Viktor Mayer-Schönberger, "The Dictatorship of Data," in *MIT Technology Review*, May 31, 2013.

65 **"Nixon's Axe-Man":** Christopher Moran, "Nixon's Axe Man: CIA Director James R. Schlesinger," in *Journal of American Studies* 53, no. 1 (February 2019), 95.

65 **"if one were writing":** *Deputy Secretary Lawrence H. Summers Testimony before the Senate Budget Committee*, 105th Congress (1998) (statement of Lawrence H. Summers, Deputy Secretary of the Treasury).

66 **grew more predictably:** Burnham, 117–18.

66 **"the fact is that in modern society":** Peter F. Drucker, *Management: Tasks, Responsibilities, Practices* (New York: Harper & Row, 1973), 325.

67 **"there is one and only one":** Milton Friedman, "The Social Responsibility of Business Is to Increase Its Profits," *The New York Times*, September 13, 1970.

68 **employed around forty workers:** P. L. Payne, "The Emergence of the Large-Scale Company in Great Britain, 1870-1914," in *Economic History Review* 20 (1967), 525–27.

68 **were employed by companies:** Office of Business Economics, *Survey of Current Business* (Washington, DC: US Department of Commerce, 1950), 13.

68 ***Fortune Magazine* began to publish:** "1955 Full List" and "2023 Fortune Global 500," *Fortune Magazine*, retrieved June 1, 2024.

69 **"what organizations really have":** Henry Mintzberg, "Musings on Management," *Harvard Business Review* 74, no. 4 (July-August, 1996).

71 **Perhaps the most infamous example:** Final Amended Opinion at 1498–527, *United States v. Philip Morris USA, Inc.*, No. 1:99-cv-02496-GK (D.D.C., August 17, 2006).

72 **During the meeting, they agreed:** *United States v. Philip Morris USA Inc.*, 449 F. Supp. 2d 1 (D.D.C. 2006), *aff'd in part & vacated in part*, 566 F.3d 1095 (D.C. Cir. 2009) (per *curiam*), *cert. denied*, 561 U.S. ___, 130 S. Ct. 3501 (2010).

72 **"the products we make":** Allan Brandt, "Inventing Conflicts of Interest: A History of Tobacco Industry Tactics," *American Journal of Public Health* 102, no. 1 (January 2012), 66.

72 **fat operating margins:** Jeremy Bulow and Paul Klemperer, "The Tobacco Deal," *Brookings Papers on Economic Activity 1998* (1998): 339–40.

72 **cigarette sales were growing:** K. Michael Cummings, Robert N. Proctor, "The Changing Public Image of Smoking in the United States: 1964-2014," *Cancer Epidemiology, Biomarkers & Prevention* 23, no. 1 (January 1, 2014), 32–36.

72 **a peak of 636 billion cigarettes:** Laverne Creek, Tom Capehart, Verner Grise, *U.S. Tobacco Statistics, 1935-92* (Washington, DC: Economic Research Service, 1994), 14.

72 **The industry only had to pay:** Jeremy Bulow, Paul Klemperer, "The Tobacco Deal," Nuffield College, University of Oxford, Department of Economics Working Paper no. 1998-W15&147 (November 1998).

73 **"the MSA did no major harm":** F. A. Sloan, C. A. Mathews, and J. G. Trogdon, "Impacts of the Master Settlement Agreement on the Tobacco Industry," in *Tobacco Control* 13 (2004) 356.

73 **"If the tobacco companies really stopped":** Final Amended Opinion, *United States v. Philip Morris USA, Inc.*, 974.

73 **annual deaths from lung cancer:** Steven G. Mann, "Epidemiology of Lung Cancer," in *Lung Cancer: Diagnostic Procedures and Therapeutic Management with Special Reference to Radiotherapy*, ed. Charles W. Scarantino (Berlin: Springer-Verlag, 2012), 1–7.

73 **nearly eighteen thousand tons of it:** Kenneth S. Davis, "The Deadly Dust: The Unhappy History of DDT," *American Heritage* 22, no. 2 (February 1971).

74 **"benefactor for all humanity":** Pennsalt DDT, "DDT Is Good for Me-e-e!" advertisement in *Time Magazine*, June 30, 1947.

74 **other diseases such as polio:** Elena Conis, "A Misfire in Fighting Polio Provides Clues as to How We'll Beat Covid," *Washington Post*, April 14, 2022.

74 **"render walls effective against stable-flies":** G. A. Campbell and T. F. West, "Persistence of D.D.T. in Oil-Bound Paint," in *Nature* 154 (1944), 512.

74 **Domestic production increased fivefold:** *Environmental Health Criteria for DDT and Its Derivatives* (Geneva: World Health Organization, 1979); Gerald Markowitz and David Rosner, "Monsanto, PCBs, and the Creation of a 'World-Wide Ecological Problem,'" in *Journal of Public Health Policy* 39 (November 7, 2018), 487–88.

74 **an alarming amount of the nation's food supply:** "U.S. Seeks to Keep Milk Free of DDT," *New York Times*, April 23, 1949.

75 **"This is an era of specialists":** Rachel Carson, *Silent Spring* (New York: Houghton Mifflin, 1962), 13.

75 **they continued to fight:** Robert Gillette, "DDT: In Field and Courtroom a Persistent Pesticide Lives On," *Science* 174, no. 4014 (December 10, 1971), 1108–10.

75 **those incontrovertibly improved:** Atul Gupta et al., "Owner Incentives and Performance in Healthcare: Private Equity Investment in Nursing Homes," *The Review of Financial Studies* 37, no. 4 (April 4, 2024), 1029-1077; Sarah Pringle, "Nursing Homes Still a PE Challenge," *Axios*, November 22, 2022.

CHAPTER 3: AS RELIABLE AS RUNNING WATER

79 **the entire gig economy:** Josh Dzieza, "Revolt of the Delivery Workers," *The Verge*, September 13, 2021; Andrew J. Hawkins, "Uber and Lyft Finally Admit They're Making Traffic Congestion Worse in Cities," *The Verge*, August 6, 2019; Lisa Pollack, "Feeling Uber-Guilty for Using Uber," *Financial Times*, August 30, 2016.

79 **more than ten thousand cities:** "Uber Is Now in over 10,000 Cities Globally," Uber press release, February 29, 2020.

79 **transportation as reliable as running water:** "Transportation Everywhere, For Everyone in Chicago," Uber blog, May 3, 2016.

79 **hundreds of premade lunches:** Jessi Hempel, "The UberEATS Standalone App Has Nothing to Do with Riders," *WIRED*, December 9, 2015.

80 **scrappy little moonshot:** Andrew Sheivachman, "Uber's Quest to Hit on Another Moonshot Product," *Skift*, September 28, 2018; "A Closer Look at Uber Eats, Uber's Fastest Growing Business," *NASDAQ*, September 3, 2019.

82 **police raids and taxi driver protests:** Hannah Jane Parkinson, "Uber Offices Raided in Paris by French Police in 'Car-Pooling' Controversy," *The Guardian*, March 18, 2015; "Uber Drivers Attacked Outside Mexico City Airport as Taxi Drivers Demonstrate," *Associated Press*, July 29, 2015; Gwyn Topham, "Black-Cab Drivers' Uber Protest brings London Traffic to a Standstill," *The Guardian*, February 10, 2016.

84 **fourteen cultural norms:** Oliver Staley, "Uber Has Replaced Travis Kalanick's Values with Eight New 'Cultural Norms,'" *Quartz*, November 7, 2017.

85 **$6.5 billion in revenues:** Biz Carson, "Uber Booked $20 Billion in Rides in 2016, but It's Still Losing Billions," *Business Insider*, April 14, 2017; "Uber Lost $4.5 Billion in 2017, but Its Revenue Jumped," *Associated Press*, February 14, 2018; Heather Somerville, "Uber Posts $1 Billion Loss in Quarter as Growth in Bookings Slows," *Reuters*, November 14, 2018.

86 **a superlative startup:** Sara Ashley O'Brien, "Uber Is the Most Valuable Startup in the World," *CNN Business*, July 31, 2015.

87 **This legal loophole:** A few places have attempted to reclassify Uber drivers as employees; California's attempt to do so was repealed by an Uber- and Lyft-backed voter referendum, although New York's minimum wage requirements are still in effect as of this writing.

87 **"a ride-sharing network that is far cheaper":** Biz Carson, "Travis Kalanick on Uber's Bet on Self-Driving Cars: 'I Can't Be Wrong.'" *Business Insider*, August 18, 2016.

88 **One year earlier:** Michael Ballaban, "Tesla's Autopilot System Is Awesome and Creepy and a Sign of a Beautiful Future," *Jalopnik*, October 14, 2015.

88 **nothing more than vaporware:** Chris Smith, "World's First Self-Driving Taxi

Is Operational in Singapore, and It's Not Uber," *BGR*, August 25, 2016; Matt Richtel and Conor Dougherty, "Google's Driverless Cars Run Into Problem: Cars With Drivers," *New York Times*, September 1, 2015.

88 **About the only place:** Mike Ramsey, "Car Makers Hunger for Self-Driving Tech," *Wall Street Journal*, March 24, 2016.

88 **Everyone who said otherwise:** Mark Harris, "How a Robot Lover Pioneered the Driverless Car, and Why He's Selling His Latest to Uber," *The Guardian*, August 19, 2016; Nick Bilton, "The Looming Threat to Uber's Plan for World Domination," *Vanity Fair*, August 30, 2016.

89 **one out of every ten:** Harry Campbell, "How Many Uber Drivers Are There?" *Rideshare Guy*, March 17, 2023.

89 **"slogging":** Geoff Weiss, "Inside 'Operation SLOG,' Uber's Plan for Crushing Competitors," in *Entrepreneur*, August 27, 2014.

90 **$7 billion in cash on hand:** Timothy B. Lee, "Uber Lost $2.8 Billion in 2016. Will It Ever Become Profitable?" *Vox*, April 15, 2017.

90 **built Uber's new Advanced Technologies Group:** "Uber Launches First Self-Driving Taxi Fleet in US," in *Financial Times*, September 14, 2016.

90 **purchased an abandoned chocolate factory:** Cecilia Kang, "No Driver? Bring It On. How Pittsburgh Became Uber's Testing Ground," *New York Times*, September 11, 2016.

90 **just to smooth things over:** "Uber and Carnegie Mellon University: A Deeper Partnership," Uber press release, September 9, 2015.

92 **he won himself a job:** Burkhard Bilger, "Auto Correct," *The New Yorker*, November 17, 2013.

92 **the first-ever fully autonomous drive:** Nathaniel Fairfield, "On the Road with Self-Driving Car Number One," *Medium*, December 13, 2016.

92 **"We're loosing [sic] our tech advantage":** Anthony Levandowski, email to Larry Page, "Chauffeur: 'Team Mac' Urgently Needed," January 9, 2016.

93 **bought it for $680 million:** Mark Harris, "How Otto Defied Nevada and Scored a $680 Million Payout from Uber," *WIRED*, November 28, 2016.

93 **"brother from another mother":** Sarah Jeong, "Uber Is Just too Underhanded to Play the Underdog Against Waymo," *The Verge*, February 7, 2018.

93 **Uber had signed an agreement:** Volvo Cars, "Volvo Cars and Uber Join Forces to Develop Autonomous Driving Cars," press release, August 18, 2016.

94 **additional radar emitters:** Steve Crowe, "How Uber Self-Driving Cars See the World," *The Robot Report*, March 19, 2018.

94 **"see" in three dimensions:** Darrell Etherington, "Uber's Self-Driving Cars Start Picking up Passengers in San Francisco," *TechCrunch*, December 14, 2016.

94 **$20 million a month:** Mark Harris, "Uber's Self-Driving Car Unit Was Burning $20 Million a Month," *TechCrunch*, March 12, 2019.

95 **cost an estimated $85,000:** Steve LeVine, "What It Really Costs to Turn a Car

into a Self-Driving Vehicle," *Quartz*, March 5, 2017; Ryan Felton, "LIDAR Maker Velodyne Shifts Away Blame in Fatal Uber Self-Driving Crash," *Jalopnik*, March 23, 2018.

95 **"the laser is the sauce":** Cyrus Farivar, "Here's How to Use Kalanickspeak at Your Next Jam Sesh, Bro," *Ars Technica*, February 10, 2018.

95 **another $10,000 total:** Alex Davies, "Turns Out the Hardware in Self-Driving Cars Is Pretty Cheap," *WIRED*, April 22, 2015.

95 **a cost improvement:** Heather Somerville et al., "Uber's Use of Fewer Safety Sensors Prompts Questions After Arizona Crash," *Reuters*, March 28, 2018.

95 **happens on Uber's cloud:** "Building Uber's Fulfillment Platform for Planet-Scale Using Google Cloud Spanner," Uber Blog, September 29, 2021.

95 **5.2 billion trips:** "10 Billion," Uber Blog, July 24, 2018; Mansoor Iqbal, "Uber Revenue and Usage Statistics (2024)," *Business of Apps*, March 1, 2024.

95 **$221 million in server capacity:** Sebastian Moss, "Uber IPO Filing Reveals Data Center Details," *Data Center Dynamics*, April 12, 2019.

96 **four terabytes of information:** Patrick Nelson, "Just One Autonomous Car Will Use 4,000 GB of Data/Day," *Network World*, December 7, 2016.

97 **a 1948 paper entitled "Intelligent Machinery":** Alan M. Turing, "Intelligent Machinery," in *The Essential Turing: Seminal Writings in Computing, Logic, Philosophy, Artificial Intelligence, and Artificial life plus The Secrets of Enigma*, ed. B. Jack Copeland (Oxford: Oxford University Press, 2004), 412–15.

98 **"would probably take the form":** Turing, "Intelligent Machinery," 429. This discussion strongly foreshadows his formal proposal for his famous, and eponymous, test of whether a computer exhibits intelligent behavior, which he made in his 1950 paper "Computing Machines and Intelligence."

98 **single most important safety task:** Hongyu Li et al., "Automatic Unusual Driving Event Identification for Dependable Self-Driving," in *The 16th ACM Conference on Embedded Networked Sensor Systems (SenSys '18), November 4–7, 2018, Shenzhen, China* (New York: Association for Computing Machinery, 2018).

99 **the sheer volume of potential data:** Shenlong Wang et al., "Deep Parametric Continuous Convolutional Neural Networks," in *Proceedings of the IEEE Conference on Computer Vision and Pattern Recognition* (Los Alamitos, CA: Conference Publishing Services, 2018), 2589.

99 **To relieve some of the processing burden:** National Transportation Safety Board, *Collision Between Vehicle Controlled by Developmental Automated Driving System and Pedestrian, Tempe, Arizona, March 18, 2018* (Washington, DC: National Transportation Safety Board, 2019), 13.

100 **merely an expression of mathematical relationships:** Mercedes Bunz, "The Calculation of Meaning: On the Misunderstanding of New Artificial Intelligence as Culture," *Culture, Theory, and Critique* 60, no. 3–4 (September 2019), 272.

100 **recognized only four categories:** "Inside Uber ATG's Data Mining Operation; Identifying Real Road Scenarios at Scale for Machine Learning," Uber blog, June 2, 2020.

100 **The operator in the passenger seat:** Matt Ramney, "Self-Driving Cars as Edge Computing Devices," (presentation, QCon San Francisco, San Francisco, CA, February 10, 2020).

101 **Unlike automotive radar:** Holger H. Meinel et al., "Automotive Radar: From Its Origins to Future Directions," *Microwave Journal*, September 13, 2013; "History," Velodyne Lidar corporate website, accessed May 30, 2024.

101 **pedestrian who wore a shirt:** James Ochoa, "These Pranksters Exposed a Hole in Waymo's Autonomous Driving System," *The Street*, April 23, 2024.

102 **Now, a single person:** NTSB, *Collision*, 41.

105 **several "rider-experience" goals:** Julie Bort, "Uber Insiders Describe Infighting and Questionable Decisions Before its Self-Driving Car Killed a Pedestrian," *Business Insider*, November 19, 2018.

106 **According to a 2010 study:** D. C. Richards, *Relationship Between Speed and Risk of Fatal Injury: Pedestrians and Car Occupants* (London: Department for Transport, 2010).

106 **as a *BuzzFeed News* reporter:** Nicole Nguyen, "My Not Too Fast, Not Too Furious Ride in a Self-Driving Uber," *BuzzFeed News*, December 12, 2017.

106 **The computer could only display:** Kerry Flynn, "Uber's Driverless Future," *Mashable*, September 14, 2016.

107 **It was therefore imperative:** Daisuke Wakabayashi, "Uber's Self-Driving Cars Were Struggling Before Arizona Crash," *New York Times*, March 23, 2018.

107 **An operator named Rafaela Vasquez:** Lauren Smiley, " 'I'm the Operator': The Aftermath of a Self-Driving Tragedy," *WIRED*, March 8, 2022.

107 **The hundreds of thousands of miles:** "Engineering Uber's Self-Driving Car Visualization Platform for the Web," Uber blog, August 28, 2018.

107 **"irony of automation":** Lisanne Bainbridge, "Ironies of Automation," *Automatica* 19, no.6 (1983), 775.

108 **we used Slack like this:** Uber also had an internal chat tool called uChat until late 2017, which was based on Atlassian's Hipchat. But it was slow and buggy, and contractors did not have access to it. We used Slack as a workaround.

109 **engineers would hold "triage" meetings:** Bort, 2018.

109 **thirty-five times more crash-prone:** National Highway Traffic Safety Administration, *Traffic Safety Facts: 2021 Data* (Washington, DC: US Department of Transportation, 2023); David Shepardson, "US Driving Hits New Record in 2023, Topping Pre-COVID Levels," press release, February 8, 2024. Nearly 6 million traffic accidents occur each year against nearly 3.2 trillion vehicle miles traveled.

109 **there was no one whose job it was:** Uber Technologies, *Uber Advanced Technologies Group: A Principled Approach to Safety* (San Francisco: Uber Technologies, Inc., 2018), 66–68.

109 **"crushing miles":** Smiley, "I'm the Operator."

109 **forced ATG employees to really believe:** "Now, Next, and Future: Timothé Adeline," UberATG blog, September 30, 2019.

109 ***the* Anthony Levandowski:** Nick Statt, "Former Google Exec Anthony Levandowski Sentenced to 18 Months for Stealing Self-Driving Car Secrets," *The Verge*, August 4, 2020.

110 **Despite the fact that:** Kate Taylor and Benjamin Goggin, "49 of the Biggest Scandals in Uber's History," *Business Insider*, May 10, 2019.

110 **the average tenure at Uber:** Kaylee Fagan, "Silicon Valley Techies Get Free Food and Dazzling Offices, but They're Not Very Loyal," *Business Insider*, April 16, 2018.

110 **never spoke publicly:** Catherine Shu, "Report: A Manager at Uber's Self-Driving Unit Warned Executives about Safety Issues Just Days before Fatal Crash," *TechCrunch*, December 10, 2018.

110 **"what it means to keep on living":** Lauren Berlant, *Cruel Optimism* (Durham, NC: Duke University Press, 2011), 24.

110 **the Tempe Police Department built their case:** *The State of Arizona v. Rafael Stuart Vasquez*, Indictment 785 GJ 251 (Arizona, Superior Court, Maricopa County, August 27, 2020).

111 **Vasquez pled guilty:** David Shepardson, "Backup Driver in 2018 Uber Self-Driving Crash Pleads Guilty," *Reuters*, July 28, 2023.

111 **in order to settle:** Connie Loizos, "Uber Has Settled with the Family of the Homeless Victim Killed Last Week," *TechCrunch*, March 29, 2018.

111 **Then it sold the division:** Krystal Hu, Tina Bellon, and Jane Lanhee Lee, "Uber Sells ATG Self-Driving Business to Aurora at $4 Billion," *Reuters*, December 7, 2020.

111 **the company has yet to generate:** Rebecca Bellan, "Autonomous Vehicle Company Aurora Sells $820M Worth of Stock," *TechCrunch*, July 20, 2023.

111 **ATG's former head:** Max Chafkin, "Even After $100 Billion, Self-Driving Cars Are Going Nowhere," *Bloomberg Businessweek*, October 5, 2022.

CHAPTER 4: ALTERNATE REALITIES

116 **a literature PhD turned computer scientist:** David C. Brock, "The Improbable Origins of PowerPoint," *IEEE Spectrum*, October 31, 2017.

116 **"There was utterly no value":** Robert Gaskins, "Forethought Restart Completed (A Brief History)," email to Forethought Directors, May 25, 1987, 1.

117 **"better prepared, more professional":** Robert Gaskins, *'Presenter': New Product Summary and Review* (Sunnyvale, CA: Forethought, Inc., 1986), 9.

117 **This presentation software:** Robert Gaskins, *Presenter: Product Marketing Analysis* (Sunnyvale, CA: Forethought, Inc., 1986), 2

118 **"entertainment value":** Gaskins, *Presenter: Product Marketing Analysis*, 18.

118 **"familiar with computers":** Dennis Austin, *Beginnings of PowerPoint: A Personal Technical Story* (Mountain View, CA: Computer History Museum, 2009), 9.

118 **The prototype was meant:** Robert Gaskins, *Sweating Bullets: Notes about Inventing PowerPoint* (San Francisco: Vinland Books, 2012), 121.

118 **twenty-eight slides long:** Gaskins, *'Presenter': New Product Summary and Review.*

118 **twice the length of the average front-page newspaper:** Kevin G. Barnhurst and John C. Nerone, "Design Changes in U.S. Front Pages, 1885-1985," *Journalism Quarterly* 68 (December 1991), 799.

119 **largest consumer software companies:** Andrew Pollack, "Microsoft Has It All—Almost," *New York Times*, September 4, 1985.

119 **In the span of five years:** "The History of Microsoft," Microsoft Corporation, video series, accessed May 31, 2024.

119 **kept getting delayed:** Tim Anderson, "Windows Hits 25," *The Register*, November 20, 2010.

120 **He assumed control:** *Sweating Bullets*, 172, 190.

120 **a "business-oriented mindset":** Bill Gates, "Transcript of a Video History Interview with Mr. William 'Bill' Gates, Winner of the 1993 Price Waterhouse Leadership Award for Lifetime Achievement, Computerworld Smithsonian Awards," David Allison, Bellevue, WA, September 27, 1994.

120 **"be the leader in doing lots of products":** Gates, "Transcript of a Video History Interview."

120 **"dominate" and "crush" rivals:** Laurie Flynn and Rachel Parker, "Extending Its Reach," *InfoWorld* 11, no. 32 (August 7, 1989), 46; Victor Luckerson, "'Crush Them': An Oral History of the Lawsuit That Upended Silicon Valley," *The Ringer*, May 18, 2018.

120 **he emphasized profitability above all:** Computer History Archives Project, "Computer History: Rare Talk—Bill Gates on Competition, Lotus, IBM and the Future of Microsoft 1987," July 24, 2021; Andrew Pollack, "Apple Declines 27.3% as Lotus Burroughs and Cray Also Fall," *New York Times*, October 18, 1985; "Cullinet Software Inc. Reports Earnings for Qtr to July 31," *New York Times*, August 21, 1985.

120 **He bullied hardware vendors:** Rajiv Chandrasekharan, "Microsoft Bullied IBM, Court Told," *Washington Post*, June 7, 1999; European Committee for Interoperable Systems, *Microsoft's History of Anticompetitive Behaviour and Competitive Harm* (Brussels: European Committee for Interoperable Systems, 2009), 3–4.

121 **He scared venture capitalists:** Stratford P. Sherman, "Technology's Most Colorful Investor," *Fortune*, September 30, 1985. Lotus itself only received venture money from a firm that had invested in a rival spreadsheet maker, Visicalc, and was smart enough to move its money to the winner before it was too late.
121 **"hostagelike":** Flynn and Parker, 45.
121 **Its offer for the full market value:** *Sweating Bullets*, 198.
121 **"administration, finance, and operations areas":** Robert Gaskins, *Lessons from the Experience of the Restart* (Sunnyvale, CA: Forethought, Inc., 1987), 2.
121 **the competition was already circling:** *Sweating Bullets*, 186.
122 **Forethought officially became a part of Microsoft:** "Microsoft Buys Software Unit," *New York Times*, July 31, 1987.
122 **a market ten times larger:** Bill Gates, memorandum, "Market Share of Applications in the United States," February 19, 1991.
122 **"Wet Paint" signs:** *Sweating Bullets*, 358.
122 **"chart junk":** *Sweating Bullets*, 348.
123 **most of his original cohort:** *Sweating Bullets*, 390.
123 **fifty times as many units:** Priyanka Sen, "Disruption, Innovation, and Endurance: A Brief History of PowerPoint," Hult International Business School blog, June 13, 2018. The lower revenue per unit is due to the way Microsoft attributed revenue to each product line in the Office bundle.
123 **750 million PowerPoint presentations every month:** Stephen M. Kosslyn et al., "PowerPoint® Presentation Flaws and Failures: A Psychological Analysis," in *Frontiers in Psychology* 3 (2012).
123 **an hour a day:** *The Big PowerPoint Study* (New York: Made in Office, 2015), 2.
123 **Beginning in 1992:** Michael Davis, "Enron: Making of the Market-Maker," *Houston Chronicle*, April 15, 2001.
123 **complex shell game:** Enron Corporation, *Enron Annual Report 2000*, January 2001.
123 **clever accounting tricks:** "Timeline: A Chronology of Enron Corp.," *New York Times*, January 18, 2006.
124 **These presentations featured:** Nathan Gregory, "Why Believe in Enron," December 10, 2014, video, 33:30; Nathan Gregory, "Enron Employee Meeting Part 1," March 20, 2009, video, 8:56; various exhibits from *United States v. Kenneth L. Lay* and *United States v. Jeffrey K. Skilling*: "Presentation: 'DPR Overview—Presented by Mike Moscoso'" (Exhibit 002613, April 26, 2006); "Email dated August 24, 2001 From: Chris Loehr To: Anne Yaeger Subject: some random files—with attachments" (Exhibit no. 007810); "Presentation: Enron Energy Services—All Employee Meeting—March 27, 2001" (Exhibit no. 006619).
124 **"from the world's leading energy company":** Gabel305, "Enron Employee Meeting Part 4," March 20, 2009, video, 8:55.

124 **the largest corporate bankruptcy in history:** Richard A. Oppel Jr. and Andrew Ross Sorkin, "Enron's Collapse: The Overview; Enron Corp. Files Largest U.S. Claim for Bankruptcy," *New York Times*, December 3, 2001.

125 **"You're the only financial institution":** Enron Corporation, "Q1 2001 Earnings Call," April 17, 2001.

125 **"Iraq: Failing to Disarm":** US State Department, *U.S. Secretary of State Colin Powell Addresses the U.N. Security Council*, February 5, 2003.

126 **"known fabricator":** Walter Pincus, "Panel Seeks Intelligence Culpability," *Washington Post*, April 1, 2005.

126 **According to a postwar assessment:** Iraq Survey Group, *Comprehensive Report of the Special Advisor to the DCI on Iraq's WMD, Vol. 1* (Alexandria, VA: GlobalSecurity.org, 2004), 63–66.

126 **"dead wrong":** "Panel Says 'Dead Wrong' Data on Prewar Iraq Demands Overhaul," *New York Times*, March 31, 2005.

126 **statements opposing an invasion:** Julia Preston, "U.N. Envoys Said to Differ Sharply in Reaction to Powell Speech," *New York Times*, February 7, 2003.

126 **joint American, British, and Spanish resolution:** "U.S., U.K., Spain Introduce New Iraq Resolution," *CNN*, February 24, 2003.

126 **the majority of Americans:** Carroll Doherty and Jocelyn Kiley, "A Look Back at How Fear and False Beliefs Bolstered U.S. Public Support for War in Iraq," report for Pew Research Center, March 14, 2023.

126 **President George W. Bush:** US Congress, House, "Authorization for Use of Military Force against Iraq Resolution of 2002," H.J. Res. 114, 107th Congress, October 16, 2002.

127 **"I didn't lie":** Karen DeYoung and Missy Ryan, "Iraq War Was a Stain on Powell's Record—One He Said He Regretted," *Washington Post*, October 18, 2021.

128 **One such exercise:** "McKinsey in Advanced Talks with US States to Settle Opioid Claims," *Financial Times*, January 28, 2021.

128 **"$$$$" to "$":** Walt Bogdanich and Michael Forsythe, "McKinsey Proposed Paying Pharmacy Companies Rebates for OxyContin Overdoses," *New York Times*, November 27, 2020; Maisie Wiltshire-Gordon, "How Euphemistic Corporate Language Aided Purdue Pharma's Role in the Opioid Crisis," *Current Affairs*, January 14, 2023.

129 **tens of thousands of slides:** Mollie Reilly and Max J. Rosenthal, "Insurance Claim Delays Deliver Massive Profits to Industry by Shorting Customers," *Huffington Post*, December 13, 2011.

129 **"detention savings opportunities":** McKinsey & Company, "Summary of detention savings opportunities," presentation to US Immigration and Customs Enforcement, published in Ian McDougall, "How McKinsey Helped the Trump Administration Detain and Deport Immigrants," *ProPublica*, December 3, 2019, 184.

129 **"low cost beds":** McDougall, "How McKinsey Helped the Trump Administration," 191.

130 **budget nearly $1 billion:** Sara Fischer, "Big Cuts Coming for CNN+ after Slow Start," *Axios*, April 12, 2022.

130 **2020 launch and collapse:** Julia Alexander, "11 Reasons Why Quibi Crashed and Burned in Less than a Year," *The Verge*, October 22, 2020.

130 **90 percent of whom:** Sara Fischer, "Scoop: CNN+ Looks Doomed," *Axios*, April 19, 2022.

130 **a $300 million mistake:** Fischer, "Scoop."

130 **"comparable to 'gold standards'":** Dan Primack, "Exclusive: Theranos 2006 Pitch Deck," *Axios*, December 15, 2017.

131 **let alone the thirty:** Nicole Wetsman, "Theranos Promised a Blood Testing Revolution—Here's What's Really Possible," *The Verge*, December 15, 2021.

131 **a tight eleven-slide presentation:** FTX Trading, Ltd., "FTX," 2021.

131 **$1.8 billion from investors:** "FTX," *Crunchbase*, accessed May 30, 2024; Berber Jin, "Sequoia Capital Apologizes to Its Fund Investors for FTX Loss," *Wall Street Journal*, November 22, 2022.

131 **falsified org charts:** Kia Kokalitcheva, "Sequoia Capital partner says firm was 'misled' by FTX," *Axios*, January 13, 2023.

132 **appropriating customer deposits:** Emma Roth, Elizabeth Lopatto, and Makena Kelly, "The many lies of Sam Bankman-Fried," *The Verge*, December 13, 2022.

132 **"working closely" with regulators:** *United States v. Samuel Bankman-Fried*, Superseding Indictment S5 22 Cr. 673 (New York, Southern District Court, New York, March 28, 2023).

132 **"one of the biggest financial frauds":** Alexander Saeedy, "FTX Says $8.9 Billion in Customer Funds Are Missing," *Wall Street Journal*, March 2, 2023.

132 **The foam measured:** *Columbia Accident Investigation Board Report Vol. 2* (Washington, DC: Government Printing Office, 2003), 11–14.

133 **"didn't look like a big enough piece":** *Columbia Accident Investigation*, 141.

133 **no high-resolution images:** *Columbia Accident Investigation*, 152–54.

133 **"hazard analysis":** *Columbia Accident Investigation*, 188.

134 **"Crater overpredicted penetration":** *Columbia Accident Investigation*, 191.

135 **largely correct:** *Columbia Accident Investigation*, 66.

135 **"rapid catastrophic sequential structural breakdown":** *Columbia Accident Investigation*, 77.

136 **Facebook's user count had doubled:** "Facebook Users Up 89% Over Last Year; Demographic Shift," *TechCrunch*, July 6, 2007.

137 **70 percent of Facebook users:** "Bambi Francisco Interviews Mark Zuckerberg in 2005," *Dow Jones Marketwatch*, date unknown.

137 **supposed user backlash:** Mark Zuckerberg, "Calm Down. Breathe. We Hear You." Facebook post, September 6, 2006.

137 **early Facebook profile:** Jillian D'Onfro and Megan Rose Dickey, "Facebook Looked Completely Different 10 Years Ago—Here's What's Changed over the Years," *Business Insider*, February 4, 2014.

137 **"we simply want to ensure":** Matthew Peter Nagowski, "A Conversation with Mark Zuckerberg," *The Current*, October 2005.

137 **"Right now we have 30 million users":** Laura Locke, "The Future of Facebook," *Time*, July 17, 2007.

137 **$85 per month:** Rip Empson, "Facebook's First Server Cost $85/Month," *TechCrunch*, October 20, 2012.

138 **signed a contract with Microsoft:** David Kirkpatrick, "Facebook's plan to hook up the world," *Fortune*, May 29, 2007.

138 **new feature called Social Ads:** "Facebook Unveils Facebook Ads," Facebook blog, November 6, 2007.

138 **The company originally designed:** "People You May Know," Facebook Help Center, accessed May 29, 2024.

138 **they would soon find themselves:** M. J. Franklin, "'People You May Know' Is the Perfect Demonstration of Everything That's Wrong with Facebook," *Mashable*, May 15, 2018.

138 **a history of talking on the phone:** Amelia Tait, "People You May Know: Is Facebook's Friend-Finding Algorithm Putting You at Risk?" *New Statesman*, September 5, 2016.

138 **Microsoft put a stop:** "Facebook Connect Is No Longer Available," Microsoft Support, accessed May 30, 2024.

138 **surface you as a potential "friend":** Kashmir Hill, "Facebook Is Using Your Phone's Location to Suggest New Friends—Which Could Be a Privacy Disaster," *Splinter*, June 28, 2016.

139 **That number has increased:** Facebook, Inc., *Annual Report 2012*, January 2013, 47; Meta Platforms, Inc., *Annual Report 2023*, January 2024, 69.

139 **Facebook salespeople worked out agreements:** Sarah Aisher, "Myanmar Coup: How Facebook Became the 'Digital Tea Shop,'" *BBC News*, February 4, 2021; Aleksander Deejay and Tamas Wells, "How Activists Are Using Facebook in Myanmar for Democratic Ends, But Facebook Itself Also Facilitated Hate Speech," *LSE Blog*, June 23, 2021.

140 **just under half the population:** Simon Kemp, "Digital 2021: Myanmar," DataReportal, February 12, 2021.

140 **"'Friends' on Facebook":** Craig Mod, "The Facebook-Loving Farmers of Myanmar," *The Atlantic*, January 21, 2016.

141 **varying levels of intimidation and violence:** UN Human Rights Council Independent International Fact-Finding Mission on Human Rights in Myanmar, *Report of the detailed findings of the Independent International Fact-Finding Mission on Human Rights in Myanmar* (Geneva: United Nations, 2018), 6–9.

141 **These sock puppet accounts:** Paul Mozur, "A Genocide Incited on Facebook, With Posts from Myanmar's Military," *New York Times*, October 15, 2018.

141 **"extinction of Buddhism":** UN Human Rights Council, 170–71.

142 **calling for a ban on beef slaughtering:** Swe Win, "With Official Help, Radical Buddhists Target Muslim Businesses," *The Irrawaddy*, September 17, 2015.

142 **"breaking laws":** Center for Advanced Defense Studies, *Sticks and Stones: Hate Speech Narratives and Facilitators in Myanmar* (Washington, DC: C4ADS), 21–22.

142 **the appearance of organically "viral" content:** *Sticks and Stones*, 16–17.

142 **By late 2015:** *Sticks and Stones*, 22–26.

142 **"clearance operations":** "Burma: Four 'Race and Religion Protection Laws' Adopted," *Global Legal Monitor*, September 14, 2015; " 'Hundreds of Rohingyas' Killed in Myanmar Crackdown," *Al Jazeera*, February 3, 2017.

143 **over one thousand malicious posts per day:** Steve Stecklow, "Why Facebook Is Losing the War on Hate Speech in Myanmar," *Reuters*, August 15, 2018.

143 **three times the volume:** Casey Newton, "The Trauma Floor," *The Verge*, February 25, 2019.

143 **a series of investigations:** Oliver Holmes and Emanuel Stoakes, "Fears Mount of Myanmar Atrocities as Fleeing Rohingya Families Drown," *The Guardian*, September 1, 2017.

143 **"coordinated inauthentic behavior":** "Removing Myanmar Military Officials from Facebook," Facebook Newsroom, August 28, 2018.

144 **around the world:** "Sri Lanka: Facebook Apologises for Role in 2018 Anti-Muslim Riots," *Al Jazeera*, May 13, 2020; Emmanuel Akinwotu, "Facebook's Role in Myanmar and Ethiopia Under New Scrutiny," *The Guardian*, October 7, 2021; Sheera Frenkel and Davey Alba, "In India, Facebook Grapples With an Amplified Version of Its Problems," *New York Times*, October 23, 2021.

144 **first five seconds:** Paul Doncaster, *The UX Five-Second Rules: Guidelines for User Experience Design's Simplest Testing Technique* (Burlington, MA: Morgan Kaufmann, 2014).

144 **On average, 60 percent:** Laura Ceci, "Average Three Month User Retention and Churn Rate of Mobile Apps Worldwide as of 2nd Half 2018," Statista, August 25, 2023.

144 **TikTok leads off:** WSJ Staff, "Inside TikTok's Algorithm: A WSJ Video Investigation," *Wall Street Journal*, July 21, 2021.

144 **about 5,400 videos:** Dan Slee, "CLIPPED: I watched the 100 best TikTok videos to find the optimum length of a clip," personal blog, January 21, 2020; Raitis Purins, "How to TikTok: 4 Key Steps as Told by a Brand," *AIThority*, January 15, 2021.

145 **One *Wall Street Journal* test:** "Investigation: How TikTok's Algorithm Figures Out Your Deepest Desires," *Wall Street Journal*, July 21, 2021.

145 **glorifying extreme diets and anorexia:** Tawnell D. Hobbs et al., "'The Corpse Bride Diet': How TikTok Inundates Teens with Eating-Disorder Videos," *Wall Street Journal*, December 17, 2021.

145 **advocate self-injury and suicide:** "Investigation," *Wall Street Journal*.

145 **"what I eat in a day":** Shannon Herrick, "'This Is Just How I Cope': An Inductive Thematic Analysis of Eating Disorder Recovery Content Created and Shared on TikTok Using #EDrecovery," *International Journal of Eating Disorders* 54, no. 4 (December 2020), 517–19.

146 **moderation removes only about 1 percent:** Amanda Silberling, "TikTok Removed 81 Million Videos for Violations in Q2, Representing 1% of Uploads," *TechCrunch*, October 13, 2021.

CHAPTER 5: WHAT IT IS LIKE TO BE A COMPUTER

158 **"low-intensity, low-technology" civil war:** *Final Report of the Panel of Experts on Libya Established Pursuant to Security Council Resolution 1973 (2011)* (Geneva: United Nations, 2021), 17.

158 **"the advancement towards the heart of the capital":** "Libyan Commander Haftar Orders Forces to Advance on Tripoli in 'Final Battle,'" *Reuters*, December 12, 2019.

158 **secret flights began to ferry:** United Nations Support Mission in Libya, *UNSMIL Statement on Continued Violations of Arms Embargo in Libya*, January 25, 2020.

159 **"automatic target recognition system":** STM, "KARGU®: Combat Proven Rotary Wing Loitering Munition System," sales brochure, accessed May 30, 2024.

159 **One such system, called "Lavender":** Yuval Abraham, "'Lavender': The AI machine directing Israel's bombing spree in Gaza," *+972 Magazine*, April 3, 2024.

160 **A third system, "the Gospel":** Yuval Abraham, "'A Mass Assassination Factory': Inside Israel's Calculated Bombing of Gaza," *+972 Magazine*, November 30, 2023.

160 **"world leading Facial Intelligence technology":** Robert Watts, "Please Join Us Next Week in Farnborough," LinkedIn post, April 2024.

160 **"help the intelligence analysts":** "Israel Defence Forces' Response to Claims about the Use of 'Lavender' AI Database in Gaza," *The Guardian*, April 3, 2024.

161 **videos uploaded to YouTube:** Alleydefence, "STM KARGU-2 Kamikaze Drone," June 5, 2023, video, 1:04.

161 **"Are you sure you want to go to the mission point?":** STM, "STM KARGU (Autonomous Tactical Multi-Rotor Attack UAV)," April 28, 2018, video, 0:52. Translation via Google Translate.

161 **"indiscriminate attacks":** International Committee of the Red Cross, *Customary International Humanitarian Laws*, accessed May 29, 2024.

161 **less time than the average social media moderator:** Newton, "The Trauma Floor"; Mosab Abu Taha, "A Palestinian Poet's Perilous Journey Out of Gaza," *New Yorker*, December 25, 2023.

161 **According to the British nonprofit Oxfam:** Oxfam International, "Daily death rate in Gaza higher than any other major 21st Century conflict – Oxfam," press release, January 11, 2024.

162 **one out of every hundred:** Victoria Kim, "Death Toll in Gaza Passes 30,000," *New York Times*, February 29, 2024.

162 **The British medical journal *The Lancet*:** Zeina Jamaluddine, "Excess Mortality in Gaza: October 7-26, 2023," *The Lancet*, November 26, 2023.

162 **only Germany has issued a blanket ban:** Federal Republic of Germany Foreign Office, *Group of Experts on Emerging Technologies in the Area of Lethal Autonomous Weapons Systems of the Convention on Prohibition or Restrictions on the Use of Certain Conventional Weapons Which May Be Deemed to Be Excessively Injurious or to Have Indiscriminate Effects*, March 26, 2019.

162 **"autonomous weapon systems should remain under meaningful human control":** Sandra de Jonogh, "Statement of the Netherlands," statement presented at the *Group of Experts on LAWS Conference*, Geneva, April 26, 2019.

162 **"human control should be considered":** United Kingdom, "Statement at Meeting of Group of Governmental Experts on Emerging Technologies in the Area of Lethal Autonomous Weapons Systems," statement presented at the *Meeting of Group of Governmental Experts on Emerging Technologies in the Area of Lethal Autonomous Weapons Systems*, Geneva, March 25–29, 2019.

162 **"in a secure, credible, reliable and manageable manner":** "Working Paper of the People's Republic of China on Lethal Autonomous Weapons Systems," July 2022, trans. United Nations Office for Disarmament Affairs.

163 **"broader human involvement in decisions":** Kelly M. Sayler, "Defense Primer: U.S. Policy on Lethal Autonomous Weapon Systems," report for Congressional Research Service, March 27, 2019.

163 **$30 billion:** *Autonomous Weapons Market 2021* (Allied Market Research, 2021).

163 **relative to the $2.2 trillion:** Nan Tian et al., *Trends in World Military Expenditure, 2022* (Stockholm: SIPRI, 2023).

163 **little previous experience:** Sam Biddle, "Google Won't Say Anything about Israel Using Its Photo Software to Create Gaza 'Hit List,'" *The Intercept*, April 5, 2024.

164 **"only slightly removed from pure thought-stuff":** Frederick P. Brooks Jr., *The Mythical Man-Month: Essays on Software Engineering* (Reading, MA: Addison-Wesley, 1975), 7.

165 **"human beings are not accustomed to being perfect":** *Mythical Man-Month*, 8.

167 **Russian soldier Ruslan Antinin:** Stephen Kalin, Isabel Coles, and Ievgeniia Sivorka, "The Russian Soldier Who Surrendered to a Ukrainian Drone," *Wall Street Journal*, June 14, 2023.

CHAPTER 6: CALCULATIONS IN AN EMERGENCY

171 **chaos cannot be predicted:** Bruce M. Boghosian et al., "A New Pathology in the Simulation of Chaotic Dynamical Systems on Digital Computers," *Advanced Theory and Simulations* 2, vol. 12 (September 23, 2019).

171 **common but usually not dangerous:** John R. Allan, "The Costs of Bird Strikes and Bird Strike Prevention," in *Human Conflicts with Wildlife: Economic Considerations* (Lincoln, NE: DigitalCommons@University of Nebraska-Lincoln, 2000).

172 **rivaling that of a car crash:** "Aircraft Certification for Bird Strike Risk," *SKYbrary Aviation Safety*, accessed May 29, 2024.

172 **There was no time:** Narrative adapted from National Transportation Safety Board, *Loss of Thrust in Both Engines After Encountering a Flock of Birds and Subsequent Ditching on the Hudson River, US Airways Flight 1549, Airbus A320-214, N106US, Weehawken, New Jersey, January 15, 2009* (Washington, DC: National Transportation Safety Board, 2010).

173 **flowed down the intakes:** NTSB, *Loss of Thrust*, 81.

173 **"digital fly-by-wire":** Barnaby J. Feder, "The A320's Fly-by-Wire System," *New York Times*, June 29, 1988.

173 **Without engine power:** NTSB, *Loss of Thrust*, 13, 170.

175 **stand out in three ways:** "Fly-by-wire (1980–1987)," Airbus blog, accessed May 29, 2024.

175 **half a ton of heavy steel:** Bryce L. Horvath and Douglas P. Wells, "Comparison of Aircraft Conceptual Design Weight Estimation Methods to the Flight Optimization System," presented at *2018 American Institute of Aeronautics and Astronautics Aerospace Sciences Meeting*, Kissimmee, FL, January 7, 2018.

176 **more than two out of three:** George E. Cooper, Maurice D. White, and John K. Lauber, eds., *Resource Management on the Flightdeck: Proceedings of a NASA/Industry Workshop* (Moffett Field, CA: NASA-Ames Research Center, 1980).

178 **irreverent call sign:** Dawn Gilbertson, "'Cactus' Call Sign Fades into US Airways History," *Arizona Republic*, April 10, 2015.

181 **the prison of top-down logic:** Karsten Rauss and Gilles Pourtois, "What Is Bottom-Up and What Is Top-Down in Predictive Coding?," *Frontiers in Psychology* 4 (May 17, 2013).

181 **billions of parameters:** Jonathan Frankle, "Do Neural Networks Really Need to Be So Big?" MIT-IBM Watson AI Lab blog, February 12, 2021.

184 **the airplane's radar:** NTSB, *Loss of Thrust*, 177.

185 **the gift of focus:** *Loss of Thrust*, 48.
186 **9.5 degrees:** *Loss of Thrust*, 75.
188 **"We were always ready":** Bernard Ziegler, *Les Cow-boys d'Airbus* (Paris: PRIVAT, 2008), 27. The translation is my own.
190 **people began to boycott:** Nick Statt, "#DeleteUber Reportedly Led 200,000 People to Delete Their Accounts," *The Verge*, February 2, 2017.
190 **"as well as diversity and inclusion":** Dan Primacy, "Was Uber Smart to Hire Eric Holder?" *Axios*, June 20, 2017.
191 **demanded to know:** Johana Bhuiyan, "Travis Kalanick Discussed Compensating the Driver He Berated in That Viral Video," *Vox*, January 16, 2018.
191 **All this was caught:** Eric Newcomer, "In Video, Uber CEO Argues with Driver over Falling Fares," *Bloomberg News*, February 28, 2017.
191 **began to leak:** Sam Levin, "Uber's Scandals, Blunders, and PR Disasters: The Full List," *The Guardian*, June 27, 2017.
191 **His only excuse:** Michael Safi, "Uber Executive 'Had No Reason to Obtain Rape Victim's Medical Records,'" *The Guardian*, June 8, 2017.
191 **unanimously accepted by the Board:** Darrell Etherington, "Uber's Board Votes Unanimously to Adopt All Recommendations of Holder Report," *TechCrunch*, June 11, 2017.
191 **Only twenty employees:** Kia Kokalitcheva, "Uber Details Changes, Including Time off for CEO Kalanick," *Axios*, June 13, 2017.
192 **David Bonderman:** Nicholas Varchaver, "One False Move," *Fortune*, April 4, 2005.
193 **"a new Uber [to] emerge":** Kara Swisher, "Arianna Huffington's Speech to Uber Staff: A 'New Uber' Will Emerge from Crisis," *Vox*, June 13, 2017.
194 **dumb and sexist joke:** Mike Isaac and Susan Chira, "David Bonderman Resigns from Uber Board after Sexist Remark," *New York Times*, June 13, 2017.
195 **a standard feature of corporate boards:** Franklin A. Gevurtz, "The Historical and Political Origins of the Corporate Board of Directors," *Hofstra Law Review* 33, no. 1 (2004): 100–102.
195 **"material suffering, even short of death":** See *In re Caremark International Inc. Derivative Legislation*, 698 A.2d 959 (Delaware Court of Chancery, 1996).
195 **Negligent boards have been successfully sued:** Edward B. Micheletti, "The Risk of Overlooking Oversight: Recent *Caremark* Decisions from the Court of Chancery Indicate Closer Judicial Scrutiny and Potential Increased Traction for Oversight Claims," *Insights: The Delaware Edition*, December 15, 2021.
196 **helped the company:** "How Much of Boeing's Revenues Comes from the U.S. Government?" *Forbes*, January 2, 2020; Veronique de Rugy and Justin Leventhal, "Ex-Im: Still 'Boeing's Bank,'" report for Mercatus Center at George Mason University, August 31, 2018.

196 **never held a dedicated session:** The Boeing Company, "Boeing Chairman, President and CEO Dennis Muilenburg and Boeing Board of Directors Reaffirm Company's Commitment to Safety," press release, September 25, 2019.

196 **The second was in April 2019:** *In re The Boeing Company derivative litigation*, C.A. 2019-0907-MTZ (Delaware Court of Chancery, 2021), 77–80.

196 **"Press is terrible. Very tough":** "Boeing board reeled from 'terrible' press after first Max crash," *Crain's Chicago Business*, March 4, 2021.

196 **supermajority:** Microsoft, Inc., "2,795,000 Shares, Microsoft Corporation Common Stock," IPO prospectus, March 13, 1986, 30.

197 **likely the largest proportion:** By contrast, Larry Page and Sergey Brin together control about 52 percent of the Alphabet shareholder vote; Warren Buffet controls about 31 percent of Berkshire Hathway; and Jeff Bezos controls about 16 percent of Amazon.

197 **"novel articulation of internet governance":** Kate Klonick, "The Facebook Oversight Board: Creating an Independent Institution to Adjudicate Online Free Expression," in *Yale Law Journal* 129, no. 8 (June 2020), 2418.

197 **wave of bad actions:** Nicholas Confessore, "Cambridge Analytica and Facebook: The Scandal and the Fallout So Far," *New York Times*, April 4, 2018.

200 **"considerations related to the interaction":** Federal Aviation Administration, *Operational Use of Flight Path Management Systems*, September 5, 2013, 91.

200 **no idea what they were looking at:** US Department of Transportation Office of Inspector General, *Timeline of Activities Leading to the Certification of the Boeing 737 MAX 8 Aircraft and Actions Taken After the October 2018 Lion Air Accident* (Washington, DC: Office of Government and Public Affairs, 2020), 8.

200 **"there is no confidence":** Boeing internal email from anonymous Aero-Stability & Control & AR Advisor, "RE: For 2pm," February 25, 2016.

200 **"The DCGA":** Instant messages from anonymous Boeing employee to (former) 737 Chief Technical Pilot, May 29, 2015.

200 **"led to a significant misunderstanding":** US Department of Transportation Office of Inspector General, *Weaknesses in FAA's Certification and Delegation Process Hindered its Oversight of the 737 MAX 8* (Washington, DC: Office of Government and Public Affairs, 2021), 2.

200 **the end of 2025:** *Aircraft Certification: Comparison of U.S. and European Processes for Approving New Designs of Commercial Transport Airplanes* (Washington, DC: Government Accountability Office, 2022), 46.

201 **Facebook's user agreement "sucks":** Abdi Latif Dahir, "'English not Swahili': The Ill-Placed Call from a US Senator on Rewriting Facebook's User Terms," *Quartz*, April 12, 2018.

201 **"collecting medical data":** *Facebook: Transparency and Use of Consumer Data, Hearing before the Committee on Energy and Commerce*, 115th Congress, 101 (2018) (question from Katherine Ann Castor, Representative from Florida).

201 **"Senator, we run ads":** "Transcript of Mark Zuckerberg's Senate Hearing," *Washington Post*, April 10, 2018.

201 **$2 million:** Marianne Bertrand et al., "Hall of Mirrors: Corporate Philanthropy and Strategic Advocacy," *NBER*, December 2018.

201 **a combined $96 million:** "Industry Profile: Internet," "Industry Profile: Electronics Mfg & Equip," "Industry Profile: Defense," *OpenSecrets*, accessed May 30, 2024. Company list includes Alphabet/Google, Amazon, Apple, Boeing, ByteDance, Meta/Facebook, and Uber.

201 **more in 2023 by itself:** "Client Profile: Meta," *OpenSecrets*, accessed May 30, 2024.

202 **"cultural consensus around the 'public interest'":** Wendy Y. Li, "Regulatory Capture's Third Face of Power," in *Socio-Economic Review* 21, no. 2 (April 2023), 1221.

202 **attack on "free speech":** Jeffrey Rosen, "The Deciders: Facebook, Google, and the Future of Privacy and Free Speech," report for the Brookings Institute, May 2, 2011.

202 **a 2020 California ballot measure:** Nicole Karlis, "Uber and Lyft Launch Anti-Labor Misinformation Campaign in Response to Historic California Bill," *Salon*, September 11, 2019.

202 ***Gonzales v. Google:*** Hailey Fuchs and Brendan Bordelon, "Google Tries to 'Astroturf' the Supreme Court," *Politico*, February 17, 2023.

202 **"divest-or-ban":** April Rubin, "'My Livelihood at Stake': TikTokers Revolt against Potential Ban," *Axios*, March 13, 2024.

202 **The Honest Ads Act:** For the People Act, H.R. 1, 117th Congress (2021).

202 **"dominant online platforms":** Platform Competition and Opportunity Act, H.R. 3826, 117th Congress (2021).

202 **$180 million campaign:** Nicole Karlis, "Uber-Funded Ballot Measure in California Would Create 'Permanent Underclass of Workers,' Expert Says," *Salon*, October 1, 2020.

203 **"deceiving users about their ability":** Federal Trade Commission, "FTC Imposes $5 Billion Penalty and Sweeping New Privacy Restrictions on Facebook," press release, July 24, 2019.

203 **one of the largest civil penalties:** Office of Public Affairs, US Department of Justice, "Facebook Agrees to Pay $5 Billion and Implement Robust New Protections of User Information in Settlement of Data-Privacy Claims," press release, July 24, 2019.

203 **three weeks to earn enough money:** Meta Platforms, Inc., "Facebook Reports Fourth Quarter and Full Year 2019 Results," press release, January 29, 2020.

203 **more than $800 million:** "Uber Technologies" and "Lyft Inc.," Violation Tracker, *Good Jobs First*, accessed May 30, 2024.

203 **"maximum amount of damages":** Matthew Barakat, "Google Wants Judge, Not Jury, to Decide Upcoming Antitrust Case in Virginia," *Associated Press*, May 17, 2024.

203 **"Magna Carta of data protection":** Michal Gal and Oshrit Aviv, "The Competitive Effects of the GDPR," *Journal of Competition Law and Economics* 16, no. 3 (September 2020), 349.

204 **ten times more reprimands:** Seb Joseph, "Five Years In, the GDPR Has Had a Double-Edged Impact on the Ad Market," *Digiday*, May 25, 2023; Johnny Ryan, "Don't Be Fooled by Meta's Fine for Data Breaches, Says Johnny Ryan," *The Economist*, May 24, 2023;

204 **$300 billion and growing:** *Global Data Broker Market Size, Share, Opportunities, COVID-19 Impact, and Trends by Data Type (Consumer Data, Business Data), by End-User (BFSI, Retail, Automotive, Construction, Others), and by Geography—Forecasts from 2023 to 2028* (Uttar Pradesh: Knowledge Sourcing Intelligence, 2023).

204 **To paraphrase Peter Reinhardt:** Peter Reinhardt, "Replacing Middle Management with APIs," personal blog, February 3, 2015.

CHAPTER 7: THE MIMICS

208 **"When you feel like":** Barifelps, "This Is All the Ads Currently Being Promoted by Replika's Company on Facebook and Instagram in the USA—Thrusday [sic], 15/02/2023," Reddit post, February 15, 2023.

208 **"Two reasons to download":** daytonim, "Found an Instagram ad for Replika. These Are the First 2 Reasons They Gave for Downloading the App," Reddit post, November 5, 2022; WalrusLimePie, "Replika AI—ads vs gameplay | Badvertising," January 22, 2023, video, 9:30.

208 **GPT-2 and GPT-3 models:** "How Does Replika Work?" Replika blog, accessed May 30, 2024.

209 **erotic roleplay:** Samantha Cole, "Replika CEO Says AI Companions Were Not Meant to Be Horny. Users Aren't Buying It," *Vice*, February 17, 2023.

209 **so-called loneliness epidemic:** *Our Epidemic of Loneliness and Isolation: U.S. Surgeon General's Advisory on the Healing Effects of Social Connection and Community* (Washington, DC: US Public Health Service, 2023), 72.

211 **entire monthly cell phone plan:** Jeannine Mancini, "What is the Average Cell Phone Bill per Month?" *MoneyLion*, March 29, 2024.

211 **permission to track you:** Mozilla Foundation, "Replika: My AI Friend," *Privacy Not Included*, February 7, 2024.

212 **"emotional and sexual relationship":** Tom Singleton, Tom Gerken, and Liv McMahon, "How a Chatbot Encouraged a Man Who Wanted to Kill the Queen," *BBC News*, October 6, 2023.

214 **fastest-growing software application in history:** Jon Porter, "ChatGPT Continues to Be One of the Fastest-Growing Services Ever," *The Verge*, November 6, 2023.

216 **"As the dawn of generative AI":** Bernard Marr, "Generative AI: The Mindset Divide That Will Determine Your Success," *Forbes*, November 14, 2023.

216 **"Study after study":** "Generative AI Generates Tricky Choices for Managers," *The Economist*, November 27, 2023.

216 **"substantial impacts on marketing":** Thomas H. Davenport and Nitin Mittal, "How Generative AI Is Changing Creative Work," *Harvard Business Review*, November 14, 2022; Govind Bhutada, "Visualizing U.S. GDP by Industry in 2023," *Visual Capitalist*, November 28, 2023.

216 **Deloitte first projected:** Brenna Sniderman, Diana Kearns-Manolatos, and Nitin Mittal, "Generating Value from Generative AI," *Deloitte Center for Integrated Research*, October 26, 2023.

216 ***Bloomberg Intelligence*'s prediction:** "Generative AI to Become a $1.3 Trillion Market by 2032, Research Finds," *Bloomberg*, June 1, 2023.

216 **McKinsey put the number:** Michael Chu et al., *The Economic Potential of Generative AI: The Next Productivity Frontier* (New York: McKinsey & Company, 2023).

216 **a nice round $7 trillion:** Goldman Sachs, *Generative AI Could Raise Global GDP by 7%* (New York: Goldman Sachs, 2023).

217 **"have a high or extremely high impact":** KPMG, "KPMG U.S. Survey: Executives Expect Generative AI to Have Enormous Impact on Business, But Unprepared for Immediate Adoption," press release, April 24, 2023.

217 **ratio surpassed nine in ten:** Brenda Sniderman, Diana Kearns-Manolatos, and Nitin Mittal, *Generating Value from Generative AI* (New York: Deloitte Center for Integrated Research, 2023).

217 **either "expert" or "advanced":** Heather Ferguson, "New Research: What Boardroom Leaders Think about Generative AI," *Alteryx*, October 5, 2023; Frithjof Lund et al., "Four Essential Questions for Boards to Ask About Generative AI," *QuantumBlack by McKinsey*, July 7, 2023.

217 **"mass extinction event":** Yuliya Chernova, "More Startups Throw in the Towel, Unable to Raise Money for Their Ideas," *Wall Street Journal*, June 9, 2023.

218 **it had become more of an also-ran:** Jordan Novet, "Satya Nadella's First Decade as Microsoft CEO Was Defined by Cloud. What's Next?" *CNBC*, February 4, 2024.

218 **Microsoft "is the place":** "Yammer Advances with Microsoft Backing," *Financial Times*, April 2, 2013.

218 **He revitalized the company:** Behnam Tabrizi, "How Microsoft Became Innovative Again," *Harvard Business Review*, February 20, 2023.

219 **more than $100 billion cash on hand:** Microsoft, "Acquisition History," Calendar Year 2014, 2022, and 2023; https://www.microsoft.com/en-us/Investor/acquisition-history.aspx, accessed May 30, 2024.

219 **an estimated $10 billion in cash:** Jeffrey Dastin, "Microsoft to Invest More in OpenAI as Tech Race Heats Up," *Reuters*, January 23, 2023.

219 **The announcement came:** "Microsoft and OpenAI Extend Partnership," Microsoft Corporate blog, January 23, 2023.

219 **market share above 3 percent:** "Search Engine Market Share in 2024," *Oberlo*, accessed May 30, 2024.

219 **Microsoft Copilot:** Charles Duhigg, "The Inside Story of Microsoft's Partnership with OpenAI," *The New Yorker*, December 1, 2023.

220 **their own secure version:** "Introducing ChatGPT Plus," ChatGPT blog, February 1, 2023.

220 **an astronomical $7 trillion:** Keach Hagey, Asa Fitch, "Sam Altman Seeks Trillions of Dollars to Reshape Business of Chips and AI," *Wall Street Journal*, February 8, 2024; Organization for Economic Co-operation and Development, "Venture Capital Investments," *OECD Statistics*, accessed May 30, 2024.

220 **a new set of AI-powered business tools:** Jeffrey Dastin, "Amazon Steps up AI Race with Anthropic Investment," *Reuters*, September 28, 2023.

220 **lost share to Microsoft's Azure:** Dave Vellante, "What Leaked Court Docs Tell Us about AWS, Azure and Google Cloud Market Shares," *Silicon Angle*, July 29, 2023.

220 **$6 billion in annual sales:** "Large Language Model (LLM) Market Size to Grow USD 40.8 Billion by 2029 at a CAGR of 21.4% | Valuates Reports," press release by Valuates Reports, September 25, 2023. Revenue projections taken from Google, Amazon, and Microsoft 2023 annual reports.

221 **80 percent share:** Philipp Wegner, "The Leading Generative AI companies," *IOT Analytics*, December 14, 2023.

221 **"is tasked with advising the President":** "National AI Advisory Committee," accessed May 30, 2024.

221 **less accurate by every measure:** Lingjiao Chen, Matei Zaharia, and James Zou, "How Is ChatGPT's Behavior Changing Over Time?" *ArXiv*, July 18, 2023.

221 **they lack an epistemological connection:** James Vincent, "Microsoft's Bing Is an Emotionally Manipulative Liar, and People Love It," *The Verge*, February 15, 2023.

221 **case precedents that never existed:** Wes Davis, "A Lawyer Used ChatGPT and Now Has to Answer for Its Bogus Citations," *The Verge*, May 27, 2023.

221 **It forgot how to write basic computer code:** Thomas Claburn, "ChatGPT's Odds of Getting Code Questions Correct Are Worse than a Coin Flip," *The Register*, August 7, 2023; Untrustedlife2, "I Have Never Seen ChatGPT Fail to Write Code So Hard," Reddit post, February 5, 2023.

222 **handsomely formatted outputs and inputs:** Jacob Clemente, "Ways to Use ChatGPT's Data-Analysis Tool," *Charter*, September 27, 2023.

222 **random, unpredictable, and hard-to-spot:** NeedsAPromotion, "Bing ChatGPT Too Proud to Admit Mistake, Doubles Down and Then Rage Quits," Reddit post, June 22, 2023.

222 **If you ask it to generate an image of a tree:** I've made up these examples myself.

As a matter of principle, I have not used generative AI text at any point throughout this book.

222 **"I know a person":** Nitasha Tiku, "The Google Engineer Who Thinks the Company's AI Has Come to Life," *Washington Post*, June 11, 2022.

223 **a rumored 1.7 trillion parameters:** Maximilian Schreiner, "GPT-4 Architecture, Datasets, Costs and More Leaked," *The Decoder*, July 11, 2023.

223 **it gets outsourced to places:** Billy Perrigo, "Exclusive: OpenAI Used Kenyan Workers on Less Than $2 Per Hour to Make ChatGPT Less Toxic," *Time*, January 18, 2023; Alex Hern, "TechScape: How Cheap, Outsourced Labour in Africa Is Shaping AI English," *The Guardian*, April 16, 2024; Shakshi Jain, "Top-5 Indian IT Firms to Train over 4 Lakh Employees in AI-Specific Roles," *Deccan Herald*, December 17, 2023; Rebecca Tan and Regine Cabato, "Behind the AI Boom, an Army of Overseas Workers in 'Digital Sweatshops,'" *Washington Post*, August 28, 2023.

224 **it tends to use certain words:** "The 10 Most Common ChatGPT Words" and "The 15 Most Common ChatGPT Phrases," *AI Phrase Finder*, accessed May 30, 2024.

224 **"*aren't anywhere near good enough*":** Cory Doctorow, "Bullies Want You to Think They're On Your Side," *Pluralistic*, March 13, 2024.

225 **"openai now generates":** Sam Altman, "openai now generates about 100 billion words per day," Twitter post, February 9, 2024.

225 **bizarre tangents, and invented words:** See Janelle Shane's blog *AI Weirdness* for some superlative examples of bizarre AI output, such as a recipe for "Crimm Grunk Garlic Cleas" or "Beef Soup with Swamp Peef and Cheese."

225 **major book publishers:** Jess Weatherbed, "Artists Are Making Creative Companies Apologize for Using AI," *The Verge*, January 9, 2024.

226 **Nicki Minaj:** Ky Stewart, "Why Does Nicki Minaj Keep Using AI Art?" *Junkee*, January 15, 2024.

226 **AI-generated cover art and illustrations:** Charlie Warzel, "I Went Viral in the Bad Way," *The Atlantic*, August 17, 2022.

226 **AI-generated "fashion models":** Elena Cresci, "From Instagram to Balmain: The Rise of CGI Models," *BBC News*, September 12, 2018; Jenna Rosenstein, "People Can't Tell If This Fenty Model Is Real or Fake," *Harper's Bazaar*, February 9, 2018.

226 **Some content aggregators:** Peter Kafka, "You're Going to See More AI-Written Articles Whether You Like It or Not," *Vox*, July 18, 2023; Mia Sato, "CNET Is Overhauling Its AI Policy and Updating Past Stories," *The Verge*, June 6, 2023.

226 **incorrectly calculated compound interest:** Paul Farhi, "A News Site Used AI to Write Articles. It Was a Journalistic Disaster," *Washington Post*, January 17, 2023.

226 **the review website that plagiarized:** Maggie Harrison Dupré, "Sports Illustrated Published Articles by Fake, AI-Generated Writers," *Futurism*, November 27, 2023.

226 **Air Canada chatbot:** Kyle Melnick, "Air Canada Chatbot Promised a Discount. Now the Airline Has to Pay It," *Washington Post*, February 18, 2024.

227 **even movie studios:** Emma Keates, "Netflix and A24 Both Land in Hot Water over Apparent AI Stuff," *AV Club*, April 18, 2024.

227 **One listing in Brazil:** Grintern, "AI Image Graphic Designer," LinkedIn job posting, accessed January 12, 2024.

227 **researchers at Cornell, UC Berkeley, and the University of Washington:** Milad Nasr et al., "Extracting Training Data from ChatGPT," *ArXiv*, November 28, 2023.

227 **researchers could trace those phrases:** Milad Nasr et al., "Scalable Extraction of Training Data from (Production) Language Models," *ArXiv*, November 28, 2023.

228 **"these models are truly approximating their datasets":** James Betker, "The 'It' in AI Models Is the Dataset," *Non_Interactive*, June 10, 2023.

228 **It has scraped the *New York Times*:** Joe Pompeo, "Inside the Legal Tussle between Authors and AI: 'We've Got to Attack This from All Directions,'" *Vanity Fair*, October 18, 2023.

228 **The company argues:** Kyle Wiggers, "OpenAI Claims New York Times Copyright Lawsuit Is Without Merit," *TechCrunch*, January 8, 2024.

229 **the law has precious little to say:** Katrina Zhu, "The State of State AI Laws: 2023," *Electronic Privacy Information Center*, August 3, 2023.

229 **pales in comparison to the licensing fees:** Erin Griffith and Cade Metz, "'Let 1,000 Flowers Bloom': A.I. Funding Frenzy Escalates," *New York Times*, March 14, 2023.

229 **it appears to be able to raise money:** Reed Albergotti, "OpenAI Has Received Just a Fraction of Microsoft's $1 Billion Investment," *Semafor*, November 18, 2023.

230 **In January 2024:** Gary Marcus and Reid Southen, "Generative AI Has a Visual Plagiarism Problem," *IEEE Spectrum*, January 6, 2024.

230 **Midjourney did not just imitate:** *Andersen v. Stability AI Ltd.*, "Exhibit J: Midjourney Name List," 3:23-cv-00201-WHO (District Court, Northern District of California, November 29, 2023).

231 **"At some point":** JonLamArt, "Midjourney Developers Caught Discussing Laundering," Twitter post, December 31, 2023.

231 **nearly twenty thousand jobs:** Angela Fu, Ren LaForme, and Tom Jones, "Media Industry Cuts Top 20,000 in 2023, Report Finds," *Poynter*, December 8, 2023; "Number of Job Losses in the Media Industry in the United States from 2000 to 2023," *Statista*, accessed May 30, 2024.

231 **Freelance work is drying up:** Society of Authors Policy Team, "SoA Survey Reveals a Third of Translators and Quarter of Illustrators Losing Work to AI," press release, April 11, 2024.

CONCLUSION: OPTING OUT

234 **once claimed to work 130 hours:** Max Chafkin, "Yahoo's Marissa Mayer on Selling a Company While Trying to Turn It Around," *Bloomberg Businessweek*, August 4, 2016.

234 **"Don't expect that you'll get":** Sheryl Sandberg, "Why We Have Too Few Women Leaders," *TEDWomen 2010*, December 2010.

234 **working forty hours a week:** Elon Musk, "There are way easier places to work," Twitter post, November 26, 2018.

234 **"you can work long, hard, or smart":** Mark Abadi, "Jeff Bezos Once Said That in Job Interviews He Told Candidates of 3 Ways to Work—and That You Have to do All 3 at Amazon," *Business Insider*, August 12, 2018.

237 **90 percent of startups fail:** Marcus Cook, "The Biggest Misconception on Why Startups Fail," *Inc.*, August 27, 2021.

237 **more detailed studies:** Tom Eisenmann, "Why Start-ups Fail," *Harvard Business Review*, May 1, 2021; Deborah Gage, "The Venture Capital Secret: 3 Out of 4 Start-Ups Fail," *Wall Street Journal*, September 20, 2012.

244 **six-part code of ethics:** "AIA's Professional & Ethical Standards," *The American Institute of Architects*, accessed May 30, 2024.

245 **the English economist Charles Goodhart:** Peter Coy, "Goodhart's Law Rules the Modern World. Here Are Nine Examples," *Bloomberg*, March 26, 2021.

246 **Facebook got rid:** Billy Perrigo, "How Facebook Forced a Reckoning by Shutting Down the Team That Put People Ahead of Profits," *Time*, October 7, 2021.

246 **Microsoft its ethics:** Zoë Schiffer and Casey Newton, "Microsoft Lays Off Team That Taught Employees How to Make AI Tools Responsibly," *The Verge*, March 13, 2023.

246 **Amazon and Google dismissed:** "Big Tech Companies Cut AI Ethics Staff, Raising Safety Concerns," *Financial Times*, March 29, 2023.

247 **"fly at all costs, in all conditions":** Adam Cohen, "Delivering the Mail Was Once One of the Riskiest Jobs in America," *Smithsonian Magazine*, May 18, 2018.

247 **not so much to protect their jobs or wages:** "Price Guide 1939," *Paper Dragon*, accessed May 30, 2024.

247 **They refused to work:** "APA History: The First 25 Years," *Allied Pilots Association*, accessed May 30, 2024.

247 **a common network of air traffic control:** "A Brief History of the FAA," Federal Aviation Administration, accessed May 30, 2024; Clinton M. Hester, "The Civil Aeronautics Act of 1938," *Journal of Air Law and Commerce* 9, no. 3 (1938): 454–55.

247 **a 90 percent reduction:** James L. Gattuso, "Air Travel: A Hundred Years of Safety," *Mackinac Center for Public Policy*, October 6, 2003.

249 **"perpetual non-disparagement clause":** Hayden Field, "OpenAI Sends Internal Memo Releasing Former Employees from Controversial Exit Agreements," *CNBC*, May 23, 2024.

249 **Theranos whistleblower Tyler Shultz:** John Carreyrou, "Theranos Whistleblower Shook the Company—And His Family," *Wall Street Journal*, November 18, 2016.

249 **more mundane forms of abuse:** Reed Albergotti, "She Pulled Herself from Addiction by Learning to Code. Now She's Leading a Worker Uprising at Apple," *Washington Post*, October 14, 2021.

250 **demand is positively historic:** Steve Lohr and Trip Mickle, "As Silicon Valley Retrenches, a Tech Talent Shift Accelerates," *New York Times*, December 29, 2022; Bill Fahey, "Four Tips on Lowering Your Engineering Team's Turnover," *Forbes*, April 21, 2021.

250 **Dr. Timnit Gebru:** Casey Newton, "The Withering Email That Got an Ethical AI Researcher Fired at Google," *Platformer*, December 3, 2020.

250 **Amazon's sale of facial recognition:** Hannah Denham, "'No Tech for ICE': Protesters Demand Amazon Cut Ties with Federal Immigration Enforcement," *Washington Post*, July 12, 2019.

251 **Google's contracts to provide cloud computing services:** Scott Shane and Daisuke Wakabayashi, "'The Business of War': Google Employees Protest Work for the Pentagon," *New York Times*, April 4, 2018

251 **Microsoft's work with oil companies:** Colin Lecher, "Microsoft Employees Are Protesting the Company's 'Complicity in the Climate Crisis,'" *The Verge*, September 19, 2019.

INDEX

Pages numbers after 255 refer to notes.